W9-BGQ-476

Surviving

Bipolar's

Fatal Grip

David Mariant
with Diane Mariant

Surviving

Bipolar's

Fatal Grip

The Journey to
Hell and Back

DOWNEY _____ LIBRARY
D____ _____

MARIANT
ENTERPRISES

Mariant Enterprises, Inc.
Santa Clara, California

Surviving Bipolar's Fatal Grip: The Journey to Hell and Back

Copyright © 2006, David Mariant and Diane Mariant. All rights reserved.

Published by Mariant Enterprises, Inc., P.O. Box 2026, Santa Clara, CA 95055
www.Mariant.com

MARIANT
ENTERPRISES

Authors:	David Mariant
	Diane Mariant
Editor:	Jean Vengua http://rhizomatous.blogspot.com/
Production Editors:	Arlene Mariant
	Dave Bolick
	Thomas Brown
Professional Review:	Jonathan Russ, M.D., Adjunct Associate Professor Emeritus, Stanford University School of Medicine
Pastoral Review:	Pastor John Shirey
Book Design:	R. Anne Hernandez www.inkandtea.com
Cover Designer:	Cathi Stevenson
Printing History:	August 2006, First printing and E-book
Printed by:	Delta Printing Solutions, Inc.
Printed in:	The United States of America

No part of this publication may be reproduced or distributed in any form or by any means, or stored in any data base or retrieval system, without the prior written permission of the author. If you purchase this book without a cover be aware that this book may be stolen property. For further information, contact the publisher, Mariant Enterprises, Inc.

The authors of this book, are not psychiatrists, doctors, or therapists and do not dispense medical advice or prescribe the use of any treatment for physical or medical problems. Always seek the advice of a qualified professional. The views of this book are the authors' alone and are in no way intended to replace or substitute for professional medical care. The authors are strong advocates of comprehensive illness management through psychiatric care, therapy, medication and self-management.

Scripture quotations marked (NLT) are taken from the Holy Bible, New Living Translation, copyright © 1996. Used by permission of Tyndale House Publishers, Inc., Wheaton, Ill 60189. All rights reserved.

Note to the Reader: The content of the book reflects a true account of one individual with bipolar disorder and may be upsetting to some. The names of some people have been changed to protect their privacy.

Library of Congress 2006927627

ISBN 13: 9780977685905   Tradepaper
ISBN 10: 0-9776859-0-X

ISBN 13: 9780977685912
ISBN 10: 0-9776859-1-8   E-book

Please visit our website :

www.SurvivingBipolar.com

SURVIVING
BIPOLAR

In Memory of My Brother

Michael Joseph Mariant

Your life has forever inspired mine!

1965 – 1997

To My Loving Children

Janae, James, Jacob, Rachel and Renee

I am sorry for the rough times and I want to thank you for your love that has seen me through my most difficult of days. I love you more than there are stars in the heavens and drops of water in the sea. Your love, hugs and kisses have been my heart's delight.

Love, Daddy

To My Loving Wife Diane

Your life has had the greatest positive impact on mine. You have stood beside me during my greatest difficulties, depression, and manic highs. Your love has been unfaltering, and you have been my safe haven. I have let you down many times, and yet your grace and love have always been there. I have often wondered what life would be like without your love, friendship, and support. I have concluded that without you, I would likely have missed the opportunity to know love's full meaning. You are my love, my life, my wife, my breath, my air, and I love you. It is with great honor that I dedicate this book to you.

I Love You... David

To My Mom and Dad

Thank you for your love and support,

and for giving me the gift of life.

CONTENTS

Foreword   p.   xiii

PART 1   **MY BIPOLAR JOURNEY**   p.   1

Chapter 1   A Personal Journey   p.   3
Chapter 2   My Diagnosis   p.   13
Chapter 3   From Depression to Manic Relapse   p.   39
Chapter 4   My Journey to Hell and Back   p.   65

PART 2   **SURVIVING BIPOLAR DISORDER**   p.   85

Chapter 5   Surviving the New Diagnosis   p.   87
Chapter 6   Managing Bipolar Disorder   p.   97
Chapter 7   Danger—Traumatic Overload   p.   121
Chapter 8   Emotional Healing and Codependency   p.   139
Chapter 9   Forgiveness and Hope   p.   149
Chapter 10   The Family Perspective and the Bipolar Child   p.   163
Chapter 11   The Journey Continues   p.   179

PART 3   **BIPOLAR SURVIVAL ESSENTIALS**   p.   187

Chapter 12   Bipolar Disorder   p.   189
Chapter 13   Understanding Sleep   p.   211
Chapter 14   Introduction to Stress Management   p.   219
Chapter 15   Codependency   p.   231
Chapter 16   Post Traumatic Stress Disorder (PTSD)   p.   247
Chapter 17   Eye Movement Desensitization and
                Reprocessing (EMDR)   p.   253
Chapter 18   Neurofeedback   p.   259
Chapter 19   Frequently Asked Questions about Suicide   p.   265

Acknowledgements   p.   273

Bibliography   p.   275

Visit Our Website   p.   277

How to Order   p.   281

POETRY

Chapter 1	One Day at a Time	p.	11
Chapter 2	Bipolar Experience	p.	37
Chapter 3	A Knight's Pledge	p.	63
Chapter 4	Twisted Fire	p.	83
Chapter 5	Questions of My Life	p.	95
Chapter 6	Learning to Fly	p.	119
Chapter 7	Where is My Anchor	p.	137
Chapter 8	Priceless Masterpiece	p.	147
Chapter 9	Enemies of Love	p.	161
Chapter 10	Thoughts of My Wife	p.	175
	Legacy of Promise	p.	177
Chapter 11	Gentle Breezes Ahead	p.	185

FOREWORD

by Diane Mariant

"It helps, I think, to consider ourselves on a very long journey: the main thing is to keep to the faith, to endure, to help each other when we stumble or tire, to weep and press on."

—Mary Caroline Richards

David's eyes were fixated on the freeway, as I sat in the passenger seat and our five children sat behind us. They were uncharacteristically quiet, and I could tell that they were scared. They didn't understand what was wrong with their daddy. I kept asking my husband why he was behaving the way he was, and why it was so important that we go to his sister's house right at that moment. His only answer was, "Just pray that God will show you." It made no sense to me. In fact, very little that had gone on over the past couple of days had made much sense at all. David drove on, crying, preaching and talking in riddles.

David had called an impromptu family meeting for reasons unknown. Everyone had agreed to drop what they were doing and go to David's sister's house immediately. His tearful call had scared them, their concern was evident on their faces when we arrived. They were expecting to hear the worst—that one of the children had a terminal illness or something equally dire.

When we arrived at Sheryl's house, I told her that something was terribly wrong with David, but that I had no idea what the problem was. I thought he might be having a nervous breakdown. I myself was a nervous wreck and decided not to stay. I took the children home and would pick up David after the meeting. We were all emotionally and physically exhausted.

Several hours later, Sheryl called to tell me that David was acting very strangely. He had raced through a speech at her house, then insisted that past family problems be resolved right then and there before he left. Everyone cooperated, with a lot of apologies and tears. Perhaps that was the one good thing that came out of this very odd situation.

David's father was going to bring him home, but Sheryl thought he really needed to be taken to a hospital. If David would not let his dad take him, she pleaded with me to do so. I agreed, but wondered how we would explain to David why we thought he needed to go to the hospital. He had already said earlier that he'd never felt better in his whole life. He seemed to think that he had been given a special gift from God, that he suddenly had acquired the ability to get by on only two or three hours of sleep. He would spend several hours at the park in the middle of the night deep in prayer and experiencing "deep meaningful insights" from the Lord.

It was very late when my father-in-law called with the details of what had transpired since he and David left Sheryl's house. David had insisted that he and his Dad go to our church and talk with the elders. When they met with the church leaders, the leaders could see that something was not right with David, and tried to convince him to go to a hospital and be examined. David instead insisted that it was more important that they listen to what he had to say.

After meeting with the church leaders, David and his dad went to get something to eat. After a time, David suddenly got up and ran out of the restaurant saying that he could not trust anyone. His dad called the police at this point, fearing for his son's life. Soon after, David called me and said he could not trust anyone and it soon became apparent that he did not even trust me. Several hours after David had abruptly fled from the restaurant and with no one aware of his whereabouts, my father, who David had always admired, went out and found him, but David ran again. My father, also fearing for David's safety, called the police.

I was becoming increasingly frantic. How could all this happen in the course of a single day? The answer came from the hospital the following day. I was soon to learn that David would be diagnosed as having bipolar disorder and was on a "manic high." The doctors told me it was most likely brought on by a lack of sleep. They also told me that bipolar disorder is likely hereditary, something that some people are born with. It was not a difficult diagnosis. He had all the symptoms of mania. It was all new to me. I had never heard of any information associated with bipolar disorder before. As a result of the diagnosis by the psychiatrist, David was put on a 72-hour hold.

Since that day, our worlds—the children's and mine, and of course my husband's—have never been the same. We would see more strange behavior in David, including severe depression. David has accused me of killing his brother and asked if I planned to kill him as well. I've been accused of being a witch and putting spells on our house. He thought that I had set trip hazards around our house intentionally, so that if there were ever a fire, we would have no way out.

If you have a loved one with bipolar disorder, I can identify with your pain. I know what it feels like to fear someone you love with all your heart, and how it feels to make love to a man who sometimes seems like a complete stranger. If you have been diagnosed with bipolar illness, please don't give up—there is hope.

This book is David's story. It is like no other book on the subject of bipolar disorder that I know of. It was not written by a doctor, but by someone who has not only learned to survive—but to thrive—despite his illness. David's story will sound familiar to many bipolar patients as well as their loved ones, and it will give anyone who reads it a better understanding of this heart-wrenching illness. Most importantly, his story offers hope in the face of this illness, and it may even save lives.

If I was going to live with bipolar disorder, I needed to learn all that I could about it. The struggles that it brings to our lives are significant, but they are not insurmountable. I love my husband, and I know that he is not the illness; rather, he is a person who happens to have this illness.

Our family has been through several bipolar episodes. David understands now that he needs to take daily medication consistently, and I thank God for that. There was a time early on, when he did not think he needed medication. Without it, he suffered a full-blown psychotic manic episode within days. I'll never forget the wild look in his eyes and the fear that gripped me when I spoke to him. David has never hurt us or been violent, however, I had no idea in the beginning what he might be capable of in the state of mind he was in.

I can only imagine some of David's feelings and experiences that I have been unable to view; he has only shared some. Others he will share for the first time in this book. He will also share our struggles with one of our children, who we believe may also have bipolar disorder. It is very difficult to diagnose children with the disease. We have learned that it could be bipolar combined with one or more other disorders. It is heart wrenching to see one's child handcuffed and taken away by the police and to see the looks on our other children's faces, as they realize that they won't be seeing their sibling for a while. Being told if and when we can visit our child has also been difficult. We also have experience with the Juvenile Justice system and several group homes for children where intense counseling and therapy are available.

Bipolar disorder has taken a significant toll on our family, and yet we have found a higher purpose to our burden. The goal is not only to provide hope to others whose lives have been touched by the illness, but also to suggest ideas and strategies for actively managing it and minimizing its impact. Our hope is for a brighter tomorrow for all of us who live with this very challenging illness.

Make no mistake, bipolar disorder is a very serious illness. If you have bipolar disorder or know someone who does, we hope you will read this entire book. The suggestions in it could possibly save your life or that of your loved one. When a bipolar episode first occurs, the worst part for the individual and the family members is not knowing. Information and understanding can make all the difference.

This illness can make a person feel like they are literally in hell, but they do not have to feel that way forever. There are viable and healthy options too. After many email polls, chat groups, therapy groups, and discussions with patients, family members, doctors and counselors, David now believes that surviving bipolar disorder requires more than just medical intervention. Surviving bipolar disorder requires active self-management by the patient and the patient's family.

Self-management may hinge on increasing awareness of the disorder. There are many excellent books, articles and websites on the subject of bipolar disorder, and we urge you to learn as much as you can to gain a deeper understanding of the illness. Knowledge, as they say, is power. You don't have to let this illness control your life. You can take control of it. It will take a significant amount of effort and courage, but if you can learn from some of the insights and strategies that David has found through his struggles with the illness, you won't regret it.

Living with bipolar can be very challenging, but life can also be happy and fulfilling.

—Diane Mariant

Part 1

My Bipolar Journey

"Success is to be measured not so much by the position that one has reached in life as by the obstacles which he has overcome while trying to succeed."

—Booker T. Washington

CHAPTER 1

A Personal Journey

"Success consists of getting up just one more time than you fall."
—Oliver Goldsmith

I have seen psychiatric wards from the inside. I have felt like a freak. I have been scared, confused, ashamed, frustrated, claustrophobic, and mad as hell. I've seen people struggling and fighting, their eyes swollen with tears. I have seen people who tried to take their own lives or end someone else's. I've seen people in their deepest depressive lows and their highest manic highs, their wrists thick with bandages. And I have seen myself reflected in their faces.

I have been at death's door. I've seen the depth of my own fear, all consuming depression and blood-boiling anger. I have felt unbearable sorrow. I've experienced dizzying mania and deep depression—and even both at the same time. I have been tied to a bed in four-point restraint. I have endured others looks—fearful, pitying, uncomprehending—and suffered the sting of discrimination, all from fear and lack of understanding. There have also been bright spots. I have experienced kindness and compassion, people shining through for me like loving angels at my time of greatest need. Diane, my wife of twenty one years, has stood by my side during the most difficult of times. Love is important to everyone, but for those of us with bipolar, it is essential to our survival. Diane's sustaining love has been the greatest example of love I will ever know.

It is necessary for me to be completely transparent with you, without reservation or inhibition. I am surviving bipolar disorder and it is important that you see deep within me so you can understand my life saving strategies of success. Grasp hold of my life story and the strategies I discuss in this book and your life will be better for it. I want to convey my daily struggles and successes, both internally and externally, to help you see the danger in your own life, and the possibility for a safer and more joyous future. My experience may be similar to yours or that of a loved one. Ultimately, I want you to know that there is hope.

Many times I have referred to bipolar disorder as a "bomb," yet the "detonator" may actually be the more significant component. The bomb itself is the genetic predisposition to the disorder that passes from one generation to the next. The detonator comprises one's life experiences and may include unhealthy relationships, co-dependencies, and other issues. The detonation itself often results from a traumatic event that ignites the fuse. In my case, the sudden death of my younger brother began the countdown to the detonation that would occur some months later, and begin my journey to hell and back. Fortunately, I learned that there are ways to defuse the detonator and reduce and even eliminate the overall risk. Even after removing the detonator, however, the bomb still has to be handled with care.

Bipolar disorder in years past was usually referred to as manic depressive illness or depressive disorder. In this book I use the term "bipolar," "bipolar disorder," "bipolar illness" and "the disorder." I use these terms interchangeably, and will often use the term "bipolar" for easier reading.

In 1999, at age thirty-five, I was diagnosed with bipolar disorder. I have constantly been reminded of the person I was at the time of my diagnosis and the desperation I felt. It is for those who find themselves in similar circumstances that I have returned, to provide relief from the despair and confusion I know all too well. My suffering is a bit of a paradox because the suffering is part of what helped me get through my crisis; reliving the pain actually became part of my healing process. I want to reach those with bipolar (especially the newly diagnosed), as well as their families, friends, doctors, therapists, and anyone else who has the interest and desire to understand this life-threatening illness. If you are where I was—or know someone who is—know that there really is hope for survival and a full life worth living. We need not be destroyed by our condition. You too can learn, as I have, how to be strong and how to set boundaries for our emotional protection. I have learned how to survive.

You may be surprised that bipolar disorder has actually taken on some very positive meanings for me as I have learned more about it in the past several years. I find it fascinating how many leaders, artists—all expressive and intelligent people—are believed to have suffered from depression or bipolar disorder. Here are a few names: King David of Israel and Job (biblical figures); Presidents Andrew Jackson, Thomas Jefferson, Abraham Lincoln, Richard Nixon, Theodore Roosevelt and George Washington; Prime Minister Winston Churchill; astronaut Buzz Aldrin (the second person to walk on the moon); the father of modern psychoanalysis, Sigmund Freud; scientist Isaac Newton; the philosopher, Plato; authors Jack London, Virginia Woolf, Mark Twain, Edgar Allen Poe and Ernest Hemingway; actors Drew Barrymore, Jim Carrey, Cary Grant, Ben Stiller and Vin Diesel; artists Vincent Van Gogh, Michelangelo and Norman Rockwell; composers Ludwig van Beethoven and Frederic Chopin. I have seen hundreds of familiar names that I really admire who suffered from depression or bipolar disorder. If you suffer from bipolar disorder or severe depression like me, we are in good company. We are counted among the greatest of great people to have ever walked the earth.

In the last few years, I have encountered many who suffer from bipolar and many who have family members or friends who suffer. So many with bipolar disorder have touched my life along the way. I hope that you will find much in this book that will resonate within you—echoing not only your pain and fear, but also your success.

Most bipolar sufferers seem to travel a similar journey. Mine was an emotionally wrenching experience that is very difficult to fully convey. I share my personal journey so that you can see the relationship between life's difficulties and the onset of bipolar symptoms. My intention to work through my life issues has been critical to my own mood stabilization and mental health. Your "life review" will surely prove helpful to you as well.

It is difficult for me to listen to others label bipolar disorder sufferers as though we and the disorder are synonymous. I cannot speak for everyone, but I can say that being labeled as "bipolar" is something I do not appreciate. "Bipolar" does not define us. We are people first, individuals who happen to have an illness called bipolar disorder. We are not the disorder itself. On the day I was first diagnosed, I felt ashamed. I was hurting badly, and feeling broken. The doctor explained that I had a chemical imbalance in my brain. What he did not do was emphasize that I am a person with value, nor did he acknowledge my feelings and the stigma associated with the diagnosis.

The doctor assured me that bipolar disorder was not a mental illness, but rather a chemical imbalance of the brain. This did not ease the stigma of mental illness I was feeling. I had seen others look at those with mental challenges in hurtful ways and I did not want to be labeled like that too. Stigma comes from lack of understanding, misinformation and what seems like an absence of empathy. Perhaps not everyone with bipolar disorder experiences the mental illness stigma, but I know far too many who do.

During those first difficult days, after my diagnosis, it would have meant a great deal to me to hear a fellow bipolar sufferer tell me that I was still a worthwhile person. It would have surely given me the strength and courage to press forward. I want to encourage you to press forward—to tell you that you are a unique and magnificent, worthwhile person. Self-acceptance has been significant to me, and I think it will be important to others as well. Similarly, a book such as this—by someone who has been there and understands the anguish—would have made a world of difference to me when I was first diagnosed. And that is why I have written this book.

I have carried feelings of brokenness and shame, feelings that you may also be experiencing. Many friends with bipolar continue to be challenged by these feelings, even years after being diagnosed. Just remember, you are not alone. As you journey with me through my own traumatic life, codependencies and what I call "the journey to hell and back," you will see that the brokenness had already established itself deep within me at an early age. In some ways, bipolar disorder magnified and mirrored my inner broken heart and mind.

Following the sudden and tragic death of my brother, I was completely devastated. Bipolar magnified my grief, intensified my feelings, and left me vulnerable to the worst mood swings of my life. I have learned that the disorder distorts the reality of who we are. However, there is hope in shedding these disabling feelings, and as you read this book, you will learn how.

Feeling broken and ashamed, I was in complete denial about having bipolar disorder and, in the beginning, refused to take medication. It wasn't until my second hospitalization and manic episode that I finally began to accept bipolar as an illness rather than my identity. My dignity had been stripped away and yet I needed to go forward in my life with strength. It was Dr. Russ, who was the first doctor to treat me with respect. He was different from all the other doctors I had known at the time. What makes Dr. Russ special to me is that he treats me with respect, like a whole person. Since then, I have found more people who treat me with kindness and respect.

Bipolar disorder is a very serious condition. Statistics show that about 20% of individuals with bipolar disorder take their lives by suicide[1]. The disorder has the highest morbidity rate of all mental illnesses, with most deaths resulting from suicide. By working to achieve health in all aspects of our lives, we can gain a much stronger chance of survival.

I encourage you to look beyond the psychiatric scope of

---

1 See Muller-Oerlinghausen B., Berghofer A. and Bauer M., "Bipolar Disorder," in *Lancet* 2002 Jan 19; 359 (9302): 241-7

bipolar illness and its treatments, most of which involve medication. If I succeed in my message to you, you will see bipolar disorder in a new light. You will see how important it is to address the entire person as a whole.

Drugs are important and can certainly minimize the effects of bipolar and address the acute need, but unfortunately, they are not a cure. There are a large number of drugs used to treat the disorder in varying dosages and combinations to correct the chemical imbalance in the brain. However, as important as drug therapies are, this should be just one element of treatment, not the entire treatment.

Doctors and researchers are still trying to better understand bipolar disorder so they can develop more consistent treatments. And, although I have yet to meet a doctor who has expressed any faith in the possibility of a cure for bipolar symptoms, I believe that a cure will be found some day.

I am optimistic that researchers will enter the field with open minds, without being bound by earlier discoveries. It is my view that we are more than simply chemical organisms, it is important to recognize that our journey involves every aspect of who we are—the physical, emotional and the spiritual. To minimize the dangers of bipolar disorder, it is extremely important that those with bipolar and their health care providers address each of these aspects, rather than simply prescribing or taking drugs.

One thing I have noticed that I have in common with so many of my friends with bipolar—we all have had significant emotional and spiritual issues in our lives. This is not to say that we don't have a physical issue with the chemical imbalance of our brains. However, drug therapy is important, but it is not enough. I don't believe that I would be alive today without having learned how to *actively manage* my illness to augment the drug therapies. When diagnosed, it seemed as though all the doctors wanted to do was give me medication and send me on my way. Very little attention, if any, was given to the stressors in my life, or the life events that brought me to the breaking point of mania and, ultimately, to the hospital. All elements of who we are must be taken into account. If stress aggravates your bipolar, then it is vital to reduce as many stressors in your life as possible in order to improve your emotional well being and chances of survival.

Painful details of my life prior to my bipolar diagnosis, including a traumatic upbringing and my brother Michael's death, are revealed within the pages of this book. I survived my psychotic, manic, and depressive episodes, as well as other frightening experiences. My stories often hinge on scary and sometimes bizarre events, but they also emphasize the importance of triumph, love, and above all, faith. I look closely at my traumatic background and how you may also benefit from your own life review. Life issues may not play a part in the disorder for everyone. However, I believe that everyone with bipolar illness should at least consider the possibility. Traumatic events and codependent issues can certainly impact anyone's life; adding bipolar to the mix can have serious, even life-threatening consequences. Surviving bipolar disorder may ultimately depend on how successfully we work through these issues, as has been true for me.

Throughout my journey, I have encountered many people with bipolar. Since I began writing this book on bipolar disorder it seems like the topic of bipolar is always coming up. When it does, it seems as though nearly everyone I talk to has it, or knows someone with it. Many have heard of the name bipolar, however rarely does anyone understand the staggering statistics of fatality for this illness; it can be deadly, and should be regarded as such.

I agree with modern medicine that there is a genetic component to bipolar disorder. I came to this understanding reluctantly, after an informal online poll revealed that about half the respondents with bipolar also have family members with bipolar. The other half reports that they are the only diagnosed case in the family; however, many indicated they had relatives who exhibited behaviors suggestive of bipolar, even though they had not been diagnosed.

Not long ago, my life took some turns that resulted in the most difficult and painful years of my life. It was during those years that I began to write poetry. Some of that poetry is included in this book. At the time, I was in a stable bipolar mood state. I thought I was recovering. I was feeling very good about the future. I had even thought about writing a book about surviving bipolar disorder some day. Little did I know that my greatest difficulties of depression and mania were yet to come. Writing poetry and writing this book have been invaluable to me and have helped me to process the sea of disturbing emotions that have hindered my life and have helped me not only heal but survive.

With bipolar disorder, we never know what might be hiding just around the corner waiting to hit us head on. My descent was painful, but it also helped identify my illness, and once something is identified it can be addressed. "My Journey to Hell and Back" was a terrible time in my life, and yet it also represents a time of the greatest healing I will probably ever know.

As you read this book, my hope is that you will gain insights for yourself and for someone you care about. I am convinced that your life will be richer for having done so. Most of all, this book represents my heart, the heart of a person with bipolar who has faith that there is hope not only to survive bipolar illness, but to do so joyfully and with a high quality of life. Thank you for giving me the opportunity to share my journey with you.

And now, buckle up and let the journey begin ...

ONE DAY AT A TIME

My soul tires of the battle
The battle that continues on
Night after night
Day after day

I am weary of the fight
The fight to breathe
Breath after breath
Sigh after sigh

Trapped within the confines
My body, soul and mind
Waiting patiently for relief
One day at a time

—David Mariant

CHAPTER 2

My Diagnosis

"Where does one go from a world of insanity?
Somewhere on the other side of despair."

— T.S. (Thomas Stearns) Eliot

My diagnosis for bipolar disorder followed my first full-blown manic episode. My life was turned upside down and would never be the same. How could this be? What was happening to me? I was told I had bipolar disorder by a doctor who did not even know my name. How could he know that after such a brief evaluation? The diagnosis was triggered by a series of traumatic events. These events built up the stress to such a level that it acted as the detonator to set off my "bipolar bomb."

I believe it was the death of my brother, Michael, that put me over the edge, emotionally. I had no idea that a person could grieve so intensely. Even though I had experienced many painful losses, when he died, it felt like part of me died with him. My brother's sudden death and the mystery surrounding it were shocking, and the experience still haunts me, nine years later. The cause of death was unknown, and there were many unanswered questions. Was it murder, suicide or did his heart just quit beating? No one could tell us what happened. The coroner's report gave no cause of death. There were so many unanswered questions that left so much unsettled. As we searched for clues, my family and I got so worked up that I became paranoid and fearful for my life. At one point, I just had to give up, as the unending speculation was taking a huge emotional toll.

As a kid growing up, I had always felt like Michael's protector. I was two years older than him and much more responsible and mature. We were very close, and we were closer in age than any of our other siblings. I remember playing with Michael, riding our bikes, pretending we were army soldiers—I could go on and on. The upshot was that I felt responsible for him, and felt as though I had failed in some way when he died, even though we were both adults by then and he had been on his own for years. The combination of shock from Michael's tragic death and my feeling that I had failed him not only stressed me to the point of overload, but also led directly to my first psychotic manic episode and hospitalization.

A year or so after Michael's death, about six months before the manic episode, I had taken a new job with a professional services company. It was the best job I had ever had. I had been assigned to a global management position for a major account, and I was very excited. The company's philosophy was to respect ideas and encourage collaboration. I thrived in this type of work environment, and felt right at home. I was respected by my manager and the vice president, and that felt good.

I had been with the company for nearly six months when we acquired a twenty million dollar service contract. The challenge was to deliver the services under serious time constraints. I was in a little over my head, and my stress levels increased rapidly. The vice president of engineering services could see that I was overwhelmed, so he invited me to meet with him in Chicago to discuss planning for the project.

The Chicago trip was significant in the onset of my illness; it was at the beginning of the trip that I began to notice unusual changes. For example, my creativity and speed of thought increased noticeably while I was flying. It was as though I was flying metaphorically as well as literally. I wasn't sure if it was from lack of rest, being at a high altitude, or some other reason. I worked on various projects as well as on "personal vision writing." It was an election year, and I was thinking about becoming the president of the United States—not something I normally thought about. I also thought about making a movie, along with other fantastic plans. Such thoughts are termed "grandiose," and

14

they fulfill one of the diagnostic criteria for mania.

I later learned that traveling across time zones can put me at an increased risk of mania due to the sleep pattern disturbances. I had noticed mood swings in the past a few times while traveling, but thought I was just tired from "jet lag." While flying at an elevation of 30,000 feet my creativity and speed of thought increased noticeably. Now in Chicago I was having the same mood swings, coupled with ideas that were flowing out of me faster than I could process them. For several days after arriving in Chicago, I was unable to sleep until 4:00 a.m. or later in the morning. Worse, the VP liked to start meetings at 7:00 a.m. so my sleep deficit built up rapidly. I now know that adequate sleep is absolutely essential in preventing the onset of mania. Effective sleep management is as critically important to my well being as my mood-stabilizing medications.

(Refer to "Bipolar Disorder" in Part 3, Bipolar Survival Essentials, for excellent information about bipolar.)

It was fifteen degrees below zero when I arrived in Chicago, the coldest weather I had ever experienced. From the airport, I had been instructed by the hotel operator to wait curbside for a bus. I was glad that I had brought my winter gear, but I did not have protection for my face which was burning with cold, and when it's fifteen below, this makes a difference.

While waiting outside the snow began to fall as the wind forcefully blew it along the walkway at an angle. It was extremely cold. No one was outside except a black man who came up to me from afar and asked if I needed help, and I said, "Sure." The man was obviously homeless because both he and his clothes seemed a bit worn and tattered. He was also wearing a bright orange down jacket which had been out of style for dozens of years. He was a humble man, friendly and somewhat quiet. He carried my bag several blocks for me and he led me to the bus stop that I needed to get to my hotel. We made small talk for a while, and then I asked what it was like to be homeless in such

15

brutal weather. It seemed like such a desperate predicament. I will never forget his words. He said, "Some days God provides what I need, and other days he provides me a little bit more." He expressed to me that God always provides enough. It meant a lot to me then, and it still means a lot to me today. I took a twenty dollar bill from my wallet and handed it to him. We shook hands, and he told me his name was "Isaiah."

I met Isaiah just days before I was first diagnosed with bipolar disorder. The few years that followed were the most difficult of my life, but Isaiah was right. Even during the hard times, God did provide just enough strength to get by. It's funny that this man's words resonate in my mind to this day. As I think about my life these past several years, I thank God for also providing a little bit more when I need it.

Late that night, I began to work at my computer. At around 4:00 a.m. I began sending instant messages to friends who were online. Normally at that hour, I would have been asleep for several hours. I just could not stop thinking about new ideas and found it impossible to sleep. I didn't even feel tired. I did finally manage to get a few hours of sleep, but my mania had begun to escalate dangerously.

In the morning, at the next meeting, my ideas were flowing freely—a common occurrence when I am in a manic state. My ideas led to others, and we came up with some outstanding plans. I still think that my manic behavior had a positive outcome on our task. Unfortunately, the tremendous sense of creativity associated with mania often fools the person with bipolar into thinking that all is well. During the flight home, my ideas continued to run wild—everything from becoming a spokesperson for the Boy Scouts, to becoming a great world leader.

Back at work the next day and throughout the week, my thoughts were still racing, and ideas were coming to me that were just plain odd—for example, a detailed plan of how I was going to become the President of the United States. I was agitated too, but I didn't realize it at the time, and I made a few enemies that week at work. As the week progressed I found myself keeping later hours at work and staying up late at night doing prayer walks.

I felt like I had a newfound "gift" from God that allowed me to function well on just a few hours of sleep. Every day that week I woke up at around three o'clock in the morning. That Sunday, I headed over to the local park to pray. Prayer walks were common for me, and this day was no different, or so it seemed at the time. Suddenly, while I was praying in the park, I heard my wife, Diane, scream out to me in panic. I ran all the way home, fearing the worst, but when I got there everyone was sleeping soundly, including Diane.

I chalked it up to an overactive imagination and woke everyone up to get ready for church. During the service, I felt a need to be heard, so I went forward to the podium and began to pray for President Clinton. I felt that Clinton needed our prayers because of his impeachment troubles. The pastor asked me to step down. Of course neither the pastor nor anyone else understood that I was experiencing mania.

When I left the church things started getting really weird. I took my five children to one of the Bible study rooms. While we were there, one of the kids wanted to use the restroom, but none was accessible. I checked the sanctuary of the main church building, but it was locked. Someone had probably accidentally locked it as they left. I was disappointed that the church would be locked, and my mind became fixated on that thought. In my mind, I related the locked door to access to God. I could not conceive of any reason to prevent access to the church, even during non-church hours. I believed that the sanctuary of a church should be available because access to God should always be available too.

Outside, I felt a sense of dread, for some reason, and became afraid for my son's life. I also felt that I needed to get a copy of a Barbie game on CD for my daughter. She had been talking about the game, and it seemed linked to saving my son's life somehow. I called several stores from my cell phone to see if the CD was available, with no luck. I called my sister to ask if her daughter had a copy of the CD. I was told that she did, so I told her that I would stop by her house immediately. As we continued our conversation on my cell phone, I asked her to call the whole family together right away. She agreed. I also asked her to contact my mom and dad. My sister knew something was wrong, and was concerned that something was terribly wrong with my daughter. My wife, Diane, and our five kids proceeded with me to my sister's house. According to Diane, I was speaking in riddles for some reason, which was both annoying and scary for my family. On my trip back from Chicago, I realized that I had not one good memory of my father and mother together, so I suppose I was hoping to create a memory of them together, and I did, although not the kind of memory I was hoping for.

Arriving at her home with my family, I was determined to get the Barbie game on CD. After the family showed up, I tried to explain what was going on, and asked all my family to hug one another. I'm sure I sounded confused, and everyone except me knew that something was very wrong. It was the classic mania scenario—we often feel fine when we're manic, and we don't see the problem otherwise.

That day was one of the few times I can remember my father caring in an important way, and in fact he may have saved my life that night. Following the visit at my sister's house, my father and I drove off and talked. I practically bludgeoned him with the good news of the gospel as I forcefully tried to convert him to Christianity. The gospel was written to tell us of the good news that Jesus Christ died to pay for our sins and give us eternal life and hope. Despite my obviously agitated state, he was very patient with me, and even seemed understanding.

We drove to the Catholic Church that I had attended until I was about the age of twenty. My dad wanted me to talk to a priest, thinking a priest would help convince me that I needed to see a doctor. I then did an about face and suggested we go instead to a non-denominational church that I had been attending in a neighboring city, and we drove there. The leaders seemed concerned, but I kept yelling, "My dad is going to hell for not accepting Christ." I could not understand their apparent lack of concern about him. We left the church; I was determined to talk to Sal, a church leader whom I respected. Sal met my father and me at a diner, where the three of us discussed the strange events of the day.

I did not like what I heard from my dad and Sal. They were implying that something was wrong with me because of my behavior. My pager went off, so I got up to return the call. It was Diane, who wanted me to get milk on the way home. She was hoping the request for milk would get me right home, without letting on that she suspected that something was terribly wrong with me. I went to the diner register, picked up a small milk to go, then ran from the building and down the street. I felt a strong urgency to get home immediately. Diane's page was actually for me to go to the grocery store and pick up a large carton of milk for the family, and I don't know why I responded like I did.

As I ran down the main street, Sal pulled up beside me and asked me to get into the car. I agreed, but only if he would take me home. When I got in, Sal said he was taking me back to see my dad, and that I needed to talk to him. I told him if he didn't stop and let me out, I would jump. It wasn't until I opened the door that he realized I was serious, so he stopped the car. I was angry that he didn't take me home like he said he would. It felt like betrayal, a theme that would cause me to mistrust every-one that night.

Sal pulled over and I got out, but the encounter did not end there. As I continued down the road—walking this time— Sal began yelling at me to get into the car. He said they had called the police. There was great anger in his voice, and I was shocked to see what looked like a "demon" in his face. I had seen the same look in the faces of all of the church leaders that night. I had not seen it in my father's face, though. It's interesting that they and I were all "born again" Christians and my father was not.

I ran across the main road, right in front of a big truck. I waved for it to stop, hoping for a ride. The driver just drove on, no doubt wondering who this waving, yelling maniac was. I ducked into a post office. I felt like a fugitive. More than anything, I just wanted to go home and sleep. I tried calling a friend from the pay phone at least a dozen times, but kept getting an unfamiliar out-of-service tone that I had never heard before that night or after. I don't even know which events of that day actually occurred, but I remember them like they were all real.

I called Diane and asked her to pick me up. She sounded very worried, but she promised to come. She sent her father instead. I was determined to go to a street called "The Lord's Way." I'm pretty sure my father-in-law thought I was out of my mind, but there really is a street called "The Lord's Way," which is located in a city about two hours from my home. I had friends who had considered buying a house there. Weeks later, after my release from the hospital, I even went there and took pictures of the street sign, just to prove that I had not made it up.

To my father-in-law's credit, he is a man of his word, and he refused to promise to take me to "The Lord's Way", so I ran from him, too. I started looking for a place where I could hide and sleep. I found a quiet street where I could lay down behind a house beside some bushes. I tried that for awhile, but got too impatient and decided to try to find someone to let me use their phone. I went from house to house seeing which one might let me use their phone and no one ever answered their doors. I even found a house with its front door wide open but no one was home, it seemed. I resisted the temptation and did not go in. After awhile with no success, I decided to leave and go to another street because I was afraid someone would notice me and call the police.

It wasn't long before the police found me. When the police officer got out of the car he asked me to identify myself and I refused. I did not do this to give him a hard time; I just wanted him to make a commitment to me first. I asked the officer if he would promise to take me home. I told him that I was tired and needed rest, which was all true. I said that if he promised to do that, I would tell him who I was. I was somewhat afraid at that point and really just wanted to go home and sleep. He was reluctant, and after I repeated my request, over several minutes and at least a half dozen times, he finally agreed and promised he would take me home. I reached out to shake the officer's hand, and that's when the trouble began. The handshake to me represents a man or woman's word that they will do as they say, sort of a pledge, so to speak. I already felt betrayed by the church, its leaders, my wife and my father-in-law. I wanted desperately to trust the police officer to take me home and to shake on it. I was relieved that he finally agreed to do so, verbally. I then needed the confirmation of his word and I wanted him to shake on it.

As I reached out to shake the hand of the officer, he then unexpectedly reached for my hand and then quickly drew back. I think I shouted out, "Who can I trust in this city?" As far as I was concerned at the time, there was absolutely no one. The officer then lunged at my throat with his hand. I could feel the nails of his fingers dig in as he throttled my neck. I was afraid he wanted to kill me and I was desperately full of terror. I had never experienced anyone do such a thing to me like this. I began to feel a choking sensation and thought I was going to be strangled. At the same time several other police officers grabbed me from behind, pulling my arms forcefully to the left and to the right while removing my jacket and frisking me in search of a weapon. I hadn't even noticed that they were there. It was at this point that I was certain they were going to kill me. I saw such a horrible look of evil in the face of the officer who had grabbed my throat. The police were yelling at me, trying to get me to acknowledge my identity. I had never seen police officers in person that were as angry as they were, especially the one who gripped my neck. I refused to speak to him. I was afraid my life would be taken from me if I did. I was handcuffed and put in the back of the police car. As I got into the car, I literally thought, "Today my life will be taken from me," and I wondered if that was God's plan.

As I sat down on the cold, hard seat of the police car, my hands hurt as the handcuffs tightened. My instinct told me I needed to be quiet. I believed that if I revealed my identity, something would happen to my son by an evil source. This was similar to my concerns earlier in the day about my son. I finally agreed to talk to one of them. I said I would speak to the officer who restrained me on my right. Somehow I knew he was safe and that he would understand. The officer was, in fact, a Christian and spoke to me as though he knew that I was also a Christian and that I was familiar with the Apostle Paul from the Bible, who endured many hardships from authorities and handled each incident in an accepting and humble way.

I can appreciate that the police officers who showed up at the scene had no idea what to expect. Their challenge was to apprehend me safely. What they knew was that it was after midnight and I was a man dressed in a suit who was resisting arrest; I was wandering around a quiet neighborhood and I was extending my hand from my side as if to brandish a weapon. I was where I was not supposed to be. As officers go out on calls, it must create a great deal of anxiety and fear at times. Law Enforcement has some very serious challenges to provide safety for everyone involved and to do so in a respectful way. They had no idea whether I had a weapon or not and they did not know if I would provoke them in some way, which could result in a lethal response to my actions.

My encounter with the police turned out to be relatively benign, however the very same type of incident could have been deadly. I am thankful to be alive. There have been several shootings by officers in different areas of the United States, in which persons suffering from bipolar disorder have been killed. My mom's friend had a brother who had bipolar disorder, and he was shot to death in my own city a few years ago. His bizarre behavior resulted in a dangerous situation and ultimately he was shot by a law enforcement person. I think this happens because our behavior in a manic state is sometimes erratic and unpredictable and most assuredly scary to the officers who are protecting us.

I was once at a community mental health reform meeting to help the mentally ill and heard a police captain shout out in a moment of compassion, "We don't shoot criminals!" What he meant was that it is the *mentally ill* or those with bipolar, like me, who end up getting shot. I think this is due to lack of understanding. The meeting was geared toward creating a greater awareness of mental health needs and providing new and innovative solutions.

By now you have no doubt noticed the recurring spiritual references and symbolism throughout my manic episode. It is important to note that, for twenty years, my life has had a strong religious and spiritual theme. Many persons who have been manic have also had highly spiritual experiences and encounters with God while manic; interestingly, some of these individuals did not even believe in God.

The policeman I chose to speak to asked me some questions, then took me to the county emergency psychiatric facility. I told him I would not enter the building voluntarily, that he was taking me there against my will. I yelled at the attending doctor, "How can you, a blind person, give sight to the seeing?" which I think made her angry. A linebacker-sized security guard came out to greet me. He pulled me gently past the doorway. Again I felt it necessary to honor my conviction and not comply with their requests. I did not mean to cause trouble. I felt that I had to offer at least token resistance or I would somehow be in danger.

What happened next surprised and confused me. I was taken to a solitary room, containing only a narrow bed fitted with restraining straps. I could not understand why they wanted to tie me down like an animal. I cooperated nonetheless and lay on the bed so they could strap down my hands and feet. Once strapped in, it was nearly impossible to move. I don't like to feel confined and I was scared.

I concentrated on ignoring the fact of being tied down, which is not an easy thing to do. The bright fluorescent lighting kept flickering, and I was becoming very agitated. I just wanted to go to sleep. I asked if they would turn the light out so I could sleep, but they refused. Hospital protocol apparently requires that the lights stay on when patients are restrained so they can be monitored by staff.

After about an hour, they took me out of the restraints and let me out of the room. I asked where I would sleep. They told me I could sleep on the floor, on a four-inch pad. I was angry; how could they treat people this way? I lost what little composure I had managed to regain and told the staff what I thought of them. I felt that what they were doing to me was inhumane. I told them that if I were a dog the humane society would close them down. To this day, I cannot understand why I was treated so disrespectfully. Losing control of our mental faculties doesn't mean we don't deserve to be treated with respect and dignity. Patients have the right to be informed as to what steps are being taken on their behalf and why. Recently I learned that the hospital now has beds for the men's emergency psychiatric services, "EPS" intake.

My complaining and resisting did not improve my situation. Later that day, I was moved to a hospital in a nearby city. As a precautionary measure, they tied me to the gurney while transporting me. I was determined to make a point that I was being moved against my wishes. A person named Peter, who admitted me to the EPS unit and had treated me kindly, said he thought I was going to be released. When the doctor told me otherwise, I became upset. I asked the doctor to bring Peter in and said that if Peter agreed with the doctor, I would accept their assessment. When my request was denied, I asked for a second opinion from another doctor, which was also denied. I could not understand why; second opinions are always available for physical illnesses and diagnoses. I thought the doctor had it in for me because I wasn't nice to him. It seems as though patients suffering from bipolar and others with mental illnesses are treated with less respect compared to patients with physical illnesses.

Later, a man came up to me and shook my hand. He was a handsome young man whose name I never learned. His kindness moves me to tears even now, as I type these words. I was so incredibly scared and felt so abandoned by everyone. This young man told me that everything would be OK. It's amazing how much a simple handshake can mean. It symbolizes a bond of trust. I reached out to shake the policeman's hand to offer my trust, which was immediately violated. As this young man reached out to me, I felt as though an angel of love had finally been sent to offer me encouragement. He appeared to be a humble man. Peace was evident on his face and apparently he was being dismissed after occupying the very room that was to become my own. It was because of his simple act of kindness that I began to trust again. My life has often been touched by individuals I refer to as "angels." I will never forget them, and hope to be an angel to others.

Late that first evening, I was desperately looking for a sign as to what I should do next. I was scared and very confused; I didn't know I was in a manic state. I felt an urge to strip naked and mark my body with toothpaste and soap. I carefully marked my chest and stomach with symbols of the cross as if preparing my body for a ritual of the dead, then lay down on the bed under a single sheet, thinking that the building was going to burn down. I eventually fell asleep.

The next morning I felt as though I were paralyzed. No matter how hard I tried, I could not regain consciousness. It was as though I were dead. It was a frightening moment. I felt as if I had risen from the dead. I had many experiences with illegal drugs in my youth, including a few bad ones. Strangely, it was legally prescribed drugs that created the worst of all my experiences and seemed to nearly cost me my life, at least, it felt that way to me. I had been given mood stabilizing drugs and a sleeping pill the previous night. I believe that an interaction between the drugs — or perhaps simply receiving excessive dosages — was responsible for my severe reaction.

The next day, I looked for a Bible. I searched high and low, but could not find one in the ward library. There were several hundred books, but not one Bible. What I did find shocked me: a book entitled *How to Get Away with Murder*. Many of those with whom I later shared this discovery thought I might have been delusional. Diane even questioned whether I remembered it clearly. So, after my hospitalization, I did an internet search for the book and found that it does in fact exist. Perhaps it was a fictional story or a mystery novel. At one point during my stay, I met a man who tried to kill his wife prior to being admitted. It seemed like a highly inappropriate book for a psych unit, the title alone could spark ideas.

When I showed the murder book to the staff, they took it away from me and someone returned later with a small Gideon's Bible. I believe that this Bible may have belonged to someone in the hospital. I loved that Bible. When I opened it, I found that particular scriptures had been underlined, and they all had such profound meaning to me. It has been the only Bible that I ever considered stealing. It was quite precious to me. It was also the only Bible I saw in the ward during my stay.

Once I had the privilege to help a friend distribute Bibles to high school students. My friend told me that hotels welcome Gideon Bibles because they want to avoid suicides, and they figure Bibles might be that last thread to which someone experiencing a profoundly depressive moment might cling. It was amazing to me that Bibles were not available in a psychiatric hospital, as so many who wind up there are suicidal. Perhaps this is something the medical profession might consider. I recommend having the Bible on hand as a preventive measure in your own bipolar management, and that is why one of the chapters in this book includes Bible scriptures that may be meaningful to you.

The patients in the ward were wonderful. It seemed as though, through their emptiness, they met a need inside me. It's difficult to explain, but they were a wonderful blessing. The people I met and talked with were some of the finest people I have ever met. They were very open, eager to listen and offer helpful advice.

After my "three day hold" in the Psych unit was over, and since I was on "good behavior," I was allowed to go outside to a less secured environment. Being confined indoors had been very difficult. I was used to being outside every day and walking a lot, and I was annoyed that the ward did not have a secure area outside. There was no way to get outdoors for those three days.

While in Chicago I had smoked my first Cuban cigar with a friend from work. In the hospital I dreamed about having a great cigar like that again. I didn't even smoke much, but I wanted a cigar. Cigars somehow had a new meaning in my mind, probably symbolizing freedom.

Each morning in the hospital, we had a morning check-in after breakfast. One morning I heard one of the staff mention to someone who had a drinking problem that a video tape was available that might help that person better understand alcoholism. I asked if there was a tape on bipolar disorder, and there was. I thought it was odd that I was not offered this video earlier, given that I was newly diagnosed. It was all part of what I perceived as less than acceptable patient courtesy. A friend suggested that even if they had offered the tape to me, I probably wouldn't have understood what I was viewing. The comment was troubling. I imagine a cancer patient would have trouble viewing a tape on cancer the first time, too.

I watched the tape on bipolar disorder, and I did benefit from it. I still had not completely accepted my diagnosis, but for the first time I realized that I might actually have bipolar disorder. Acceptance was a difficult process, but here was a source of objective information describing my illness. I could watch the tape and make my own decision instead of having people with unknown qualifications tell me what was wrong with me. It was perhaps the first step in the process that helped me recognize that I might have bipolar disorder. I also realized that other bipolar patients could benefit from viewing this videotape, as many of them were also newly diagnosed. No doubt they, like me, were also grappling with little or no understanding of their illness.

Whenever a new bipolar patient joined the ward, I suggested that they watch the video with me. One day, five people joined me. We even had a group meeting afterward which I led. I was simultaneously proud of my efforts and confused as to why the ward staff was doing nothing. Since my hospitalization,

I have shared this video with many people. I encourage you to seek out videos, books, and whatever additional information you can find to help you to better understand your illness.

Since my "three day hold" began following my Sunday admission, I was expecting to leave on Wednesday. What I did not know is that "three day hold" does not necessarily imply release on the third day. The doctors decide whether you're well enough to leave. At about ten o'clock that evening, dressed and ready to leave, I went to the front desk for discharge. I went through my entire story with the night shift personnel, beginning with my being detained by police, up through the present moment.

The people behind the desk called security. I was civil, but they were not about to let me leave. I was confused and afraid. I was at the end of my rope. I cried and I prayed to God for help. Right on cue, one of the security guards came over to talk to me. He reminded me that the Apostle Paul had to accept his situation. I agreed to do likewise, believing that this man spoke with what I perceived as God's truth. He was another one of my angels. He even bought me a Coke. The staff workers seemed irked that I would listen to the security guard but not to them. People just don't understand the power of kindness and respect.

On Friday, my fifth day at the hospital, the doctor encouraged me to stay for fourteen more days. I could not even bear the thought and refused outright. I had learned that I had a legal right to a hearing on the matter, with a patient's advocate present. A judge would hear my "grievance" and decide whether my interests would be served by allowing a doctor to hold me against my will. During my hearing, the doctor had no legal reason to deny my right to refuse treatment. Although the judge had some concerns, she determined that there was no compelling reason for my further detainment.

Looking back, I can understand the doctor's concern; I was in fact quite ill at the time, with both mania and psychosis. Patient advocacy is important because there is always a risk of mental health providers abusing patients. Advocacy provides an important check on potential abuses and helps ensure patient safety. As the saying goes, information is power. Familiarize yourself with patient rights information in your state, so you'll be better prepared to protect your rights if the worst should happen. It is also important to have someone you trust to exercise good judgment and to be frank with you on matters of your safety and well being.

After the advocacy meeting, I was preparing to be released. I called Diane and asked her to come and get me. She said she would, but she did not. The doctor had called her and encouraged her to convince me to stay longer, while he tried to find a legal reason to keep me longer, against my will. When she finally showed up two hours later, I was very angry. She would not tell me why she was so late. I decided I would leave the hospital on my own. Diane was trying to talk me into staying, and she became hysterical. I had never seen my wife that way before.

At one point, Diane tried to physically prevent me from leaving. She grabbed me and would not let me go. I called for the security guard, insisting that I had a right to leave because I had already been released from the hospital and that she needed to be restrained so that I could leave. I told the security guard that we were going to get a divorce, so he complied with my request. As I was leaving, my doctor came in. Diane shouted in a horrified and panicky voice, "Don't let him go!" The doctor told her that she could call the emergency line, 9-1-1. The hospital could not hold me legally, but in an emergency situation, I could be brought back. The security guard restrained her. Later I learned that she was horrified and thought that she would never see me again because I was still manic.

I fled the hospital, once again feeling like a fugitive. I was confused because I had had a hearing, and the doctor's order to extend my stay for fourteen days had been overturned. I did not understand my rights, but have since learned that the police cannot automatically detain a person because of a wife's concern. However, I did not know it at that time, and my reserve of trust for any type of official was extremely low at that point.

As I expected, Diane did call the police. I boarded a near-by train headed toward my home and discovered that the police had even notified the train crew. Onboard the train, I heard a dispatch alerting the crew. I got off at the station near my home and called a friend that I trusted. I told him I needed his help and he came to pick me up. We then met another friend. I shared with them my recent experiences and told them I needed to get out of town. They were quite sympathetic. I asked them not to tell anyone that I was there and they agreed. They supplied me with a briefcase and another small bag.

My friend, Frank, took me to the airport where I rented a car. I then headed to a cell phone store and bought a Motorola StarTAC phone with all the bells and whistles. I was determined never to be without a cell phone again so I could get help when I needed it. Then I headed for the mountains. I stopped on the way to get a new set of clothes to make it harder for the police to identify me. I was not sure to what extent police in surrounding areas would be notified. My concerns manifested from my paranoia and fear and, of course, the events of the day.

It was late in the day when I arrived in Rescue, California. I had visited the town a week before I was hospitalized, and there I had encountered a wonderful feeling of the Lord's presence. It felt peaceful and calm, and on the following day I visited a realtor. She took me to a large ranch that overlooked the Sierra Nevada. Looking out the kitchen window, I was enthralled by the gorgeous view. It was the nicest home and property I had ever seen. I put an offer on the house immediately. The asking price was 1.1 million dollars, and I offered them one hundred thousand dollars over the asking price, another result of my mania. The sellers had had no other offers, and the market was in a slump. I convinced them that the house was worth their previous selling price and that I would not pay them any less than its true value. Of course they did not argue with me, and they were happy to accept the higher amount. Fortunately my wife was able to withdraw my bid a few weeks later, after realizing the impracticality of my purchase.

After buying my dream house, I checked into a motel. I called Diane and told her I would be home the next day, but did not tell her where I was. I told her I had purchased a lottery ticket and expected to win with absolute certainty—another mania-fueled grandiose idea. That night I left the TV on all night. I half expected it to speak to me personally. I was feeling paranoid, worried that the police would get me and that someone might hurt me.

The next day, I went to find Frank's sister. I had visited her in the hospital a week or so earlier. She was dying of cancer. Even though I had no idea where she lived, I drove all over the area, winding up just a few blocks away from where she was staying. As I was driving, I would hear clues. The most frequent clues seemed to come from my CD player; as the song played, the track would skip, causing a word to play over and over again. This seemed to happen when I needed another sign and I would identify the word as a clue. Sometimes I went into shops or even asked people for directions.

I stopped at a church for a morning service and put all of my cash into the offering plate, as well as the lottery tickets that I "knew" were going to win. At another point, I went into a movie theater and watched a movie I felt I needed to watch for some reason, and then left after watching it for only half an hour. Both the movie and the church seemed to be related to my quest to find my friend's sister. After leaving the theater, I called Frank and asked him how to get to his sister Francine's house. Then I called him again to get her number so I could call and ask if I could stop by. She was surprised that I managed to go across several cities to wind up just a block or so away from where she lived. She said I could stop in. While we visited I shared my situation and she prayed for me. Her kindness and prayers were comforting, and I felt at peace when I left her home.

After leaving the house, I became concerned about my blood pressure because I felt unusual. I could feel my heart racing, something I had never noticed before, so I went to a hospital emergency room, still in a manic delusional state. I waited at the hospital for hours and never did get in. While there I talked with numerous people and prayed for them. I met a police officer whose partner had been injured, so I prayed for her. Another person I talked with had a loved one who was having emergency heart surgery. Another was looking at some lottery tickets. I just knew he was one of the winners. I never confirmed it, but I did learn that the winner of that week's lottery was from that area. It was interesting. It was as though my manic state gave me special perceptual abilities. I even escorted a blind man into the emergency patient rooms to visit another man who I assumed was his father. I felt like I had a purpose there, a purpose to touch lives.

After leaving the emergency room, I headed for home. I dropped by my sister's house, which was about half way. I wanted to smoke a cigar with my brother-in-law. I am not sure why, but since my earlier hospital stay, I wanted to smoke and celebrate with cigars. The lights were on, and it appeared that they were home, but they never answered the door. Perhaps they were not home after all.

When I got home, Diane had put on something very nice to keep me there and it seemed that she wanted to be intimate with me. She was afraid that if I left I might never return because I was still highly manic and I could easily get hurt or killed. I was highly agitated and did not want to be intimate at that time, but I did stay home and went to bed. Diane was happy that I was getting some desperately needed sleep. The next morning, my older brother showed up at my house. I didn't think anything of it, even though it was Monday morning and he should have been at work. He and I went for a ride in my rental car, had a fast-food lunch, and then went to see a psychiatrist. I actually wanted to see the doctor because I was concerned about my heart rate, which seemed a bit erratic the previous day.

I had seen the same doctor while having difficulty with a family member years earlier. I thought he could help me because he had been helpful to me before. Diane and my brother talked to the doctor, who didn't seem to even listen to me. Eventually he wrote me up for a 5150, or "three day hold." He wanted to know if I would go to the hospital voluntarily or if I needed to go in an ambulance.

I insisted that his call for another three-day hold had no merit. I believe he wrote me up as unable to take care of myself. I had just traveled to the mountains, stayed two nights, and bought clothes and food. It is also true that I had just put a bid on an expensive ranch home and was convinced that I was going to win the lottery, but I thought that the doctor had no legal right to detain me and he did so falsely. In hindsight, I believe he stretched the truth to help me as he saw fit. It does beg the question, though: should a psychiatrist violate a patient's rights to help the patient? Can there be a "greater good" that justifies violating someone's basic rights? Looking back, I realize that I was in desperate need of help. Unfortunately, while the doctor's actions may have in fact helped me, they may have also aggravated my condition. I told him that I would only go to the hospital via ambulance because I was going against my will, and I would not support his methods.

The ambulance came and took me to the hospital. I was very cooperative and was admitted; however, I was very angry with Diane. She not only called the police on me a few days earlier, she also took me to the psychiatrist and convinced him to send me back to the hospital. I was fuming with anger, and as soon as I had a chance, I called a lawyer to see about getting a divorce.

Later, I discussed my situation with some other patients. One man, Tom, told me that he had tried to kill his wife. It seemed ironic that this same person suggested that my wife was probably operating out of fear and most likely only did what she did for my own safety. A woman, Susan, who was listening to our conversation provided comforting words and recommended trying to overcome my anger. Talking with Tom and Susan helped me see where my wife was coming from. Later that evening I went to my room and prayed. My prayer was simple: "God, please take the anger from me. I am not able to do it myself." By morning my anger was gone. It felt like a miracle had occurred.

I don't remember much about the week that followed. I do remember wanting to use the shower and noticing a woman staff person go in before me with a pair of scissors. I still see those scissors vividly in memory today. I don't know whether it was a hallucination or reality. Several patients thought some of the hospital staff were playing mind games, and I had no idea whether this was true or not. The memory lines up with many of the paranoid complaints that the patients had about the hospital staff that worked on the ward.

From conversations with other patients and my wife, I realized that Diane was afraid for my life. Family members came to visit me and I noticed that my mom, my daughter, and my son all had fever blisters, and my other son had hives. I also seemed to know that I had to cooperate with the doctors so that Diane would feel comfortable bringing me home. It is important to keep in mind that loved ones do not know how to react to us when mania sets in. In my wife's case, she feared that I might hurt her or myself. By seeking help to minimize mood swings, those of us who have bipolar disorder can create a better quality of life for ourselves and for our loved ones.

After I was released, I agreed to attend outpatient classes every few days. The idea was to get training for a few basic skills to help with managing bipolar. The classes included a doctor's visit and would evaluate how I was doing and prescribe drugs as needed. The class seemed helpful, although I was unable to get into the follow-up class, "Managing Bipolar Disorder," which I would later regret.

I was on disability for about three weeks. When I returned to work I learned that I had lost my high-level management job. I was devastated. I was unable to tell my manager what was going on because I was so ashamed. Human Resources was no help at all. All I could think of was that I was now bipolar and that I just went manic. I was filled with shame and now I had lost my job. I now realize that I was fortunate just to have a job, even if it was just a run-of-the-mill management position.

I was depressed for an entire year. My boss seemed angry with me, and our relationship never returned to what it had been prior to my manic episode. I think the stigma surrounding bipolar disorder was partially to blame. The company's HR employees also seemed to judge me in an uncaring way. Human resources departments are supposed to keep this type of medical situation private, but they didn't, and in my opinion my boss was prejudiced after he learned of my illness.

My first manic episode and first diagnosis of bipolar disorder changed my life significantly. Since my youth I have carried a lot of shame, which was intensified by this episode. I also carried the results of numerous traumatic events, which were also a great burden on me. My manic episode was a traumatic event in itself, precipitated, in my opinion, by a heavy emotional load. I went into the manic experience feeling that I could trust no one. When I returned to work, I lost my job, which only added to the burden. Following my manic episode, I was not even sure I actually had bipolar disorder after all. And if I was not bipolar, I had no need for medication. It was this reasoning that, a year and a half later caused me to stop all medications, and which resulted in a nearly fatal psychotic manic episode.

BIPOLAR EXPERIENCE

I cry and I cry, how could this be?
Have I been abandoned by my God who loves me?
Medications and diagnosis, denial, pain and shame
Daunting experiences, who is to blame?

A new diagnosis; today, I am ashamed
How could God have made me this way?
Hospitals strip me of my pride and dignity
Their espoused love provokes me to insanity

Fear for my life, confusion, dignity stripped away
Tied to a bed, trapped and confined, why is this OK?
Love, where are you, why are you absent from this place?
My heart is bleeding, in need of healing, I cry for God's grace

Intensity of feeling both high and low
Feeling the glory of God while standing at the gates of Hell below
At my lowest point, God hears my cry!
Sending love to my empty soul through an angel nearby

From the depths of sorrow and tragedy
To the heights of God's heavenly throne
I learned that I am not only loved by God
But that I am one of His own

—David Mariant

CHAPTER 3

From Depression to Manic Relapse

If depression is creeping up and must be faced,
learn something about the nature of the beast:
You may escape without a mauling.

—Dr. R. W. Shephard

I was shaken after my recent manic episode, and also as a result of losing the assignment that had meant so much to me. Going manic cost me my job and it was the best job I had ever had. I was a high level manager who interacted with VPs and even the President and CEO of the Fortune 500 company I worked for. I felt like a complete failure and wondered if I would ever regain the respect I had once enjoyed in the company. I believe I was out of work for about four weeks from the time I went manic to the time I returned to work. How could I conceal the fact that I was manic and diagnosed with bipolar disorder? I was too embarrassed to tell my boss what had happened to me. Of course he was angry. I wasn't sure what the personnel department had told him about why I had been gone nearly a month. I tried to explain to the personnel department and to my boss that I had joined the company specifically for the job they had just taken away from me. I felt trapped. On one hand I felt that their taking my job was wrong and that I should leave the company. On the other hand, I felt discouraged and depressed, and I was not up to looking for another job.

In hindsight, it might have been better to have shared with my employer what had happened, but I was afraid I would look like a freak. It would have been helpful if the human resources department had been a little more sensitive to my situation and aware of how to handle a person diagnosed with bipolar disorder. I was disappointed about how things were handled, and perhaps if I had just told my boss what was going on things may have worked out better.

My boss brought in a replacement project manager while I was in the hospital. He didn't even want me in his group any longer. That hurt and further enforced the idea that I was a failure. In all fairness, I had let him down in the worst way. It was a 20 million dollar project, one of the largest contracts the company had at the time, and I was the program manager. My boss found himself in a very awkward situation, and I am sorry for that. I have often wondered what he thought happened to me—whether I was in jail, on drugs or alcohol, or who knows what. To this day, I have never told him what really happened.

With bipolar disorder, we often hurt others and our relationships, and then we move on. We often fail to reconcile the past. When we do that, we carry not only the burden of the illness, but also the havoc that we leave in our wake. At the time I was unfamiliar with the Americans with Disabilities Act (ADA), which affords some protection, but at that point and even today—I find it hard to think of myself as "disabled."

Today I am grateful that the company did not fire me, although it was hard to see it that way at the time because I was angry. Fortunately, a VP brought me into his group and created new opportunities for me, but it was difficult to get motivated to do my job. Working from home, it took a great deal of effort to even get out of bed unless there was something I absolutely had to get up for. Having obligations and appointments has always helped motivate me, and making early morning appointments helped me get my day going. Working from home was clearly a mistake because I had very little contact with people and had too much time to stew and be depressed. I also found myself taking responsibility for few if any assignments that came up and would allow my peers to take them on instead. It seemed like everything I did was setting me up for further and further despair and hopelessness, and most of all a sense that I wasn't needed and that I was a failure. Losing my high level job was very difficult for me and it took me a very long time to forgive myself.

The depression began immediately after my bipolar diagnosis a few weeks after the bizarre mania wore off. I felt that I could not face anyone, including my wife. One of the most difficult things to deal with was the sense that I no longer felt like myself. With all the medications, it was like being in someone else's mind and body. I was afraid that I would never be creative or myself again. There appears to be some connection between creativity and bipolar disorder. Mood-stabilizing medications can sometimes strip away the creativity that is a significant part of the personalities of those with bipolar disorder. Some of my friends with bipolar disorder have suggested that I might never be creative again. That certainly didn't brighten my spirits. All my life, I have been creative and artistic, and I identified strongly with those qualities. Without them, it was as though part of me had died.

It seemed as though I could not count on anything at all. I could not even count on being the person I was yesterday. It was clear that I very likely would need medication for the rest of my life. I hated myself because of the mania and for losing myself to the illness. I was depressed, and even worse, I was grieving the death of my person, my very soul, and the uncertainty of who I had become. In the course of one day, a life that seemed fine was destroyed in a blink by a manic attack — or so it seemed.

I was deeply depressed for a year. I was on lithium for mood stabilization but I was still very depressed. As a younger person I experienced the negative effects of illegal drugs including dangerous side affects, and since then, I have never wanted any substance in my body that I did not need, so I was slow to accept any medication changes. Because of this it was a much longer process for me to achieve an optimum level and combination of medications that would best help me. This probably prolonged my depression, which was deep for about a year, until my doctor added Lamictal.

Now, several years after I was diagnosed and on medication, I have slowly regained some of my creativity and a greater sense of who I am, mainly through writing and poetry. This loss of creativity is important to talk about because many people with bipolar want to stop taking their medication because of it. With regular effort though, creative talents can eventually be regained. It has happened for me, so if you are in this situation, please don't give up on yourself. Don't stop taking your bipolar medication without first having a discussion with your doctor.

Following my diagnosis, I faced a number of challenges, and I carried around a great deal of shame and guilt. When I couldn't even crawl out of bed to do my job, the guilt just kept growing. I had previously been an aggressive and a highly productive person. What on earth happened to me? At corporate and sales meetings, I would literally hide in a corner. My manic episode and sudden disappearance from work was visible to all of the higher-ups in the company, which only added to my shame and sense of being "defective." The days and months following my diagnosis were tricky and uncertain. At the time, there was no one to guide me or tell me that I was going to be all right.

Bipolar disorder has been a constant struggle to know who I am. Most people take for granted knowing who they are. I have to think about my basic identity every single day. It's unsettling to say the least. It can certainly shift my outlook on any given day. Understanding that I am not my bipolar disorder and not the sum of all my failures, has been difficult. If you or a loved one is struggling with the illness, it is useful to think about how difficult it can be to separate oneself from the illness. Later in the book, I will talk more about the topic of personal identity.

Understanding myself in a more loving and compassionate way is key to surviving bipolar disorder. If you struggle with self-acceptance, know that most of us with bipolar disorder share this challenge. I don't think a day goes by that I don't have negative thoughts rolling around in my head, thoughts that often bring me down. Ultimately, we choose the thoughts that we want to listen to. By recognizing negative self-talk and exercising self-discipline, I have achieved greater happiness simply by focusing on thoughts that bring me peace and hope. This is tough to do. It is time consuming and difficult to shut out negative thoughts and focus only on the positive ones, but it's worth the effort—even if you're only partially successful. Being involved in enjoyable activities and projects can help create positive thoughts, and positive thinking breeds more positive thinking.

It was a simple home improvement project that turned the tide for me and lifted me out of my depression. We were living in our second home, which I had fully remodeled, just as I had with our first home. We had full landscaping done, and the only thing left to do was install the perimeter watering system and plant flowers and other small plants. I don't remember what got me started. The weather was nice one day and I just started working. There was a lot of physical labor involved in digging the holes and trenches, but there was also an opportunity to be creative. I knew this project was something I could enjoy, and that's why it was so important to me.

Pursuing our passions is one of the best ways to work through depression. My landscaping project allowed me to indulge my passion, to think about how things can be improved and then go about improving them. Of course, indulging our passions means we need to know what they are, and the best time to think about them is when we are not depressed. When we are in a depression, it's difficult to see anything but darkness and hopelessness. It's hard to think about anything that ever brought us pleasure. Unfortunately, depression throws us into a "black hole" and the prospect of staying in that dark place is overwhelming, often leading to suicidal thoughts. If we can just "hang on," things can and do get brighter and better—and I hope to show you how.

The assignment I had at work following my bipolar diagnosis was winding down. I felt like I had contributed little if anything, possibly even making things more difficult for others. I don't know if that was true, but that was how I felt. When I was delegated the task of renovating our department's website, I felt like I had one last chance to redeem myself and to make a contribution.

Although at first I was very excited about the website project, it turned out to be a very tough job. I felt that the project would make a huge difference to the company's financial future, and I began planning and talking with consultants. I enjoy working with others, and unfortunately, I made the mistake of involving a woman who was already working on the company's main website. The decision to include her in discussions would end up bringing me a great deal of stress, and ultimately, precipitating a second manic episode.

Because the company website was this woman's responsibility, she was reluctant to work with me and share company survey data. One day she even confronted me and became verbally abusive. In retrospect, it's hard to understand why I even tried to put up with her. My self-worth was very low at that point, and I believed that everything she said was probably true. We all have our own issues. She no doubt felt threatened by what she perceived as my encroachment on her turf.

At one point, I tried to involve my VP. He said he would intervene, but never did. I warned him that things would get worse if he did not step in, and they did. I could clearly read the writing on the wall. I was frustrated that he wouldn't take me seriously. The problem could have easily been prevented had my role in the project been clearly specified at the very beginning, but the stress was already mounting and my mood swing was in motion.

Being in the manic state can make it difficult to separate reality from fantasy. My second manic episode is still somewhat unclear to me as I try to recall the details, so I have invited my wife to share her recollections. During this period, I would walk my dog, Nikita, late every night. She is a beautiful and loving Siberian Husky with gray and white fur, who loves to run and play. Nikita is one of my best friends. It was a time of reflection and prayer. I remember making a pledge to the Lord. The pledge was what I refer to as the "A Knights Pledge." It had to do with giving over my life's purpose to the Lord for the benefit of God and others. I may or may not have been in a manic state at the time when I made this pledge. I do know that it's not uncommon for people who aren't bipolar to make such a pledge. My life went on a downward spiral for the second time just days after making that pledge. It began when I woke up at about 3:00 a.m. one night.

Diane: It was Sunday morning, and although I was very tired from staying up almost all night talking with my husband, we began to get ready for church. A voice in the back of my head kept telling me that going to church was a mistake, but I ignored it. David was acting a bit strange, but I convinced myself that there was nothing to fear.

I recall thinking that David was on his medicine, and that he could not possibly have gone off of it. After consulting with his doctor, we had agreed that if he ever felt that he wanted to try going off his prescription, that it would be a joint decision between the two of us. Still, I knew that something wasn't quite right.

David was jumping from one subject to another, connecting things in ways that apparently only he was able to comprehend. It was similar to the first time he went manic, but I again convinced myself that I was being silly to think that it could be happening again. David was just tired, and I figured he would take a good long nap when we got home and he would be fine. Looking back, I should have listened to that inner voice that told me to stay home, but it may have just delayed the inevitable.

Sitting in the Sunday school classroom at the new church we had been attending for a few months, I kept wondering where David had gone. He had simply left the class without a word. I felt I should go find him, but again convinced myself I was getting worried over nothing. He probably bumped into someone and was talking. He could talk for hours given the opportunity and an interesting subject to discuss. I just sat there and waited for him to return, even though that nagging voice was still telling me to get up and go find him.

Our son was in his church Sunday school classroom, when David opened the door and motioned for him to come out.

I later learned that, with tears streaming down his face, David took our son into the baptismal area, and pleaded for him to baptize David. Of course our son, not even ten years old, was very confused about his dad's request. How could a small boy baptize his dad? To make matters worse, a group of people watched this whole confusing event. They weren't sure what was going on, but did not interfere. They were there to practice the morning songs, so they played their instruments and sang worship songs while David stood in the baptismal pouring his heart out to our son.

After Sunday school, I went to look for David. I ran into the pastor, who asked if he could talk to me for a moment. He described what he had heard from the band members about the baptism incident. It was immediately clear to me that David was manic again. I told the pastor about David's illness. I had a sinking feeling that I should never have left David alone. Our children were already in their classes for the second service, so I decided to just sit down in a pew and hoped David would join me. I did not know what to do and I was scared. I prayed and cried the entire time, not hearing a word the pastor was saying. I jumped a bit when I felt a slight tap on my shoulder. Looking up, expecting to see David, I was surprised to see the deacon handing me David's car keys. He told me that David had dropped them off for me so that I could get home, and gave me the message that David was leaving to go on a trip and that he would see me later.

David: After the encounter with my son I decided to run home and get my motor home; at the time I didn't even know why. I remember that I felt a need to do this quickly to prevent Diane's opposition, though. It seemed like I was so into the present moment or event that I did not know what was to come. Each event I was experiencing made sense to me. It was like movie scenes going from one scene to another.

As I arrived home I began to back my thirty one foot motor home out of my side yard parking area when the vehicle's side mirror hit the fence. I struggled with this for a while and then asked my neighbor to help me. He was about eighty years old and could barely walk. I knew he could help me because he had a rig like mine years earlier, and in fact he did help me.

I decided to return to church in the motor home to give Diane the car keys to our car so she could drive home. I had run home so I would not leave her stranded at church without a car, but I still had the car keys. Because the church service had already started, I decided to give the keys to one of the leaders to give to my wife. I left them with a message that I was going on a trip. After doing so I got into the motor home, drove around the parking lot and drove from the church. I now was determined to drive to the cemetery for some reason. As I drove closer, I suddenly knew why I retrieved my motor home and why I was headed to the cemetery. I was now on a very important mission from God.

Diane: I ran from the church, not caring what kind of spectacle I was creating. When I got out the door, I could see David in our motor home pulling out of the parking lot. I chased him, actually running down the road for about a block, screaming and waving my arms. It was no use; I could not catch him. As he turned the corner and sped off, memories of the last time he went manic flooded my mind.

I walked back to church and collapsed on the lawn. I was desperate for help. As I sat there crying, I felt a hand on my shoulder. It was a man from church. I didn't know him at all, but I poured out my feelings to him anyway. We had tried so hard to keep David's illness to ourselves and not let our church family know about our struggles. Now here I was telling the whole story to someone I had only smiled at and taken a church program from once a week. His wife was there too, and they both listened as I told the whole story and asked them what I should do.

I eventually decided to have someone else drive the children home. I would go home and call the police and ask them to find David. I hoped that they could talk him into going to the hospital for a check-up. The nice couple went with me to the house. I still remember the loving care and concern in their faces.

David: I noticed that it was a beautiful California spring day and the sun was shining and the breeze was gentle. As I drove into the enormous cemetery, I drove near the plot where my brother Michael was laid to rest and parked my enormous vehicle along the tiny street. By this time I was heaving with uncontrollable sorrow and tears. I got out of the motor home and walked swiftly toward my brothers grave. I then proceeded to lay myself flat, face down on the ground with my hands outstretched and began to pray. I could taste the dirt and grass in my mouth and felt the residue of dirt and tears on my face. My brother Michael was one of the many dead souls that I was going to round up in my motor home. I was on a mission and determined to save the lost souls. This all seemed perfectly normal to me at the time.

I then arose and quickly walked over to the rows where children were buried. I noticed a few women standing thirty feet away from me or so and I could hear them talking. I am surprised now as I think back that they seemed to think everything was fine and that my laying down in front of each of the children's head stones and crying profusely was normal somehow. I wonder if they saw my motor home or me for that matter, because they didn't seem to care at all. Perhaps they were being polite. It would be interesting to know their thoughts now.

After my emotional experience and gathering up the dead souls, I realized I was hungry. I was in luck because there was food in our rig. I had a can of chili. We often stock our rig with food that can sustain our large family for several weeks. While I was eating I listened to the radio and for some reason believed I needed to drive to a city about seventy five miles away. As I left the cemetery, for whatever reason, I decided to go home. On my way home I stopped at a garage sale, of all things, and bought a picture of two angels smoking cigarettes. This seemed to represent to me the fallen angels and it was important to buy it at this time.

Diane: We were all surprised when David pulled into the driveway in the motor home. He did not understand why we were all so concerned about him, and was confused about what the police were doing at our house. He said he felt great. In fact, he had just successfully driven the motor home through the graveyard without a problem. The graveyard has narrow roads and a lot of turns that would be extremely difficult to maneuver a thirty foot motor home through, and yet David said that he did it without a problem. For a moment, I pictured toppled gravestones and statues and flowers strewn all over the road.

David was only willing to talk to one of the policemen present, and the two of them talked for quite a while. Meanwhile, our children arrived, and they all went quickly inside. I could see that they were scared. They were no doubt reliving the memory of the first time that their dad went manic. The police were not very successful getting David to agree to go to the hospital. They had no legal reason to detain him. He was not threatening anyone, did not appear unable to care for himself, or to be a danger to himself or other's, so they had no reason to forcibly take him to the hospital.

David came up with the idea of letting our son decide whether he would go to the hospital. He told our son that it was his decision, and that he would do whatever he decided was best. It upset me that he put our son in that position. It was clearly inappropriate for a child to make such a decision.

I pleaded with my son to tell his daddy to get some help. The confusing morning in the baptismal had been more than our son could comprehend, and now he needed to tell his daddy to go with the police. His eyes filled with tears as he told David that he wanted him to go with the police to the hospital. The policeman explained that, as a matter of protocol, they were required to handcuff him. It was very difficult to watch. As the police took his daddy away, I held my son tightly and told him that he had done the right thing. I sat for a long time after everyone left, wondering what I could have done to change the events of the day. I continued to wonder throughout the following week and as

I drove to the hospital to pick David up when he was released.

I had visited David a few times at the hospital. He acted strangely each time, and his behavior bothered me a great deal. Our pastor accompanied me on our first visit because I was too upset and too tired to make the drive on my own. David did jumping jacks almost the entire time we were there and talked to us about things that made no sense. During another visit, he played a tune on the piano over and over, and acted as though it were of great importance, as if he was trying to figure out what it meant.

On another occasion, I watched David put a difficult puzzle together just by looking at the pieces on the table, selecting the right one, and putting it in. It was as if he knew every piece and its position in the puzzle, with none of the trial and error that one would normally expect for this activity. I had never seen such a thing before. It was both fascinating and a bit scary to watch, and to this day, he has not been able to do it again.

David: I was never a fan of the hospital I had stayed at when hospitalized the first time a year and a half earlier. The difference between the hospital then and the one I was about to enter was like night and day. Out of my four hospitalizations, this was the only hospitalization during which my manic-psychotic state worsened. It could be that my mental state upon admission was different this time. The nursing staff was also on strike. The fill-in nurses were unaccustomed to the various tasks required, and the level of patient care was unacceptable.

As I was being moved from the ambulance to the hospital's receiving area, I pretended I was asleep. I don't know why I did this. Although I believe I was secured to the gurney, I seem to remember that I also put my arms and legs up, as though I was convulsing. In a few days, I would do the same thing again, prior to being transferred to yet another hospital. I was taken to an isolation room and strapped down to a bed—another encounter with four-point restraints.

Note to the reader: the following section contains graphic sexual content and descriptions of demonic fantasies.

Looking out the hospital window from the bed where I was restrained, I watched a cloud formation pass by, and actually felt that I could control the speed at which it moved across the sky. After a while, I called out for help because I needed to urgently use the bathroom. I heard a young woman in the next room also calling out for help and getting no response. It was degrading to be in the position of having to ask to go to the bathroom in the first place, and all the more so given the lack of response.

The staff finally came in to administer medications. I was angry that they wanted me to trust them to give me unwanted meds, and yet they would not trust me to decide when I needed to urinate. I just wanted a little respect. I thought they were negligent to make me wait so long. After using the restroom, I climbed back onto the bed and put my feet and hands back into the restraints. It was important to me to show them that I was making the decision to allow myself to be restrained, even though I thought their actions were wrong.

This manic episode was different from past episodes. I felt "outside" of myself—like an observer. Later, after my restraints were removed, I watched television, and saw subtitles with profanities moving across the screen. The subtitles seemed completely real to me at the time. I even went over to the television to see how it was hooked up, in order to discover how they were able to display the subtitles. I wondered how that was possible since I had no awareness of such things existing, and no one has ever told me about evil subtitles. What is interesting, is that I have learned that many people experience this phenomenon with television during manic and depressive episodes. During the hospitalization I also feared for my life. I thought my roommate was the devil and that he wanted to kill me. I prayed that he would return to God and ask for forgiveness for his sinful actions. I felt important in some way too, for doing this.

I stayed at the hospital for three days. It was a frightening experience, and I felt that there was an evil presence there. I felt that my roommate was a devil who wanted to have sex with me and eventually did. One morning I remember lying on my side in bed, facing away from my roommate who was laying in the bed a few feet away from me. Suddenly I felt a penis enter my rectum and thrust back and forth and I could feel the evil presence beside me. The thrusting lasted awhile. I even rocked back and forth in reaction to the thrusting. It felt like this was an act to dominate or claim me in some evil way. It felt as if evil was being planted within me. As I rolled over I realized that my roommate was sound asleep and was in his bed. I was shocked. It was so real to me. I had imagined the experience in my psychotic state and yet even in a psychotic state I was surprised. This imagined sex act mimicked the sexual abuse I had experienced as a child.

With all the horrible things I was experiencing in my mind, I didn't sleep well, resulting in an even deeper psychotic state. I paced up and down the hall all day and night quoting a page that was torn out of my Bible. I also felt the need to do one hundred jumping jacks every time I felt that I was getting tired. I was out of touch with reality, and yet, after a few days I managed to convince the doctor to release me from the hospital. I was very paranoid, scared for my life, and very angry. This set the stage for disaster at home.

Diane: David did not trust anyone at the hospital, and he thought there was no reason to stay. He was cooperative though, and over the next several days, he did get a little better. He started back on the medication he had stopped taking two weeks earlier, and the doctor said he was stable enough to go home. David admitted later that he fooled the doctor into thinking that he was OK, and that he should go home. He also said that he knew exactly what he was doing at the time. When I picked him up, I could immediately see that he should not have been released. I could not understand why they were releasing him when it was so obvious that he was still delusional, irrational and confused.

I felt I had no choice; he was free to go. As I loaded his suitcase into the car, he got on his hands and knees, kissed the ground, and yelled, "Freedom!"

The car ride home was scary. David talked about Satan and all the demons that were at the hospital, and about the other patients. He may have been more stable, but he certainly was not thinking clearly.

At home, things were no better. At one point, he went into the children's rooms and carefully arranged piles of things on their beds into "sculptures." He was very proud of his efforts and showed the sculptures off to me as if they had some deep spiritual meaning. I obviously did not understand their meaning, and because of that, David grew very angry with me. It seemed as though I could not say anything right to him. Later, as he sat at his computer, I walked into the room and said something, apparently in a tone he did not like. He said that he saw the devil in my eyes, and that as I stood in the doorway, he felt himself get as cold as ice in my presence. He thought I was possessed.

David: After my wife picked me up from the hospital, things began to get really weird. As soon as I got home, I jumped into my car and drove off to have breakfast with my friend Frank. After breakfast, I drove around quite awhile and noticed concentration camps all around as I traveled throughout the city. What I actually saw were schools that were getting major remodeling done. There were chain link fences all around them to provide a safety barrier. That is why I thought they had the appearance of a concentration camp. I also saw several groups of children in single file walking by the schools. I later went to a fast food restaurant and ordered my usual hamburger, fries, and soft drink. While I was driving and while eating at the restaurant, I felt that Hitler's atrocities were still going on, and that kids were being marched off to concentration camps to be executed. There were children on the walkways of the restaurant, but obviously they were not going to be executed. At the restaurant, I thought the hamburger patties were made from human flesh. I thought that

I had to eat the human flesh burgers to show my allegiance to Hitler. I remember taking bite after bite and feeling the need to vomit and at the same time maintain my composure. Someone was watching me and I did not know who.

The events of this particular day were so bizarre, that it later drove me to learn how to manage my illness and survive. I never want to be psychotic again; I fear that I may lose my mind permanently. As I recall the events now, I remember feelings that were more like thoughts. It was as though I were in a dream, with disconnected thoughts that would abruptly shift to different contexts and different realities.

After leaving the fast food restaurant, I headed for the cemetery, this time to look for my Aunt Edie's grave site. I am not even sure why. When she died a few years earlier, I was filled with joy, in part because I knew she would go to a better place. My aunt had suffered terribly in her final days, and during my last visit, I had asked her to say hello to Jesus for me when she got to heaven. When I first heard the news of her death, I had such a euphoric feeling—the sense that she was with God and that God knew about me in a personal way.

The cemetery was about thirty miles away. I drove very fast, reaching speeds in excess of 100 mph, even topping 120 mph at one point. I flipped my mirrors up and swerved through traffic without concern for myself or anyone else. I remember seeing the cars and trucks on the road around me and believed that they were evacuating the city for some reason related to the Hitler theme. At one point, I slowed down quite a bit. I don't remember why. Soon afterward, I noticed a parade of highway patrol cars in front of me. It even seemed like they were leading an entourage for me.

I got off the highway and headed for the cemetery. I re-call asking several people for directions. It seemed as though I was in a time warp, like I knew what others were going to say before they said it. I attributed this to my being a second out of step with time. "Future step" is what I have called it since. I also felt that my driving speed had something to do with the time warp. It was more strangeness added to the already exceedingly strange psychotic mania I was experiencing. While driving, I even recall hearing what seemed like sonic booms, as if somehow I had broken the sound barrier. As strange as this account seems now as I write about it, my perception at the time was that nothing was wrong with me or my behavior.

I never did find my aunt's grave, but I did spend some time looking for it. Being in the cemetery made me think of the many deaths that had occurred in my family, mainly to men at an early age. My uncle died at fifty. My friend who was a big brother to me died at twenty-eight. My own brother died at thirty-one, and there were many others. At one point, in my psychotic state, I believed that my mother was responsible for these deaths.

My eldest son turned eleven years old on the day I was released from the hospital, the same day that I went to visit the graveyard. By the time I hooked up with my family, my wife and kids were at my mom's house. I was in an even more extreme psychotic state. I had had little sleep, and when I entered my mom's house I could smell the same smell that my brother's apartment had after he died. Because he had died ten days before he was found, we had to hire a special cleaning service to deodorize my brother's place. The deodorizer had a strong cherry pie smell to it. When I smelled cherry pie in my mom's house, my mind immediately linked the two things in some bizarre way, and I concluded that my mom had been responsible for my brother's death.

The kids, my wife, and my mom were all very worried. My wife and my mother knew about the risk of my being manic, and they knew my behavior was anything but normal. I didn't stay long at my mom's house, but unfortunately, I did stay long enough to ruin my son's birthday. I am certain all of the kids were quite scared at that point. As for my son, I had already saddled him with the decision to send me to the hospital. Now it was his birthday and I was still sick and getting worse.

I drove around until very late that night and then just showed up unannounced at my Godmother's house. I pounded on her door, but she would not answer. I wanted to talk to her about the death of her husband Ray, my Godfather. He died young, before I was ten years old. I believed that she could unravel the many strange deaths that had occurred in my family. After a while, I left and went back to my car.

Diane: Late that night as I was getting ready for bed, still wondering where David was, I got a call from David's Godmother. She sounded very distressed. She said that David had come to her house and was standing at her door shouting and asking her if she knew who was responsible for all the killings that had happened in the city. She had never seen David that way and would not let him in. He also asked to speak to her husband, who had been dead for many years. She was afraid, and not knowing what else to do, left him on her porch and called me.

I quickly called the police and David's dad to tell them where David was, and then raced over there myself. I arrived before the police and David's dad, and I saw David near the front door of his Godmother's house. I noticed that he had left the keys in the ignition of his car. I grabbed the keys, figuring that if I had them he couldn't go anywhere. I tried to find a place to hide them, but he saw me and came over. I still had the keys in my hand, and did not know what to do. I decided to throw them, and hope that he would not find them before the police arrived. My aim was very poor, and they landed on the grass where he could easily retrieve them.

David got into his car and started the engine, and I found myself struggling with him to get the keys out of the ignition. As we battled over the keys, he started to drive away. I was half in and half out of the car. I was terrified as the car sped up a bit, but then I saw the lights of a police car behind us. David pulled over, and the police asked us both to step away from the vehicle. I explained to the officers that David was manic and needed to go to a hospital. I told them he had been released too early and was still suffering from mania.

The police talked to me, David, and David's Godmother,

after which they decided that they had no legal grounds to detain him or take him to the hospital. They said they sympathized with me, but they had no choice but to let him drive off again, which is what he did. I stood there in disbelief, then drove home fearing that I may have seen my husband for the last time. He was not fit to be driving, and I feared for his safety and the safety of those around him.

David: When I spoke to the officer I told him I was getting a divorce from my wife and that is why she was so upset. After convincing him of my story, the police officer said I was free to leave. I left my Godmother's house and drove down the street for a few blocks. I turned the car around and drove back past my Godmother's house and where my dad and Diane were talking to the police officer. As I drove by I waved at them in a way that said I fooled them. I drove around town for awhile and eventually I drove home. At that point I was paranoid and afraid my wife was going to kill me. At a later point I realized the officer that I spoke to looked exactly like the security guard at the hospital when I was first hospitalized.

Diane: When David arrived home, I was relieved when he climbed into bed and tried to go to sleep. Later, however, he suddenly started shaking violently. I thought he was having a seizure. I had never seen one before, but he seemed to be shaking uncontrollably. His eyes had a blank stare, and he was apparently not able to talk.

I dialed 9-1-1 and told the dispatcher that I believed my husband was having a seizure. Minutes later an ambulance was in front of our house. The paramedics found no evidence of a seizure, but they also could not get a word out of David. He pointed to everything and used sign language to convey what he wanted. They asked me if he could speak, and I felt funny saying that he could, but for whatever reason, was refusing to.

The paramedics were debating about whether or not to take him to the hospital when David once again began to shake violently. I was glad they were there to witness it, but they told me that it was not like a typical seizure. It was voluntary movement, not involuntary. David's strange behavior did finally get the attention that he needed, however. They decided to check him into the hospital. I never thought I would be happy to see my husband leave the house in an ambulance, but at that moment, I was very happy that he was being admitted. I was also glad that the children had slept through the whole thing. After they drove away, I cried myself to sleep once more.

David: After arriving at the hospital, I was examined by a doctor I did not like, and immediately developed a bad attitude toward him. He wanted me to share with him what was going on and said it would be private. It wasn't private at all because the office door was open. I told him that while I was waiting to talk with him I had overheard all sorts of conversations from the adjoining rooms. He didn't like that.

After touching his stethoscope to my chest for only a second, the doctor said everything was fine. Soon after, someone brought a needle with Haldol and injected me. Haldol is an anti-psychotic, but it actually caused me to become more and more out of touch. I have no memory of the evening beyond that moment.

I was taken to yet another psychiatric hospital, where I was admitted. There I began to heal emotionally, and my mania began to subside. The medical staff on the ward was very kind and treated me with respect, which pleased me very much. The doctor assigned to my case, however, was disrespectful and manipulative. He wanted me to take Haldol, which I refused to do. I was afraid it might kill me. I did not even know that the earlier injection was Haldol. My first hospitalization had been such a scary experience because of an interaction involving a drug similar to Haldol. It created a sense of not being able to wake up, as though I were paralyzed or trying to awaken from the dead. It felt like someone was trying to kill me.

While in the hospital I got very sick with flu-like symptoms including a high fever. I slept a great deal as a result of the illness and that was probably a good thing. After a few days of sleeping I felt somewhat better. I wanted to leave, but the doctor insisted I stay longer. I refused and called a patient advocate. A hearing was scheduled. Minutes before the hearing time, the doctor released me. I think he knew he did not have any grounds to keep me there, and I believe he sensed that I might get him in trouble. In my opinion, he behaved unprofessionally. I felt that he had treated me as some kind of lab rat rather than as a person.

I had grown angry and refused when the doctor insisted I take Haldol voluntarily. Because I have had terrible reactions to anti-psychotics, I am reluctant to ever take them again unless it is absolutely necessary. My previous experience with Haldol had resulted in losing my memory for an entire day. No drug is a "magic pill," and it is up to each patient to determine which drugs work and which ones do not work. Psychiatrists are often accustomed to prescribing drugs and not being questioned about their decisions. It is up to the patient to change this status quo by making it clear to their doctors what is and what is not acceptable behavior on their part. A "Medical Directive" or "Drug ID Program," listing medications we are currently taking and those to avoid, can guide doctors' decisions, should we not be in a position to make ourselves heard. Those with medical emergencies are routinely asked if there are any allergies, or bad reactions to certain drugs. Unfortunately this same approach is not used in a psychiatric emergency. Preparing ourselves in advance with a Medical Directive or Drug ID Program can reduce our stress level should we ever find ourselves in such a situation.

It is vital to the survival of those with bipolar disorder that we be treated with respect, even when we are manic or depressed. It is enough to bear the burden of this illness. We should not have to carry the additional burden of being treated as less than worthy of respect by having our wishes denied. The staff at one hospital told me that doctors, in their experience, often have a "God complex" and treat others quite disrespectfully. I do not think that this is the case with all doctors, and it is not true of my doctor, but I have seen it with several doctors.

Diane: They kept David longer than three days and he was not released until he was over the flu and the mania had died down. I was very happy when he told me he would never again stop taking his medicine. He told me that taking a few pills a day was a small price to pay for keeping his sanity. He also told me that his shaking violently in the bed was a "test" for me, although to this day, he cannot recall what the test was. He also cannot recall why he did not talk to me or the paramedics that night.

David: My mother picked me up from the hospital and drove me home. I had a much different mind set at this point. I wanted to live. I decided that I would never allow myself to wind up in a full blown psychotic or manic state again. I knew that I needed to learn more about bipolar disorder quickly. I needed to develop safety strategies to keep from losing my mind.

Being in a psychotic state and out of touch with reality is very scary. It's like living inside a nightmare. My first priority was to contact my medical provider and enroll in a bipolar management class. I was supposed to take the class earlier, but had been turned down because I couldn't make the first session. I was determined to take the class this time around as I knew my life depended on it.

The bipolar management class was excellent. What I learned has been very helpful to my surviving bipolar disorder and has served as part of the foundation for this book. I will touch on many of the points in later chapters. If you have bipolar disorder, I strongly recommend that you take a management class and read as many books on the subject as you can. As they say, knowledge is power, and in this case, knowledge can save your life. The class, and my research on bipolar disorder, has helped me to control my mood swings on several occasions, including several potentially dangerous mood swings, particularly during the period I will describe in the next chapter.

Diane: The events that day at church and over the following weeks when David had a manic psychotic episode left scars on our whole family. Several people at church became a little wary of David. People tend to fear mental illness and behaviors they don't understand. Over time we were able to explain much of what had happened, and with David back on his medicine, things became more comfortable. However, I believe the events of that day were what led to our eventual departure from that church. A few parishioners had become close friends, but after David's manic episode, coupled with his openness and honesty about his personal life, the friendships eventually fell apart. I believe they were scared by everything he told them about bipolar disorder.

David: The year and a half that followed my last hospitalization was very good. I began to recover rapidly. The shame of having bipolar disorder was lessening, and I was thankful to be alive. After returning to work for a second time, I did become a bit depressed. I was shuffled around from job to job within the company under a succession of managers as the company downsized. About six months later, I was laid off along with some 75,000 others. I did not take it personally, in fact, I was thankful to have a break, a "paid mind break" if you will. It was the time off that allowed me to become involved in projects and charity work, and these activities made me feel much better about myself. It also gave me time to write this book.

I had always thought that I left the hospital in a psychotic state, and in fact I did. What I did not realize is that I entered the hospital both manic and psychotic as well. I realized this only after obtaining and reviewing copies of my hospital records. My doctor was reluctant to release records to me on the grounds that doing so could harm me psychologically. I had to go all the way to the CEO of the hospital to have my request granted, so don't be afraid to be persistent in seeking your records if you want them.

It's important that you know that I did not review many of my medical records until several years later. In fact I have some records that I have yet to look at and review. I may never do so. In obtaining and eventually reviewing the medical records I was able to piece together my behavior and that is helpful to me.

It is important for those of us with bipolar disorder to create a "life safety plan." I'm convinced that my full-blown illness resulted from my lack of knowledge of how to manage my condition. Mania is dangerous precisely because the patient feels terrific. Some of my family members and close friends knew things were not right with me and yet they said nothing. I have since given them permission to comment, in a loving way, when they are concerned about me. I want to live, and so I have to be willing to listen to people when they voice concerns about my behavior. An advance "life safety plan" will not necessarily prevent manic and depressive episodes, but it can reduce the chances of something catastrophic happening by making sure the appropriate intervention occurs as soon as possible. At the time of my first and second manic episodes, I did not have a life safety plan. It amazes me that I was lucky to survive intact.

Diane: In the next chapter, David will share an ordeal to help you understand how a terrible experience for our family resulted in a severe depression. Depression is on the other end of the bi-polar spectrum from mania. What David will describe is called "mixed bipolar state." It is depression coupled with the energy of mania and is very dangerous. When mixed bipolar state occurs, a person can get so desperate that they may end their own life. David has admitted to having mixed bipolar state and has felt suicidal at times. Thankfully, he has developed strategies to fight off depression when it first strikes. With mixed bipolar state and its added danger, it is even more important that he follow his life saving strategies. We hope these strategies will be helpful for you and your loved ones in managing bipolar disorder.

A Knight's Pledge

You are Jesus, my King, my Lord, my Savior
My Commander, you require everything
I raise my right hand to you God in pledge

I give you my life and my allegiance
My trust, my faith
My hopes and my dreams

I give you my gifts, my talent
My wealth, my poverty

I give you my family, my friends
My ministry and my reputation
I give you all that I have, all that I am

I have counted the cost and pledge to serve you
To the best of my abilities, forever
Your Warrior, Servant, and beloved Son

—David Mariant

CHAPTER 4

The Journey to Hell and Back

"If you are going through hell...keep going."

—Winston Churchill

The year that followed my last hospitalization was the most tumultuous period of my life. I am just glad that I survived and that I'm here to share it. During that time, I felt as though I was on an out-of-control rollercoaster and hanging on for dear life. I was not only going through the highest of highs and the lowest of lows—but often both at the same time. By then I had learned to recognize the onset of mania and was managing it pretty well, but the severe depression and unfamiliar mood state caught me by surprise.

What I did not know at the time was that I was experiencing an extremely serious manifestation of bipolar, called "mixed bipolar state." Mixed bipolar state is rarely discussed; the general public, and those with bipolar and their families, are often unaware that bipolar can manifest in this way. Worse, doctors very often miss it in their patients. Be sure to talk with your doctor about mixed bipolar state and discuss strategies that will help you best detect its occurrence. Keeping a mood chart will likely be one strategy your doctor or therapist will encourage; it will assist in accurate diagnosis and treatment of your condition.

When the elements of bipolar, depression, emotionality (even innocent enthusiasm or excitement) meet misunderstanding, lack of knowledge, prejudice and fear—the person with bipolar is at heightened risk for potentially dangerous and even lethal consequences. The extremes of this can be seen in tragedies where police and security forces have shot and killed individuals behaving erratically. Educating ourselves, families and the public is vitally important to prevent these tragedies from occurring needlessly. In some ways, lack of knowledge is an important backdrop for the problems—including past traumatic events, mania, depression and the mixed bipolar state that begin my "journey to hell" and put my life at its greatest risk.

It was a particularly dangerous time in my life journey—a time when suicide was on my mind. My family and I were completely involved in our church to the point that most of our loving friendships and activities were church-centered. The church was so ingrained in the fabric of our lives that we became unhealthily out of balance. My role in the congregation was Sunday School Teacher; I co-directed the prayer ministry not only for our church, but for other churches in the community. I also sang in the choir, participated in drama and managed the church grounds. My passion to serve and get things done was intense.

I have learned that understanding myself and identifying events or situations that might trigger my mood swings is crucial. I found that I needed friendship and acceptance in an emotionally dependent way. This created a fear that I would lose these important relationships, yet the fear fueled the destruction of the very relationships that were important to me and that I wanted to preserve. The experience during this period was intense. This point is so significant that the lessons I learned are perhaps my most valuable life saving insights of all.

Diane: A year had gone by since that last confusing, psychotic episode at the church. No one really spoke of it and for the most part everyone treated David with great respect. They looked up to him as an important leader in the church. The pastor encouraged David to participate and lead many church activities even though he knew first hand that David had bipolar disorder and had seen him at his worst. This really was commendable. It seemed that the difficult times and bipolar episodes were behind us. David was taking his medication faithfully and there was no reason to believe that he would have any more problems. We were naive to the risks that were looming.

As I looked around the church social hall, I felt very proud that David and our family had made the seemingly impossible not only possible, but a reality. Our family spent the whole summer remodeling the church fellowship hall. David worked very long days that often went past midnight and seemed to precipitate a mild mania. We were very proud because we managed to pull off a fifty thousand dollar remodel for about ten thousand dollars. We did this through our organized effort of volunteers and community donations. It was an awesome experience and we felt very good about the outcome. However, we were surprised and extremely disappointed to learn of opposition that arose from a few church leaders. We didn't understand the opposition and because of our devoted effort David took it quite personally. He felt that the opposition called into question his motivations, invalidating his desire to serve the church. This seemed to be a recurring theme as the year went by, triggering deepening depression and setting the stage for other mood states that would follow.

David: I had no idea how much the opinions of others could affect me; I felt that the opinions of others had power over me. At the same time I was intimidated by what others thought. My issue of unhealthy "needing" of others and their acceptance of me is dysfunctional—something that I will discuss later. I discovered that my emotions belong to me and I do not have to give control over them to others. This was a great revelation for me.

I felt that the service I provided would improve my standing with the pastor when the work I did for the church was called into question. I kept working harder and harder and yet I couldn't seem to make matters better. My passion to serve God and the church was out of balance to the point that I neglected my family when they needed me most. I was out of control trying to win the approval of others. Because much of my life and my personality is driven by passion, I often inadvertently step on the toes of others. My passion and desire to bring people together and to get things done is sometimes misconstrued as competitive, undermining and condescending. This misunderstanding of my passion was quite unfortunate.

Two of our good friends at the church were Angela, the music director, and her husband Justin. They had both seen me first hand when I was manic at the church a year earlier. They both loved to lead worship, write songs and help the church community in a variety of ways. I had all of these things in common with them and this is why our friendship developed and was so meaningful to me. They were both somewhat shy, yet competitive and passionate. They were caring people and loved me, even though I had bipolar disorder, and both of them had seen me at my worst. When others were negative about our renovation of the social hall, Angela and Justin had been the most supportive of all. They were excited because they could see that many in the congregation would benefit from it. We all enjoyed doing whatever we could for our church and the community at large. Their patience was unbelievable too, although it would eventually be stressed to its limit and come to an end.

Diane: A church choir practice set off a chain of events that still perplexes us today. I have often looked back and wondered what might have happened if I or someone else had been the one to help Angela, the distressed music director, instead of David. As she prepared to teach our group the musical production we had all volunteered to learn, she suddenly broke down and began to cry heavily. Everyone was stunned and did not know how to react. This was especially unusual because it was uncommon among our church members to express emotion so strongly. While very apologetic for the emotional outburst, she did not offer an explanation. David did the one thing for our friend, the right thing, that I wish I had done in hindsight. He walked over, talked with her sympathetically for awhile, and gave her a hug.

David: I had just spoken to Angela a few days earlier about some matters that were troubling her at the time and as we ended our conversation she assured me that she was okay. Although I was concerned for her, I was comforted, knowing that she felt better after the emotional outburst. However, my concern was heightened. I really had hoped my wife or one of the other ladies would talk to her after the meeting, but no one did. Since she was upset, I went over and talked with her for awhile and gave her a reassuring hug.

Angela explained that she was extremely concerned about the huge task of leading the church choir and creating the orchestra. She was depending upon others whom she felt were letting her down. Although I did not mention it at the time, I thought I recognized a "suicidal look" in her eyes—a frantic look—a look of desperation and fear. She seemed to be having some sort of breakdown and I became very concerned. But more than that, I was alarmed, and a deep fear of my own, almost a sense of panic, began to grow in me then and over the next few months. Since Michael died so young and possibly by suicide, I could easily imagine the same thing happening to her. It wasn't a vague idea, but a palpable thought. As I look back I can see that I misread the signs of what I thought was a suicidal look. This happened around the fifth anniversary of my brother Michael's death and I believe that is why I saw things in a distorted way.

Angela's emotional distress and the look I saw in her eyes almost immediately triggered flashbacks of vivid and traumatic memories of Michael's death. She reminded me of my brother in so many ways. When I saw her for the first time performing on stage, she was singing and playing the keyboard like my brother did. When she first learned of Michael's music and CD she became interested in learning more about him and the possibility of recruiting him for some of her musical endeavors. One day, I gave her a copy of his CD, and told her that Michael had died several years previously. She appeared to be deeply moved. Angela was the same age as Michael when he died; she also wrote songs just like him.

69

Since my brother's death and my own experience, I had become hyper-sensitive to signs of what I perceived as suicidal characteristics in others. My overwhelming concern was a sign of a vulnerability in my emotional well-being. Flashbacks of fear were significant stressors that began a fluctuation in my moods that occurred throughout that year. When my new fear for Angela's life resonated with the unresolved older stressors of my brother's death, the outcome detonated the bipolar bomb which nearly became deadly.

It was the fifth anniversary of Michael's death, and the feeling that my world was knocked off its axis, and that I had failed, returned to haunt me. It was awful. I had no idea that so many emotions and photographic memories were buried and would come to life just like the horror that had occurred five years earlier. I wanted the grieving for Michael to be over and yet to my utter surprise it was not. Because my life seemed to be going in a positive direction since my last hospitalization for mania, I did not anticipate that memories could emerge in this way. My overwhelming and obsessive concern for Angela began my depressive descent, trying both her and her husband's friendship and patience.

The terrible dreams about Michael's death, some of which focused on the various ways by which he may have been murdered, began to manifest again. I was thankful when I woke up to realize the nightmares were just dreams. Upon awakening my heart would pound and fear would overwhelm me. I also had repeated nightmares about Angela, who seemed in great danger and in need of help. I was afraid and confused about all of the dreams and the fear remained in the background of my mind and distorted my encounters with everyone for many months.

During this period, I was depressed, yet—though it might seem contradictory—my thoughts moved rapidly and I could not turn them off. They seemed to be related to my intense worry for Angela while the memories of Michael kept pulling me deeper and deeper into depression. I found myself returning to the cemetery a great deal to pay respects to him and to think about my concern for Angela.

Diane: David was very absorbed and could not stop talking about his fears and concerns; he couldn't sleep, fearing what might happen next. I became increasingly concerned for the drama unfolding before me, and saw potential disaster that I did not know how to prevent. He could not seem to control the emotional drive, or bring himself to just let it go. It was similar to his behavior following the death of his brother five years earlier. I didn't know what to do! It was like an out of control train that was certain to derail if it hit a curve.

David: I began to go manic in a way that I had never experienced before and did not understand. While previous manic episodes were expressed outwardly in ways that others could see as clearly "manic" and wildly erratic or dissociative, this time my feelings were mostly interior, although I had periodic outward signs of manic and depressive symptoms. Clearly Diane, Angela, Justin, the pastor of the church and a few others knew something was wrong, but did not know what it was. I had a heightened awareness of danger for myself, and for Angela. I felt like I was walking through a mine field, and exploding land mines were everywhere. Depression, racing thoughts, fear and paranoia went rampant and fueled my interior "hell." What is amazing is that although I was experiencing the "hell" of depression, I was also experiencing manic symptoms and was so excited and involved in my church activities, that I was unaware of how easily I could fall into a dangerous depressive state. I became easily lost in the emotions and concerns of the moment, and lost a larger sense of perspective.

A long series of concerned discussions and anxious emails passed between me and Angela. Out of fear for Angela I obsessed for her safety, because I wanted to create a situation I could control and trust. I was never able to do that and it only fueled more obsession and fear. I did not know how to stop my worry and I felt like I had no control over it at all. My fear for her safety began to aggravate my friendship with her, and also with the church leaders. There were many misunderstandings, and my behavior was often misinterpreted. Looking back at photos throughout that year, I was shocked that my plight was not apparent in the photographs or to many of the people in my life at the time.

Diane: I was not sure what was going on, because I saw David faithfully taking his medicine every morning and every night. I had seen manic behavior already, and he did not seem to present those kinds of symptoms. So what was happening? My oldest children were also concerned about their dad because he talked incessantly about church and church leaders and his moods flip flopped each day. David was happy one day and depressed the next day and it seemed to revolve mostly around Angela's mental and emotional state, the approval or disapproval of church leaders, and general intense anxieties that he could not shake. He couldn't sleep many nights and cried a lot. One night after sharing with Angela his deep feelings for Michael and his untimely death, David cried all night long and awoke throughout the night with his pillow sopping wet with tears. His emotional outpouring for both Michael and now Angela was unbelievable and I did not understand it. I had never seen David in such an emotionally distraught state like this before. I would often find him sitting at his computer in the middle of the night, his eyes desperately trying to close, and sobbing because he did not know what to write to Angela, Justin, or the pastor to try to fix matters.

David: By this time I had become extremely stressed. It became obvious that other church members were noticing my emotional intensity, and were bothered by it; some were anxious, others merely irritated, and yet others responded angrily. It upset me that others might notice how fearful and depressed I was and that they would think badly of me. This could jeopardize my work in the church that was so important to me. I felt both angry and ashamed and did not understand my extreme over-concern for Angela or my unexplainable need to relive Michael's death through her.

Driving home one evening, I remember feeling so depressed that my heart felt hollow. I felt drained of energy, yet my mind raced on, thinking uncontrollably of all the trouble I was going through. Thoughts of harming myself flew at me from all directions. I was so afraid that I considered checking myself into the hospital, because I wasn't sure if I would hurt myself or not. These deep waters of depression were unlike any depression I have ever felt before.

Diane: David shared everything with me and I was confident that he was faithfully taking his medication, so I reasoned that he was not in a manic state. He clearly was not healthy, but what do you call the state that he was in? The severe mood swings seemed to be brought on by the haunting past of his brother's death and acceptance or rejection from key people in his life. Acceptance would bring him a bit closer to the manic side of the spectrum, and rejection brought him a bit closer to the depressive side. I was afraid for David. His doctor increased his anti-depressant prescription at one point; however, his mental turmoil and the damage to his friendships could not be fixed with pills, and neither could David's sanity and self-esteem. I didn't know what was going on or what to do to stop his internal and external destruction.

One day I told Angela that David suspected that he saw a suicidal look in her eyes and the concern was tearing him apart. Her reaction was shock; she could not understand how he could draw such a conclusion. She claimed to never have had suicidal thoughts, and that David was mistaken. I also mentioned to her that I thought she seemed depressed, although I did not think she was suicidal, as did David. Because he had never shared his deepest fears openly, he came across all wrong. If David had been honest and shared what he thought, perhaps things would have turned out differently. In spite of the misunderstanding, Angela planned to work with and help David organize and carry out a church service for our city; this project was very important to both of them. Even with all the tension, she decided to go ahead and work with David to carry out the project. In light of everything that was going on, I thought her support was truly amazing.

David: Prior to the prayer service, I was busy working hard to bring everything together. The pastor, Angela, and Justin were also involved in this service and its preparation. I did not involve them very much, however, and in hind sight that was a mistake. Even with Angela's suggestion to involve the pastor more so, I did not. In retrospect, I was not trying to override anyone, but I think it came across that way, and I may have appeared unwilling to cooperate. This set a bad tone for what would follow later.

Sleeping at night was very difficult, and I had a lot of energy because I was so excited to have the opportunity to lead the service. All of the troubling and depressing stuff was pushed to the background of my thoughts, but not forgotten. I even remember thinking that I might be escalating to a manic state, and indeed I was—but it was confusing, because my mood could just as easily switch to depression.

Finally, the time came for me to do the service for the city churches. After my thirty minute message, I was overwhelmed with joy and excitement and was feeling especially grand. The service was awesome and I received many compliments and thanks from community pastors and attendees. I was feeling at the top of the world; this service meant so much to me. I thought things were now going to be great. I loved the experience so much that I wanted to dedicate my life to full time ministry and work for the church. I was very happy with the outcome of the service and having been allowed to pursue my passion and lead the effort; I was sure that any misunderstandings were now behind me. I thought the leaders now had confidence in me, since things worked out so well, but I was mistaken.

Diane: The church service was attended by many in the community and it went very well. David was the speaker and many said that he gave a very moving and memorable talk and prayer. David and I thought this was going to be a turning point and the church matters would soon get better. I was surprised and David was devastated when he learned that some of the leaders had serious complaints, arguing that he should not have been given permission to lead the service as an un-ordained minister. David had spent many nights and hours preparing for this important gathering. The positive feedback from community leaders and many others was so uplifting, that the negative complaints and actions by a few caused a huge fall for him, sending him into another depressive crash, and I was afraid.

David had worked so hard to shine and do an excellent job with the community service, but it now became obvious that he could do nothing to get things on track. It was terribly disappointing for him. Because of his confusion, he responded by writing an angry note telling the leaders how he felt. He wrote that their actions were hypocritical and likely done to accommodate his removal from the church, rather than to reach a mutual resolution. He explained that "far reaching consequences" were often a result of unresolved matters like this and families get hurt. David and I had already seen several other leaders and their families leave the church due to similar matters. David knew that a lot of feelings would likely be hurt including our family and church members, and he tried to make that clear. However, the words, "far reaching consequences," were taken out of context and perceived as a physical threat. This was really upsetting, because David has no history of violence or ever hurting anyone. The fear and confusion brought on by his angry note was the driving force behind the decisions that soon followed.

David: I did not understand why people I cared about assumed such bad things about me even after I explained my true intentions. I am often emotionally intense and not aware of it until after the fact – and it's natural for me to bring my emotions into any work or service that I do. My service for this church was dramatic and expressive; I suspect that the pastor did not like the style of service because it was so dramatic, and it made him uncomfortable. Later I learned that years ago a church leader such as I led a similar service and was asked to leave the church. Although some community pastors loved the service, other more conservative pastors apparently did not. I think it brought out conflicting issues of style and the use of expressive emotion in presenting church services. Not considering the needs and wishes of everyone attending was a major oversight on my part. I really should have included the pastor in the planning stages to avoid such an outcome.

After the service my friendship with Justin and Angela was further stressed. Even though Justin had been amazingly patient with me in the past, he understandably had become intolerant of my obsessive worry for his wife. I gradually learned that Angela had also become afraid of me which was a shock, because even in my worst manic states I have never even thought of violence. I did not know how to turn off the worry and wished that I could. Justin gave me a call one day, after he reviewed the note I had sent to the church leaders, and we had a heated discussion.

After the church service, the pastor also learned more about the intensity of my concern for Angela's troubled state and my heated conversation with Justin, which compounded the problem. As a result, the pastor, Justin and Angela put together a plan that involved my attending church elsewhere for six months, while attending therapy for bipolar disorder—until such time as the pastor was satisfied that I was emotionally well again. The pastor even offered to pay for this therapy during that time and yet I did not feel he was sincere; furthermore I was already seeing a professional therapist. Although Diane and the children were not asked to leave the church, Diane was asked to support their decision. Because she felt that this could cause a wedge in our marriage, which was the last thing we needed at the time, she declined to support them. My family continued to attend the church while I decided to attend elsewhere while trying to work things out with the pastor and leaders. At this time, I felt confused and was frantically trying to remedy the matter.

It seemed as if one day I was at the top of the world fulfilling my passion with the church service, and in the blink of an eye my emotions once again crashed into depression. I was already troubled with my confused and obsessive concern for Angela's emotional state and the end of important friendships, and now I had to deal with leaving a church and a community that I loved. I still held out hope that the situation might improve.

Diane: It was time for the church's annual Christmas production; we were especially excited because our oldest daughter was playing the lead role, which required changing her hair color, practicing her lines and learning the feature song. We were very proud of her. We were all happy to play roles in the production and we all anticipated a wonderful and joyful Christmas celebration. Our children were excited too; they would be dressed in costume for the event and play special parts. Our family had participated in this community event for several years and it had always been a joy. We enjoyed this event very much, although a cloud of darkness loomed over us because of the conflict with David. Unfortunately, every effort we made to talk with the pastor or anyone at the church, failed. We were told that David could not attend the performance to see his daughter perform in a dramatic role that was very important to her and to us.

David: We were unable to make any progress or even fully understand why such serious actions were taken against me. It even felt like they thought I might harm or even kill someone, judging by their actions, although I do not know if this is completely true. It was a scary time for me because I never thought such an accusation would ever be made against me. I began to feel paranoid that something else might be said that was untrue and that others would believe it just because they heard it from a leader.

Diane: On the day before the performance, both David and I came to the conclusion that we should leave the church; it had now become an unhealthy psychological environment, with all the failed attempts to fix things, and it was not good for our family as a whole. David and I were both excited and upset. David and I wanted to see our daughter's performance before we resigned. The dilemma was that David was not allowed on the church property at all. Eventually the pastor did agree that David could attend on the last day of the performance with a chaperone. David felt horrible about the restriction and the need for a chaperone; it seemed to drive home our belief that they really thought he could harm someone.

Unfortunately, the weather was expected to be horrible throughout the next several nights of the performance. Since the performance would be outdoors, we were afraid that it would be rained out, and that we would miss the important event. David decided to attend the performance on the opening night to avoid the bad weather conditions that were predicted, although neither one of us expected the outcome that followed. We quietly walked through the front gates with the children at our side. Several people at the gates warmly greeted us. Once in the open audience area David videotaped our daughter's performance. When he was eventually discovered, he handed the church leaders our letters of resignation and continued to enjoy the wonderful performance. David was causing no disturbance at all. However his attendance, watching the performance and turning in our resignations really upset the leaders.

After the show, our daughter was informed that because her dad attended the show without a chaperone, she would not be allowed to play the lead role for the remaining four nights. Our younger children were eagerly awaiting their turn to be part of the play and we expected them to be in it the following day; but now they also learned that they would never have their turn in the performance that year. Because of the church leaders' actions against us that night, our daughter was deeply hurt and emotionally distraught. Our other children were sobbing as we

78

were told to leave the performance and escorted out. I will never forget the confusion, anger, and sadness in our children's faces. We were all crying. What had happened to the loving church we had once known? Why were they so angry and afraid of David? What were they afraid of? David was right; their actions had far reaching consequences that affected everyone involved and changed the direction of our family's life forever—the night we were walked off that property.

David: It was strange; I was numb to what was happening all around me as if I really wasn't there. I felt detached from the events and the emotions of my family—everything was a blur and yet I still retained memories of what happened. My wife and kids were crying, and my daughter was screaming at the top of her lungs. My oldest boy was yelling at me that it was all my fault that this happened; in part, he was right. How could I have let it go this far? With one last glance at the pastor's face I looked away and was shocked back into reality. I looked to the heavens. My heart was heavy and my body shaking. "God, I never thought it would come to this," I spoke in prayer, "Please help me!"

As we got into the car, I had an idea. I said to my family, "Let's go get a soda." We drove to the convenience store and each picked something out all the while I was thinking to myself, "What on earth is happening to us?" I decided to drive up into the mountains, something I did often when I needed to think about things. Driving has always been such a healing thing and de-stresses me, and now more than ever before, my family desperately needed healing. As we drove off, my oldest son, who had been yelling at me, said something I will never forget, "Dad, at least you now know who your friends are." He was so right about that. We drove for what seemed like an hour. When we arrived at a lookout over the valley, I pulled over.

The night view was beautiful; however, the wind was whipping and brisk. We were all shivering as we gathered together as a family looking out over the valley. I prayed a prayer and allowed each of us to take turns to be angry and scream. After we all did this we jumped back into the car because we were freezing cold. All the way home that night we talked and cried, and most important of all, we were a family.

Diane: David experienced many sleepless nights after we left the church. He replayed the events over and over again in his mind to try to figure out what he could have done differently. The children were confused and did not fully understand why we were not able to set foot on the church property again. They missed their friends and the groups they used to attend regularly and so did we. Our house was full of mixed emotions day after day. I could see that David was in deep despair and serious depression. Although David never alluded to committing suicide, in such a state of mind it seemed like a possibility and because of this I worried that he might commit that unthinkable act.

David: Soon after I had my lithium level checked. I wanted to find out if something was wrong with me. I thought my lithium level could be at a non-therapeutic (low) level, even though I was taking my medication faithfully each day and that could possibly explain everything. Unfortunately, my lithium level was fine and the mood state I was in seemed independent of my lithium level. Because the strong emotions were not apparent during my routine doctor's appointment, my doctor thought I was okay, and so did the others around me. Yet, the world felt like it was falling apart all around me. My doctor has since mentioned that a mixed bipolar state is often missed by doctors. The mixed bipolar state can be the most dangerous and deadliest mood state of all and proved to be quite dangerous for me. I cannot overstress the potential danger I was in. I now recognize that I experienced a variety of bipolar states including mixed bipolar state, mania and depression. The mixed bipolar state is so difficult to diagnose. I did not realize I had been in that state until years later. In that state I probably came across as uncooperative, with an attitude problem. I was misinterpreted by many people. The following is an athoritative description of mixed bipolar state:

"In some people ... symptoms of mania and depression may occur together in what is called a mixed bipolar state. Symptoms of a mixed state often include agitation, trouble sleeping, significant change in appetite, psychosis, and suicidal thinking. A person may have a very sad, hopeless mood while at the same time feeling extremely energized."[1]

I now believe that my good friends, the pastor, Justin and Angela became frightened of my unexplainable behavior to the point that they thought I might harm someone. Even those who love one another can be frightened by bipolar behavior. Fear of the unknown, anger or hatred based upon limited knowledge of bipolar was what led to their actions. Strong emotions like mine don't necessarily lead to violence. Still at times I can barely understand myself, especially as I look back several years ago when these events occurred. How can I expect other people to have a greater understanding of who I am and magically respond to me in a better way than I do myself? People don't understand what they perceive as our weird behavior; they become frightened by it and when they do, they run away from it, or try to eliminate the cause of their uneasiness. Justin, Angela and the pastor were just a few of the friendships that I valued at the church and lost. My wife and family who I love dearly paid a huge price because they also incurred the same loss as I did.

After many years I have finally come to terms with what took place at the church. I eventually sent apologies, forgave the people who hurt me and my family and learned to forgive myself. I even spoke to the pastor one day and we both apologized and I shared the lessons I had learned about forgiveness. The apologies and conversation helped bring some closure to the horrible mess. My wife talked with Angela a few times too and she said she continues to pray for our family and that seems

---

1 See "What are the Symptoms of Bipolar Disorder?" in "Bipolar Disorder," NIMH (National Institute of Mental Health), http://www.nimh.nih.gov/Publicat/bipolar.cfm

very thoughtful. I don't want to make my forgiving others sound easy, because this was no simple task. For years I was angry at them for their actions and although I felt like everything was intentional on their part and that they meant to harm me—that may not be the case.

The events in this chapter, especially the accusations that I might harm or kill, caused me to go into a depression and to think about committing suicide. Even years later while recalling and writing about these events, I rebounded into depression. I may never fully get over this matter; however, I am now aware of its potential danger and can even choose to steer away from thinking about it. The loss of friends that I loved, and fear from mixed bipolar state could have also brought me to the brink of suicide. The same events drove me to write this book to help others survive bipolar illness and reduce this potential threat.

Even though we had a bad experience at a church, my family's beliefs have not faltered and our belief in God remains strong. We sincerely believe that Christian faith is responsible for both my survival and our survival as a family. We are now involved in a new, warm and friendly local church. Each day seems to bring new hope and a new sense of confidence for the days that follow. What previously devastated me and put my life in grievous danger, has made me stronger and has given me the determination and strength to share my story.

You can make it through your difficult struggles, too, and you too can survive. The most important result of my conflicts is that I am a better person today. It has taught me how to be strong by significantly overcoming both the post-traumatic stress disorder related to my brother's death, and the codependent need for approval from others. We all need to decide what we want out of life. I want to live and be prosperous, especially in loving others and being loved. The choices I've made to seek help for my bipolar disorder are why I live today. I am alive because of my choice. Armed now with new understandings of the illness, I stand a much better chance of "surviving bipolar's fatal grip."

TWISTED FIRE

Memories held so tight
They have blinded my sight

Frozen in time and space
Why am I in this place?

Through turbulence and strife
Flames burning tall and bright

Twisted fire, burn away
Impurities of yesterday

In surrender I come
Crossing my life, chasm

Fire, cleanse my offering
Return, my joy to sing

Offerings, bitter, sweet
Ashes, joyful, complete

Fixation is released
Today is unleashed

Twisted fire, life in me
Constantly make me free!

—David Mariant

Part 2

SURVIVING BIPOLAR DISORDER

"Deep into that darkness peering, long I stood there, wondering, fearing, doubting, dreaming dreams no mortal ever dared to dream before."

—Edgar Allan Poe

CHAPTER 5

Surviving the New Diagnosis

"How few of us ever emerge from such beginning! How many souls perish in its tumult!"

—Kate Chopin

Survival can mean a variety of things. This book was written to help others with bipolar disorder survive—literally—but it is also meant to enhance the survival of families, friendships, and other relationships. As I reflect on my journey, I am always conscious of the family that loves me on one hand, but who have also been very deeply wounded by me on the other. If we are to survive day-to-day with this illness, it is essential that we learn how to preserve our relationships in the process.

Earlier in this book, I wrote about my experience of feeling that I could control the weather from inside a hospital while in a four-point restraint. Thankfully I no longer have that sort of magical thinking, but I have learned there are many ways that we can control our extreme "emotional weather," and avoid leaving lasting emotional scars on those we love. By our ups and downs we either add to the energy of those around us—or we deplete it.

If we do not seek help controlling our bipolar disorder, we will likely continue to leave trails of destruction behind us. The choice really is ours to make. I have made my choice and in doing so have fought to reclaim my life, shed my abusive behavior, and save my precious relationships with friends and family.

This book is a collection of lessons that I have learned along the way. You will also find additional important information included in Part 3 Bipolar Survival Essentials . This knowledge is critical to your survival. It is not the "be-all, end-all" of bipolar disorder information; but can be a starting point to enhance your understanding that this illness can be emotionally wounding and even fatal if we don't take control.

What I am suggesting is a holistic approach. In this section, I will share important insights and practices that I have developed and use. These things can be used to support your efforts on behalf of both your own survival and that of your personal relationships. Many ideas that I will share have worked for me and for others, and I believe they will be of value to you as well.

Relationships are, paradoxically, what we need most in our struggle to control our illness and what we are most likely to have damaged along the way. We tend to misinterpret people's motivations, and because of this, we tend to have a "backward" approach to relationships. We often do not know how to express anger and other strong feelings in a healthy way, making it difficult to maintain healthy relationships.

It is easy to see why so many find it difficult to interact with us. To others, it often appears that we love them one day and hate them the next. We may succeed in hiding our feelings for long periods, then suddenly blow up, releasing all of our pent up anger and inflicting pain and trauma on our friends and loved ones.

Unresolved life issues affect many people, not just those of us with this disorder. Anyone can express their feelings by lashing out at others, or turn things inward and become depressed. We hurt others and ourselves when we do this. There is no question that unresolved issues are more difficult for those of us with bipolar because our mood swings magnify them.

My purpose is not to write a medical book, although the medical information in the Essential section is quite good and has been very helpful to me personally. But I do want to draw attention to what I believe is the most important chapter in this section, about managing bipolar disorder. I emphasize the importance of understanding one's life history, as it can very well hold the keys to understanding many aspects of the illness.

The initial diagnosis of bipolar disorder can be an extremely difficult experience. I have already touched on this in other areas of the book. Although my experience was nothing less than horrific, I have heard from others that their diagnosis was actually a blessing to them, and that it helped them in their healing process. In my case, I failed to recognize my behavior as abnormal until I wound up in a hospital ward one day. Others cannot understand why they act and feel the way they do and why they hurt so badly inside. To them, the bipolar diagnosis is a welcome relief because it explains so much.

My own diagnosis hit me like a ton of bricks; it came seemingly out of nowhere. My first manic episode brought questions, confusion, and fear about my life that I could not have ever imagined. Over the years, family members and even therapists had suspected that I might have bipolar disorder, but no one ever said anything because they weren't sure. One problem is that mania feels so good, and we feel on top of the world, so it's understandably difficult to accept that something might be wrong with that—and wrong with us.

As I address the issue of surviving bipolar disorder here, I want to begin by emphasizing two elements that are essential to effective self-management of our illness: the first is knowing our body and mind. The second is knowing the illness and how to manage it. My perspective in this chapter has been developed over the past six or seven years. Please read it carefully and thoughtfully.

If you have just recently been diagnosed with bipolar disorder, I want to reassure you that you are not a bad person and you can make it through what lies ahead. A healthy sense of personal self-worth is critical to moving forward in life, especially for a person with bipolar disorder. You are not a freak, and you are not "broken." You've probably had these thoughts because I know I did. At times I still do.

One of the most important things I can tell you is that while you may feel frightened, confused and abandoned, you are not alone. You are not the only person ever to have bipolar disorder. I don't want to minimize your feelings, but I do want to emphasize that you are not alone. When I was first diagnosed, I felt like there was a huge barrier separating me from everyone around me. It was truly one of the most difficult times of my life. It was as though everyone was talking, but no one was listening. The feeling of being invisible and alone was extremely painful. Should this happen to you, know that there is hope. I have written this book to be a friend to you, one that I hope will inspire you and encourage you to carry on.

For family and friends of a bipolar individual who read this book, you are probably very worried and concerned right now. Things may be happening that you don't understand. Your friend, child or sibling may even have been forcibly restrained and carried away kicking and screaming. I know it seems bad, but at least your friend or family member is safe from harming him/herself or others. Things can and will get better.

My bipolar diagnosis followed being taken into police custody, brought to an emergency psychiatric hospital, and then transferred to another psychiatric facility. I was terrified to say the least. I had no idea what a "three-day hold" meant. How could they hold me against my will without charging me with a crime? People talked about me as though I was not even there, and I felt highly disrespected. Of course I was very agitated at the time, and I'm sure my behavior appeared erratic if not dangerous, but I still felt that my rights were being violated—*I felt violated.*

At the emergency psychiatric hospital I was told for the first time that I had bipolar disorder. I had no clue what that meant and no idea how they could simply look at me and make that determination. It felt as though they just wanted to shove medication down my throat and stick needles into my arms to take blood samples. The experience was traumatic—horrific even—but it was actually the beginning of my recovery, and in that sense, it was a good thing in the end, although it took many years to accept that fact.

In the beginning, it would have been helpful to better understand what the illness was. It would have been helpful to understand how my family figured into the situation, too. When my family called the hospital, the doctors asked them if I was suicidal at the time of my admission, or if I'd had previous "suicidal ideation." One family member, apparently not wanting to take any chances, gave responses that were not accurate. Fear can do strange things to people's perceptions. Unfortunately, my own reports as to my condition were not taken seriously. It's easy to see why, but it didn't reduce the frustration and anger over losing control.

The doctor put me on a variety of drugs, including ones that supposedly prevent suicidal thoughts, even though I told him that I had never been suicidal. I think it's natural to become angry in this situation. Where do the patient's rights begin and where do they end? When are a patient's responses taken seriously and when are they ignored, and why? Does any mental health-related diagnosis automatically invalidate any information coming from the patient?

My story and my hope is to give you an opportunity to look into the life of a person with bipolar disorder. If you went to the hospital and you were told you had a broken arm, you would be treated and released and two months later you'd be back to normal. With bipolar disorder, everything is far more complicated. We may be depressed or manic, and we're not thinking clearly, so this diagnosis is a very scary thing. What are we supposed to do? How are we supposed to react? If you have bipolar disorder, understand that this may be what all of us experience—you are not alone. You'll get through it, and chances are excellent that you will be okay.

For patients, family, and friends, it is important to know that patients have certain rights that must be protected. Ask for a copy of the *Mental Health Patients' Rights Handbook* from your mental health provider. Patients' rights vary from state to state and from country to country, so it is important to be well informed on the subject.

I do not want to discourage mental health care because it has been very important to me. However, you should be aware that abuse may happen within the mental health care system. If you ever suspect abuse of any sort, report it immediately. I have witnessed abusive behavior by hospital staff belittling patients and treating them disrespectfully. I have also seen tremendous kindness and compassion. The unfortunate fact is that those who lack power over their own lives are easy targets for abuse. Therefore, if you suspect abuse, do not ignore your suspicion; go to your health care provider and demand that they investigate.

I have seen hospital staff members dismiss patients' complaints by attributing them to the patients' altered mental state. Family, friends, and health care providers should always respect an individual's feelings and take complaints seriously. Validation of self-worth and feelings are important to everyone. In many cases, patients simply need respect.

It is important that you or your loved one have a doctor and a therapist. They can help you begin the self-management process. Indeed, learning how to manage your illness can save your life. Seek out professionals who are respectful and caring. Make sure you're all compatible with one another. Sessions should feel like pieces of a puzzle are falling into place, or simply insightful. Don't settle for anything less, or you'll be wasting your time. Find health care providers who feel right to you.

Denial of a bipolar disorder diagnosis is very real. I have experienced denial and so have a number of my friends at one time or other, so you should expect it, too. Denial is often based on feelings of fear, confusion and low self-worth—i.e., one's already fragile self-esteem cannot handle the added burden of having bipolar—so this can add to the emotional issues you have to deal with. The diagnosis of bipolar disorder raised a great deal of questions about my life at a time when answers seemed in short supply. Keep in mind that it's not your fault that you have bipolar disorder; of course no one wants it, but you are not alone and you can lead a satisfying life if you try.

I shared my bipolar experience with a friend, who said, "You know, people with bipolar seem to have been given a broader palette of life's colors." She went on: "I don't see all the colors that you see. You've been given the gift of seeing more colors." Unaccustomed to thinking of my illness as an advantage, I realized that being bipolar can actually be a blessing. I have found that people with bipolar are the most loving and caring people that I know. Maybe it comes from the empathy that we naturally develop for each other, but it's good to know that it's there.

Whether you have bipolar disorder or not we have an opportunity to take a look at our lives and count our blessings. Do the same for yourself and take stock of the positive things that make you a special and unique person. What strengths do you have as an individual, in your family and relationships? When I focus on the good things of life including the good in myself, my outlook is transformed. I challenge you now to take a moment and see for yourself the beauty that is within you.

I'm proud to be who I am. I'm not bipolar; my name is David, and I have an illness called "bipolar disorder." I am not my illness, and that's what's important for me to believe and remember. I am a creative person, a deep feeler, a deep thinker, and I love people. I want to devote my life to helping others, and for these things I am not ashamed.

I nearly lost my life during extreme depressive and manic episodes following my bipolar disorder diagnosis. At that point I realized I had better learn about bipolar disorder and how to manage it. I knew that my life depended on it. Understanding myself, my past and inner healing have allowed me to maintain an attitude of awareness, that has enabled me to survive. The struggle is never complete. Bipolar survival is not a destination, but an attitude, one that must become part of our daily lives and our daily hope.

QUESTIONS OF MY LIFE

Why have I been made, to what purpose will I serve?
Which signs will I see?
What will they be?

What do I do with the life I've been given?
Where do I go?
What is my destination?

Who shall guide me with encouragement along the way?
When life is confusing
Who will make clear my way?

Which roads do I travel?
Which paths do I cross and what way do I go?
What will be my final destination?

—David Mariant

CHAPTER 6

Managing Bipolar Disorder

"It is only through extremes that men can arrive at the middle path of wisdom and virtue."

—Wilhelm von Humboldt

NOTE to the reader: It may be helpful to review Part 3, Bipolar Survival Essentials, at the back of the book before reading this chapter to better utilize the material, and to increase your knowledge of bipolar disorder and its diagnosis.

If you have bipolar disorder or know someone who does, this chapter probably contains the most important information you will find in the entire book. Your life or that of your friend or loved one may very well depend on implementing the strategies described here. The simple idea behind surviving bipolar disorder is to avoid out-of-control mood swings. Having a carefully planned strategy can be a powerful weapon against severe bipolar episodes. Responding immediately to signs of an impending episode can ward off full-blown mania or depression. Immediate intervention is important, as the more manic or depressed we become, the more difficult it is to bring that mood back to a safe level. In order to detect dangerous mood states it is also essential that we learn what a healthy normal mood state is so we have a good point of reference.

For the person experiencing mood swings or mood cycling between depression and mania, it is important to develop a fallback system as a safety net. We need to understand our mental and emotional health and how our bodies and minds react to the ebb and flow of everyday life. As we build our knowledge of our emotional, mental and physical selves, we become better able to recognize the triggers that bring on mania and depression. We also learn how to create new outcomes instead of waiting helplessly for the next episode to strike.

Much of what you are about to read is common sense, and yet you may not have thought about some of the potential lifesavers that I will point out. Other strategies that I have developed are a result of several years of trial and error. It's important to have your self-management strategies in place before you need them. The whole point of self-management is to learn how to identify the strategies and techniques that work for you so they will be there when you need them.

Self-managing our bipolar disorder recognizes the fact that ultimately, we are responsible for the outcome of our illness. We are the ultimate beneficiaries. Learning how to manage bipolar disorder will give you more control and allow you to live life more fully. You will gain a greater sense of power through your increased knowledge and understanding. You will learn how to anticipate bipolar mood changes and take action, rather than simply waiting for them to happen. Once I learned how to manage my bipolar disorder, I began taking my illness more seriously and found a greater sense of meaning in my life. This sense of meaning and the control I have gained over the illness are what compelled me to write this book, and I wish to share my hope with you. A quality life is not beyond your reach; there are positive steps you can take now to make it happen.

Self-management addresses the whole person. Drug therapy is highly effective for mood stabilization, and therapists can help us work through underlying issues and provide us with the necessary emotional support. What has been missing in the past, in my opinion, is a "case manager" to coordinate the multipronged effort to reduce the impact of bipolar on our lives. It wasn't until I stepped into the role of my own "case manager" and began to evaluate the needs of my "whole" self—the emotional, physical and spiritual—that my illness and my life began to turn around.

I am not a doctor or trained therapist, and none of the

suggestions presented here is meant to replace competent medical care by trained professionals. However, I have been successful in developing effective self-management techniques for my bipolar disorder, motivated out of self-preservation. Prior to learning how to self-manage, I nearly lost my life. As I continue to experience day-to-day life with all of its unavoidable conflicts and stressful situations, I continue to develop new and more comprehensive survival strategies to avoid and to minimize mania and depression. I recommend that you do the same. One way to do this is to read this book and to re-read it, until you become familiar with the strategies and are better prepared to handle anything that comes your way.

The fact that we can identify signs of an approaching bipolar episode and take steps to deal with it is actually empowering. We need not feel like we are at the mercy of our illness. The more we know about this disorder and the effects of mania, depression and mixed bipolar state, the better equipped we will be to manage our next episode. With bipolar disorder, one thing we know for sure: there is very likely to be a "next" episode. The better we can prepare for it, the better we will be able to be proactive in managing it.

One extremely helpful tool I have discovered for managing my own bipolar disorder is utilizing online support groups. Web-based support groups have become an important part of my own personal safety net. These groups give those with bipolar the opportunity to chat online and both share and support others during difficult times. The groups have been a godsend to me—so much so that I have established a Web site, "SurvivingBipolar.com" for the same purpose. Visitors to the site are encouraged to post commentary, ask questions, share thoughts and insights and explore feelings. It's a wonderful way to learn and grow in a supportive environment. Many insights that I share in this book come not only from my study and research, but from interactions with those who have bipolar. If you have bipolar or have a loved one who does, I recommend that you avail yourself of this powerful information and communication tool.

For online support refer to: www.SurvivingBipolar.com

Perhaps you have yet to experience an incident that convinces you that bipolar disorder is a serious condition. It is not unusual to be in denial about having bipolar disorder, just as I was in denial when first diagnosed. A year and a half after my diagnosis, I saw myself as generally well, so I decided to stop taking my prescribed medications. Of course I was in denial. I became convinced that I was not bipolar at all, and even thought that mania was a result of taking the medications. My doctor initially told me that my manic episode may actually have been induced by an antidepressant I had been prescribed. This provided all the rationale I needed to convince myself that I did not in fact have bipolar disorder at all. Hoping to prove I was not bipolar, I stopped taking my medications without bothering to ask for my doctor's approval. Of course this is a very dangerous and foolhardy thing to do. Never discontinue psychiatric medications without medical advice and careful consideration.

Within just days of stopping my medications, I had a psychotic reaction. Within two weeks, I was hospitalized and disoriented. After I began to recover, I recall thinking that I never wanted to be in such a state again. I feared that I might actually lose my mind permanently. I now accept that I have bipolar disorder and am perfectly willing to take a few pills every day to stabilize my moods and to protect my mental state. For my own sake, and the sake of the family that I love, I am committed to doing everything I possibly can to stay strong and healthy, and that means adhering strictly to my prescribed drug regimen.

Perhaps you or someone you love is having difficulty accepting a bipolar disorder diagnosis and taking prescribed medications, just as I did when first diagnosed. Unfortunately, many have to experience a significant psychiatric episode before accepting the seriousness of this disorder and the critical need for professional intervention. It is interesting to note that some are actually thankful for their bipolar diagnoses. Learning that they have bipolar disorder gives them an explanation for why they act and feel the way they do. I had assumed that the bipolar disorder diagnosis could only be viewed as a negative. I now realize that many are optimistic about their diagnoses. Gaining new perspectives is one example of the many benefits of participating in bipolar support groups.

It was fortunate that, shortly after my diagnosis, I found an excellent doctor. He continues to be a great help to me even now. Other doctors I met—in the psychiatric hospital—did not appear to think of me as a "real person," but rather as a defective product that needed to be "fixed." As a result, I felt broken and flawed. All mental health professionals are not created equally. You need to actively seek out doctors and therapists who you feel comfortable with, then do everything you can to keep working with them. If you are not happy with your current physician, select another until you find one you are comfortable with. It's your health and well being that's at stake, so don't settle for less. Having the right doctor can make all the difference.

Inconsiderate, dispassionate treatment is not limited to doctors. During my stays in the hospital, I observed many staff members who tended to disregard patients' attempts to communicate. They apparently saw patients as unable to understand anything or care for themselves in any way. This may actually be true in very severe cases, but certainly is not true for everyone. This is a serious problem. More than anything, people with bipolar disorder need compassion and their worth as human beings validated; clearly, treating them as "human" would be a huge step in the right direction.

Of the many people I know with bipolar disorder from various parts of the world through online interactions, some have described their care in glowing terms. Others have reported that care and consideration were significantly lacking. This is why effective self-management includes the participation of friends and family to ensure the well being of the person with bipolar disorder—to be their advocate—should that person's ability to act on their own behalf be compromised.

Someone in a manic or depressed state may exhibit distorted thinking, but it is important not to discount points that the person is trying to make. If they have a problem with the doctor, for example, it would be helpful to discuss the issue with the patient, and to talk to the doctor as well. Even if you don't agree with what your friend or loved one is saying or doing, you can still validate their concerns and feelings. In this way, you will be perceived as a friend who has their best interest at heart. Try to see things from their point of view. Even if you can't, the main thing is that you have listened to them and considered what they had to say. Consideration is valuable, even if you believe they are too ill at the time to make decisions for themselves. If you are the parent or spouse of someone with bipolar disorder, it is important to balance respect for the person with the need to act in their best interest. I would have appreciated having my feelings taken more seriously by my family when I was in the hospital. They probably thought they were helping, but I think their fear and lack of understanding may have distorted their perception. I grew very angry with my family because I thought they were undermining my well-being.

Bipolar Management Class

Another important element in managing bipolar disorder is to learn as much as possible about the illness. Once I was able to attend a class on managing bipolar disorder taught by a therapist and a doctor, I quickly realized how important the knowledge I gained about the disorder would be to my future. One of the most significant aspects of the class was emphasis on acceptance and self-respect. It was especially helpful to learn that I was not alone. Others not only had bipolar disorder, but were learning to live successfully with the illness. It helped me to accept my diagnosis and to begin the process of my healing.

If classes aren't available in your area, there are many excellent books available on bipolar disorder. Do all that you can to increase your knowledge and understanding of this illness. Doctors and therapists are also excellent resources. The Internet contains a vast amount of information on bipolar disorder, and online support groups are also available to you when you are ready.

Please review "Introduction to Stress Management" in Part 3, Bipolar Survival Essentials, at the back of this book. Stress management is important to managing bipolar disorder.

It is difficult to understand why health care providers do not require or at least strongly recommend that every person with bipolar disorder attend bipolar self-management classes. When doctors and therapists act as advocates for bipolar disorder knowledge and support, we are better served, while the government health care, HMOs and insurance companies have lower expenses for hospitalizations.

Mind and body awareness were emphasized in the class to provide advanced warning signs of an approaching episode and to mitigate its impact. Through self-understanding and learning to recognize early warning signals, we can prevent full-blown episodes and hospitalizations. Another important discovery for me was the use of personal history timelines—events that correlate strongly with manic and depressive episodes. I found it helpful to develop my own personal life history and timeline of traumatic events and codependent experiences in my life.

No matter what crowd I am in, I find that whenever I mention bipolar disorder, it seems that someone else either has the disorder or knows someone who does. Many have the disorder in their family lineage. Developing your own family history can be very important. We may learn who has the illness within the family and what strategies and medications worked for them. Another important element to consider is distortions in our thinking. We tend to respond negatively to things people say, often because we don't understand them correctly or hear them in a distorted way. Our responses, therefore, may not be as productive as we would have liked, and unfortunately relationships can be hurt.

Suicide Prevention

As difficult as it may be to think about, understanding the nature of suicide is an important part of effective self-management. What brings a person to the point of suicide? Depression can catch us off guard and can come on quickly with brute force. Even if it approaches slowly, its depth can take us by surprise. During severe depressive episodes and mixed bipolar state, I have experienced reckless behavior and have thought about death. At those times suicidal thoughts pounded away at me—seemingly "wanting" me to just give in and die. Although I never reached the point of carrying out my suicidal thoughts, I can certainly appreciate how it can happen. Remember that one in five persons with bipolar disorder takes his or her own life; therefore, it is crucial that we understand the nature of suicidal thinking. When I recently learned of this statistic, I was horrified. Bipolar really is a potentially fatal illness, and in my opinion we need to respect it as such.

If you find yourself in the depths of despair, it's hard to imagine things will ever improve or that you will ever feel better. Please don't try to go it alone; seek help to hang on until the mood passes. Talk to your therapist. Talk to someone and share how you feel. In most localities there are Suicide and Crisis telephone help lines where you can call anonymously. Often, just knowing someone cares and is there for you is all that it takes to turn the corner.

Please review "Frequently Asked Questions about Suicide" in Part 3, Bipolar Survival Essentials. Reviewing the suicide portion of the Essentials will help you become more aware of the warning signs of suicidal thinking and answer many of your questions.

Relationships

Healthy relationships are an important aspect in managing bipolar disorder. Unfortunately, not all relationships are healthy. In my case, I have learned that I cannot afford to be around people I refer to as "toxic"—those controlling and abusive people who poison me with their emotional garbage. In the past, I had the tendency to take on that garbage and poison myself, only adding to my depression. Our well-being depends on healthy and nourishing relationships. It's not easy, but I have had to eliminate friends and even family members from my life at times just to gain more strength and establish stronger boundaries.

In looking back, I found that each of my hospitalizations was preceded by a toxic relationship. One case at work involved a passive boss who did not back me up when he should have. The work relationships went awry when ideas I presented as a part of my job responsibilities were dismissed. In other instances, fault was unfairly placed at my feet, or negative interactions occurred and were misinterpreted. Inappropriate blaming generated such a strong, but repressed, emotional response, that a manic episode resulted. It is important, therefore, that we learn to control who and what we allow into our lives whenever possible.

Healthy relationships, on the other hand, are critically important, and that means showing appropriate concern. In a friendship, we inquire how our friend is doing, and let our friend know we care. The same is true should the friend happen to have bipolar disorder. It is even more important to ask because the response can reveal how they are being treated and how they are doing. Ask how they are getting along. Do they like their doctor and therapist? Are they taking their medications? How are they sleeping? How is their hospital stay? Do they feel respected? This type of support can work wonders in helping your loved one, and they will likely appreciate your interest. Always take their feedback seriously and with respect. If they don't want to answer questions, respect that as well. If you make the effort, they will at least know that the lines of communication are open.

Asking questions is especially important in an in-patient situation. Hospital patients should be asked about their doctor, the therapist, the hospital, and their general wellness. In my case I felt defective as a person. It felt as though others were looking at me in the same way I looked at myself. Since the person with bipolar disorder may already feel defective and flawed, anything that suggests defectiveness will likely be taken as a confirmation, only adding to feelings of hopelessness and despair.

Permission is important. If anyone other than my wife or a doctor or therapist were to ask if I was taking my medications, I would feel defensive and even violated. This was especially true during my early experience with bipolar when I was very sensitive to having the illness. So parents, brothers, sisters, and friends—if you don't have an agreement allowing you to ask questions and give feedback, I recommend that you ask for permission before doing so as a matter of common courtesy. If you have been asked not to inquire, then don't. Respecting another person's wishes may be difficult. However, it is important to understand that the individual with bipolar disorder likely has difficulty setting boundaries. You will be actually helping them by respecting the boundaries that they have established.

Emergency situations—a person exhibiting signs of severe depression or mania, or talking about ending their lives—are a different matter. If you know someone with a bad heart having chest pains, you wouldn't pepper him or her with questions about their condition. You would call 9-1-1. Sometimes it's necessary to intervene even without an explicit agreement, but only when it's appropriate. Even before we had an agreement, my wife called 9-1-1 because she felt my behavior indicated an emergency. Although I resented it at the time, I later realized that she probably saved my life.

Asking appropriate questions and respecting boundaries goes back to the notion of "loving support." My definition of loving support goes beyond the questions, "Did you take your medicine?" or "Did you get enough rest?" Well-meaning spouses, parents, and friends are often quick to ask these questions, especially when a person with bipolar disorder comes out of the hospital or is newly diagnosed. Of course they mean well, but these questions, asked repeatedly, may not be viewed as love at all. It quickly begins to feel that they are being treated like a child. A dilemma exists between asking questions lovingly and not asking the questions—allowing the person space. For me, it was an issue of self-respect. Bipolar disorder and any other illness is a personal matter, and the individual should be respected. Open communication is important, so ask your loved one if it's OK to ask questions, and if the questions are in any way offensive.

There was a time when, although my loved ones felt they were affirming their love for me by constantly asking me if I was taking my medication, it felt rude and demeaning. The issue relates directly to one's self-identity and self-worth. As my self-worth has grown stronger and healthier, I no longer feel so intimidated by the questions. It is also easier to answer, "it's private," if asked a question we feel invades our personal space. We have the right, after all, to decide what is personal and private and what we are willing to share. The ability to set appropriate boundaries is an essential skill for reducing stress in our lives.

Having said that, it is important to establish a relationship with a primary "loving support person." In my case, it's my wife. She needs to know that she can ask me about taking my medication and my health in general. If she thinks I'm not getting enough rest, for example, she needs to mention it to me. She is really my back-up monitor. It was difficult for me to allow anyone to be in that position until after my second hospitalization. If someone asked me about my meds (medication), I would get angry. Now that I have given my wife permission to ask, I don't get angry anymore. In fact, I appreciate her concern.

My reluctance to be asked about taking my meds changed around the time I stopped taking them for a week without telling anyone and suffered a manic episode as a result. Since then, I am much more diligent about taking my prescribed medications, and my wife is more diligent following up with me. I love her for the concern she shows, and taking a few pills each day helps me to stay alive and well. This is why it is so important to have open communication with someone in your life. If you're not bothered by people asking you personal questions, so much the better. You need to feel comfortable; but if you're a very private person, you may need to work on expanding your comfort zone.

One of the keys to self-management is accurate input from others. Give people who are close to you permission to ask if you feel all right, if you are on your meds, or provide feedback. If such comments and questions offend you, learn how to be more accepting. Talk to the people in your support network and suggest ways to approach the subject if they become concerned. In fact, I learned from friends some time later, that they thought I had been behaving strangely prior to my second hospitalization. Unfortunately, they felt awkward saying anything. When I heard this, I encouraged them to let me or my wife know if they ever notice anything that does not seem right. Had they spoken up at the time, I might have acted on it. I am no longer so self-conscious and offended. I am also more accepting about having bipolar disorder, to the point that I have been able to write this book. Please consider allowing others to give you feedback, as your life and safety may very well depend on it.

Journaling

Journaling is a good way to keep track of your day-to-day condition. Journaling has helped me to understand my own bipolar disorder more clearly, so much so that I am able to share with you what I have discovered about my own survival. A journal typically includes a mood diary, timeline of life events, list of medications, hospitalization reports, and other documents relevant to self-managing your bipolar disorder. At some point, it may be necessary to share information with your doctor or therapist. This is especially true if you and your doctor are working together to adjust your medication and fine-tune your mood stabilization.

Your journal might begin with notes about how you think

and feel each day. Other uses for your journal might include gauging your day-to-day moods, your weight, sleep and rising times, and times you take medications. Optimum mood stabilization can be difficult to establish with medication; it takes time and patience. I suggest that you record your medications daily, along with any side effects you may experience to discuss with your doctor. Psychiatrists and therapists may have mood charts available for your use.

Be consistent with your journaling, and once you get into the habit, it is useful to review your notes from time to time to look for patterns. Ask your doctor and therapist what things would be helpful to track, and bring your journal with you to your regular appointments. Your doctor and therapist will find the information helpful, but you should also try to make sense of the information on your own.

Emergency Information Card

I suggest that you keep an emergency medical card with you at all times. Use a three inch by five inch index card for this purpose. Fold the card to a size that allows you to keep the information in your wallet or purse. You might consider giving a copy of the index card and information to your emergency contacts and your medical provider to be placed in your file and perhaps your doctor and therapist. You might also consider laminating the cards to preserve them. Please note that your doctor, therapist and medical provider may want the information on a full size sheet of paper. I keep my information in my wallet. Place a note on your drivers license or I.D. card that says something like, "I have bipolar disorder, refer to the information card in my wallet for more information. The card should have several pieces of information. Consult your doctor for additional suggestions.

BIPOLAR DISORDER PATIENT INFORMATION CARD
(at the top of side one)

Patient:
 Name
 Address
 Phone Number, home and cellular

Emergency Contact: (two or more is suggested)
 Name
 Phone Numbers, home and cellular

Medical Provider:
 Name
 Address
 Medical Record Number
 Phone Number

 Doctor:
 Names
 Phone Numbers

Therapist:
 Names
 Phone Numbers

MEDICATIONS AND DIRECTIVE (at the top of side two)

Bipolar Disorder Diagnosis Date – Describe multiple diagnosis if applicable

Suicidal History - Describe

Medication Names - dosages, frequency and the date you started taking the medication.

List any allergies to medications

List any previous hospitalizations

Special Instructions: If you were detained by a police officer or a paramedic, what would you want to tell them. If there is something that you can think of then include that on the card too.

Medications

Medication is an essential element in treating most cases of bipolar disorder. Drug therapy regimens are patient specific. The various drugs and dosages available provide endless possible custom treatments. Fine-tuning drugs and dosages can take time. Recording your reactions to specific drugs and dosages can greatly reduce the time needed to discover the optimal treatment program for you.

The great variety of medications and dosages used to treat bipolar disorder also increases the potential for side effects. Your doctor will likely require regular blood tests. These tests are necessary to determine if medication levels in your blood stream are toxic or therapeutic. Don't hesitate to contact your doctor if you are concerned about any unusual side effects, and make note in your journal any reactions to your medications.

It is very important to be aware of interactions among medications. If you are taking prescription or over the counter medications for other conditions or illnesses in addition to your bipolar disorder meds, it is important that all doctors involved in your care are aware of all medications you are taking. Over the past three years, for example, I developed a serious allergy. I suffered from severe coughing attacks. My doctor prescribed Prednisone. Within just a few days I was nearly full-blown manic. Although I did not know it at the time, even those who aren't bipolar may experience mental effects and sleep disorders with Prednisone. Since then, I have been on a gradual, physician supervised reduced dosage of Prednisone. I take it at a specific time of day, which helps reduce interaction with my other medications.

Life History

Creating a life history, including traumatic events and family relationships, can be very helpful. Earlier I discussed "traumatic overload" because life traumas can be cumulative and can often trigger bipolar responses. Your journal can be useful in reconstructing your past creating your own "life history." It does not have to be done all at once. I found that it was easier to start at the beginning of my life and go forward, but it may be easier for you to start at the present and work backward or skip around. As you construct your "life timeline," make note of feelings associated with your traumatic events. It is OK if you cannot recall any traumatic life events because they may not be triggers for you. It is also possible that you have blocked painful memories from your consciousness. In any case, if you have experienced mania or severe depression, note them in your timeline. It is helpful to review your history with your doctor and therapist. In my own case, I was able to identify several areas in my life history that had a strong hold on me and even jeopardized my personal safety.

Consider talking to your doctor or therapist about creating a life history. You may want to do this with your therapist because some events that come up in your past may be very upsetting to you. I suggest that you first take out a pad of paper and jot down all of the significant events that you can think of. Skip several lines between ideas that come to mind. Do this until the ideas stop flowing. Trust me, more ideas are likely to come to the surface. If you can, assign dates to the events and do the best you can. I think life events should also include happy events like having a child, getting married or buying your first sports car.

Once you have a list, "try to number the events" so you can transfer the life events to a new piece of paper in a chronological order. Again, when you put the events down in chronological order, leave a few lines after each for the next few steps. With the new list, jot down the feelings associated with each event. It might be helpful to also write a brief summary about the event and why it is a significant event. Pay close attention to the people involved in that event and how you felt about them. Did they add joy to the event, were they toxic or did they add serious stress. Where did the event take place, where were you? Add whatever additional information you feel is important to each event. Don't limit your writing to a few lines either.

Now is the interesting part. Scan through all of the significant events and jot down on yet another blank piece of paper your answers to the following questions. Write as much as you want because this step will make all of your efforts worthwhile. It is likely that important information will emerge about your past and personal responses that can help you prepare yourself to survive bipolar disorder in the future with confidence. Take your time, perhaps you may wish to do this step over the course of a few days. Answer the following:

- What was your initial thought after scanning the significant events?
- Can you see events precipitate mania and depression?
- What events precipitate joy and happiness?
- Do you see any patterns emerge?
- What were your initial thoughts about the patterns?
- How do you feel about the patterns and how they relate to your bipolar disorder and your wellbeing?
- What insights have you gained from this exercise?
- Continue adding to your life history as new events come to mind.

You may wish to periodically review your life history for further life insight. Now that you have done this work you might want to share your insights with your therapist or doctor. Remember, you are your own doctor first. You will likely have greater insights into what will help you survive bipolar than any one else. This step has helped me tremendously and I now recognize that the toxic person is like a flame to the fire and can result in danger for my life. Try this exercise; I think it may be helpful.

Please review "Facts about Post Traumatic Stress Disorder" and "Codependency" in Part 3, Bipolar Survival Essentials. Reviewing the Essentials will help you understand the significance of life events that affect your bipolar disorder.

Monitoring Mood

Talk with your doctor and therapist about how to monitor your moods. This is key! They will be able to help you create a mood chart and develop safety strategies. The idea of the mood chart is to assign a number to how you are feeling each day and record it. The Bipolar chapter in the Essential section of the book provides definitions for moods and ratings, but it is not a substitute for consulting your own medical professional. Once you understand how to rate your moods, you can record them in your journal. Try to record your mood every day. A suggested schedule might be like mine:

-5 = Dangerously Depressed   0 = Healthy   +5 = Dangerously Manic

Moods lower than −2 (depression), or more than +2 (manic) are approaching the danger level, and I know I am at risk of full-blown mania or depression and possible hospitalization. The important thing is to work to minimize extreme mood swings. If our mood goes too far toward mania or depression, it is much more difficult to recover and stabilize. In tracking my own moods, I can tell when my mood is "ramping up" or moving from one level to another, and I can take steps to respond. If I get too little sleep for a few days in a row, for example, I know that I am moving closer to a manic state. Knowing this, I can immediately implement the sleep strategies that I have learned.

There are a number of strategies that you can develop and implement to manage your bipolar disorder in conjunction with your doctor and therapist. Mood charting is a powerful tool in surviving bipolar disorder, and does require professional involvement and guidance. Be sure to discuss your plans with your doctor thoroughly before you take action with any strategy. The most important thing to remember is that we must know our bodies and minds. We must know when depression or mania is coming on. We must be on alert and mood charting allows you to recognize the sometimes subtle changes in our moods and ultimately can save your life.

Sleep

Sleep is a matter of life and death for me and for many others with bipolar disorder. If I do not get enough sleep over the course of several days, I may go manic. In some ways, sleep is more important than anything else, including medication. Therefore, sleep is a top priority, even though it can be difficult at times. One strategy I follow is to resist the urge to get out of bed when I wake up too early in the morning, even if I feel wide awake. At the very least my body gets additional rest, and if I stay in bed, I might go back to sleep. Even a rough night's sleep is better than none at all, especially for those of us with bipolar disorder.

When I am depressed, the problem is more often too much sleep rather than not enough. When my job required that I telecommute from home, I became very depressed because of the isolation and the new diagnosis. Getting out of bed in the morning became nearly impossible. Scheduling activities ahead of time made it easier to function, especially scheduling early morning appointments and conference calls.

Knowing your sleep requirements is critical to developing strategies to get the sleep you need. Consider making daily journal entries regarding the quantity and quality of sleep you get each night.

Please review "Brain Basics, Understanding Sleep" in Part 3, Bipolar Survival Essentials. Reviewing the Essentials will help you learn the importance of sleep and strategies for sleeping better.

Therapy

Addressing codependency in my life has been vital to overcome the mood swings of bipolar disorder and reduce the risk. In a similar way a treatment called EMDR (Eye Movement Desensitization Reprocessing), has helped me address traumatic events in my life and overcome them. Traumatic events have nearly paralyzed me and have had a huge bearing on my stress load. With the stress load reduced I am safer.

I have had the privilege of exploring a number of therapy options and have done a great deal of personal research on the topic of bipolar disorder. I will describe many therapeutic options that are available that have helped me. A recent discovery was made through neurofeedback therapy. The treatment has been helpful dealing with my child who is diagnosed with bipolar disorder. Another huge benefit for me is that I learned how to fall asleep through learning a breathing technique. You will read more about my family and my child with bipolar later in the book. Through neurofeedback I have learned how to overcome the debilitating fears and I have also learned how to better control my thoughts. By controlling my mind and thoughts better, my safety is increased because uncontrolled thinking and thoughts lead to depression or mania. I also have included a chapter on NeuroFeedback in Part 3, Bipolar Survival Essentials, a contribution by my psychologist who administered the therapy.

Support Groups

Surround yourself with people who love you unconditionally. Get involved with a bipolar support group, both in person and, if possible, online. You will not regret it. I started the **www.SurvivingBipolar.com** website and forums for the purpose of online bipolar community support. It is anonymous. Family members and friends of the diagnosed person can participate online with privacy and ask the questions they otherwise might not ask.

The Challenge

Because I have written this book, it may seem that I have it "all together." I don't. Like everyone else with bipolar disorder, I struggle regularly and sometimes desperately. Managing bipolar is an ongoing challenge, and often a daunting one, but it is possible to meet the challenge. The most important thing is not to give up. Focus on arming yourself with as much information as you can find. If one strategy doesn't work for you, try something else. Get the best doctor and therapist you can find and learn as much as you can from them. Keep in mind that although they are busy professionals, they really do want to help you. If they didn't, they would be doing something else with their lives.

It is very important to remember that this book is not a substitute for professional medical treatment, including medication, nor is it a substitute for further learning about bipolar disorder. My hope is that reading this book is merely a beginning. Knowing yourself and managing your bipolar disorder is critical to your survival, so do learn as much as you can about your own life – your life history, stressors, relationships, the triggers. Doing so will put you in a much better position to preserve your life. My sincere hope is that your life will become more well balanced and meaningful as a result.

Please refer to Part 3, Bipolar Survival Essentials, at the back of this book for further detailed information on all topics discussed in this chapter.

LEARNING TO FLY

My mind is clear
My heartache gone
My face is smiling
My soul burden gone

My pain recedes
My wounds are well
I walk again
Even after I fell

I am no longer crushed
By memories of the past
I can look to the future
The glorious contrast

The new man in the mirror
I want to know
I want to be his friend
And to watch him grow

—David Mariant

CHAPTER 7

Danger — Traumatic Overload

"I hear the little children of the wind
crying solitary in lonely places."

— William (Fiona McLeod) Sharp

As I have mentioned previously, bipolar disorder is like a "bomb" — and a bomb it will always be. In my opinion, traumatic life issues can very well be the dangerous detonator that increases the risk of a life-threatening bipolar explosion. My simple definition of a traumatic event: the witnessing of, or learning of a horrible incident that leaves an image "burned" in your mind. In my case, such images brought about fear, panic and a strong sense of being out of control. Traumatic events may include, but are not limited to, seeing someone's body after they die, seeing someone killed, learning of a loved one's suicide, sexual abuse, betrayal, drugs, a child or loved one threatening to run away, breaking the law and endangering the family, and the list goes on . . .There are many significant issues that have set off my bipolar detonator. I realize that recognizing these "detonators" will be critical to my survival; this is key to minimizing the risks associated with bipolar disorder — risks that have the potential to trigger a negative mental or emotional response.

Any traumatic event in our lives is a serious issue. Many of us are unable to function in a normal way and may even become extremely disabled. Certain events that I have experienced have certainly added a huge burden to an already overburdened life. I am not suggesting that bipolar disorder is always a result of traumatic experiences, but that these types of events can add to the stress load, and could very well trigger a bipolar response in either a manic or depressive episode. Traumatic experiences during my childhood have haunted me most of my life and have affected me in negative ways. My hope is that you will see deeper meaning in relation to traumatic events that may have occurred or are occurring in your life, and the significance of addressing those events in therapy. Remember, the more baggage we can work through and unload from our lives and minds, the better off we will be.

Further along in this chapter you will see a string of events that took place from my infancy to the present. Hopefully, you will take a moment to reflect on key events and traumas during your own lifetime. As a means to instinctively protect ourselves from trauma and mental overload, it is quite common for us to protectively block out that event which may be too much to handle. This is a normal coping device. Unfortunately, a painful event previously blocked out quite commonly rears its ugly head many years later by leaking out small amounts of the lost memory. Many with bipolar have disclosed to me major traumatic events from their distant pasts and are now having to deal with these issues.

Nearly everyone has a past traumatic event or are currently dealing with one. In my observation, most people with bipolar disorder seem to have experienced very troubling situations or an extreme amount of these traumas over the years. We have been formed and molded, not only by our physical being when entering this world, but by the emotional, spiritual and additional traumatic experiences of our lives.

Why is the emotional and spiritual side of the bipolar experience so de-emphasized by the community of doctors and therapists that I have spoken to? Although I have some understanding, the answer still remains unclear to me now. At the time of diagnosis it seemed like my life history of emotional traumatizing events did not matter. Bipolar disorder often manifests itself as an emergency and the first medical response to those in need of urgent, immediate treatment by doctors is medication. Therapy is offered, as well as bipolar disorder management classes. However, so many times the doctors and therapists focus primarily on medication. This, of course, is often the key to stabilizing the onset of the mania or depression in one's life that can put one in grave danger. Medication seems to be a good first course of action to deal with both the emergency and non-emergency situation. I will share a slightly broader perspective than just medication; I present a view which emphasizes the need to address the complete self. I have found it essential in my own healing and bipolar management to address the emotional and spiritual side of myself along with medication treatment, in order to find balance in my life. I want to emphasize bipolar disorder management. I cannot stress enough the importance that we do ongoing "life work"—in other words, continued work on the stresses and problems from our past and in our every day life to find balance. I know that it was essential for my own personal survival. I hope you, as well as your family and loved ones, find comfort in knowing that although a person may have significant life issues including current or past traumas, he or she can take steps to better their lives and survive bipolar disorder.

Before I go further, I want it to be clear that I don't mean to infer that childhood trauma is responsible for bipolar disorder. However, through reviewing my own history and posing questions to those with bipolar, serious childhood trauma and an unhealthy upbringing is very common among half of the respondents. I am convinced that traumatic events played a large part in how my illness has affected me. As you continue to read through the pages of this book I hope this becomes apparent to you. How your life events have affected you and your bipolar experience may also become clearer to you. What kind of traumatic experiences do you recall in your life? Have you spent any time working through those issues? To ignore traumatic overload in your life is dangerous, and unfortunately, with bipolar disorder it can be fatal. I strongly believe that life events are significantly responsible for awakening the bipolar disorder predisposition and its resulting serious mood swings.

I suggest that you take a sheet of paper and write down

each traumatic event in your life in the order that it occurred. Including the dates or your age might be helpful. In effect, you create a "life timeline of events" and as you do so you may find yourself looking back to your own history. The unresolved harmful life events built upon each other in my case until I reached my emotional breaking point. This will become clear as you read on.

Note to the reader: The following section contains graphic material that may be upsetting.

Overdose

My earliest memory is of a traumatic experience that occurred just before my second birthday, when I overdosed on aspirin that I found in my mother's purse. Although I don't remember taking the aspirin, I do remember being in the speeding car to the hospital—and screaming for my mom while a tube was being shoved down my throat in the Emergency Room, in an effort to pump out the contents of my stomach. I have hated hospitals ever since.

Domestic Violence

At about two or three years of age, I witnessed a terrible fight between my parents and felt terrible fear that my father was killing my mother; this was only one of many fights that I recall. I remember many details... at one point I was only a few feet away when I remember loud cursing and my mother's pleading. I think that my father was attempting to strangle her, and I did not understand. I witnessed some scary things. I was horrified! I remember my dad being handcuffed and taken away by police. Although I discussed the events with my siblings and determined my memories were accurate, I don't know if they are in the right sequence. Although I was young at the time, the memories are quite vivid. This wasn't the only time I witnessed my father enraged with my mother, but I remember that it was one of the worst. Not only did I lose my dad that night, but soon after my parents divorced. I felt like I never really had a father after that point, although my sister, my brothers and I did see him occasionally. I thank God that he has changed over the years and his anger and rage have subsided.

After the divorce, the yelling and anger still continued between my parents, and so did my fears. Since the early days of my life, I have continued this "walk in fear" over having witnessed and lived through those horrific events. It seeps back into my memory from time to time—even now. Fortunately, I now have a good relationship with both my mom and my dad. It was when my dad and I discussed my early childhood memories of what it felt like for me to witness him nearly killing my mom, that something very special happened. Over the course of my life I tried to discuss this matter of the terrible fight that I witnessed between he and my mom, without any real sense of satisfaction. He was very defensive, and it seemed as though he always dismissed my feelings. However, the last time we discussed this matter I persisted in saying that they were my feelings and the way I remembered them as a two or three years old, and they were what they were. Eventually he agreed that despite the possibility of an inaccurate sense of reality I had been carrying those feelings around with me all of my life. The conversation left me with the sense that my feelings were finally validated. That really meant a lot to me, and it still does. Not only did the conversation seem to bring some closure to those events, but I also gained a caring father that day.

Sexual Abuse

At about six to eight years old I experienced perhaps the most traumatic series of events that any child can experience. In fact the events became even more traumatic as I grew older. There were two boys who were about four and six years older than I. I respected and looked up to both boys, one was like a father to me, and yet they separately sexually abused me, which still haunts me. The individuals knew one another, however I don't believe they knew that they both were being inappropriate with me. After the molestations, they would instruct me not to tell anyone. They knew what they were doing was wrong. It was a very confusing time in my life. Being a small child, I did not feel that they or I were doing anything wrong; in fact, naturally, I had no sense of boundaries and did not even think I should try to stop them. It was all a game, they told me—our secret little game. Hardcore molestation occurred over a period of about four or five years with the oldest boy who was somewhat like a father figure to me. The other boy fondled me and the molestation was more along the lines of touching. This also continued for several years.

A few years ago, I confronted my molesters. I wanted to discuss the matter of sexual abuse. I needed to understand and to begin the process of healing emotionally by forgiving them, for my own sake. The boy who was somewhat like a father figure to me was in total denial, quickly saying he had no remembrance of participating in such repeated sick events in our youth which was a rather convenient thing for him to say at the time. His words of no memory of the events hurt me as much as being molested all those years. He tried to act as though I made up everything. I understand that this is often the case for sexual violators. Perhaps he thought it would just go away or that I brought it up to damage his reputation, but that was not the case. I just wanted an apology; I wanted to understand who molested *him, to understand why this happened to me* and to move on. The other violator denied any wrongdoing but did admit to it happening. The one that denied wrongdoing was later sent to prison for five years for fondling another little boy several years after molesting me. I have heard that he has since been classified as a pedophile and has a police record. I think the boy that was a fatherly figure to me should be a registered sexual offender too, even more so. After doing some of my own research I believe this person would have received in the neighborhood of 8 years in prison or so and also be classified properly as a sexual predator.

It shocked me when I tried to discuss the wrongdoing with a close relative of the first violator; this person became very sympathetic for the *violator* and began to justify the violator's actions. By the time I left this person's home, I felt that this person not only seemed to pity my abuser, but seemed to be blaming me for being too hard and judgmental! The reaction to what I disclosed was a completely hysterical one. Perhaps the belief was that I was going to press charges; in fact I was just trying to find a way to forgive my abusers and move on with my life. I also mentioned the incident to the father of this same abuser and got NO response. It seemed like one extreme to the other, from hysteria to no response at all. However, since the father was rarely involved in his son's life, I didn't pursue the matter with him again.

My violator's close relative turned the whole event around, and that discussion became another one of the sickest, traumatic, and emotional experiences I have ever had. To try to overcome the wounds etched in me from the sexual abuse, molestation and denials, I underwent EMDR, (Eye Movement Desensitization Reprocessing). EMDR is a wonderful treatment for traumatic events and has proven helpful in healing my many wounds from the past. While undergoing the EMDR therapy, I literally felt like I was going to vomit due to the emotional energy stored up surrounding these traumatic events.

To date, I have never discussed this matter with the parents of the abuser who went to prison. I had learned from many sources, including the brother of my abuser, that the abuser had been seriously molested by *his father*.

Because sexual abuse is so prevalent, this may be an area for which you will want to seek help. "…one in three girls and one in six boys are sexually abused before age 18."[1] I know

---

1 See Russell, Diane E. H. "The Incidence and Prevalence of interfamily and Extrafamilial Sexual Abuse of Female Children," in *Handbook on Sexual Abuse of Children*, edited by Lenore E.A. Walker. Springer Publishing Co, 1988.

that a great number of my friends who have bipolar disorder have also experienced sexual abuse and most of them seemed to experience a serious degree of abuse just as I did. Because depression is a major effect of sexual abuse and depression is so dangerous, we need to seek help even though this is a very sensitive topic.

Medical Emergency

At age ten I stepped on a sewing needle at my home and it broke off and lodged itself in my foot. This required two surgeries to remove it. The first surgery was while I was awake and I have vivid traumatic memories of seeing my entire foot wrapped in gauze soaked blood. Naturally, from that point forward I have been horrified of needles.

Loss of Loved Ones

I am not alone in having had many traumatic life events. Many of them have concerned the loss of loved ones. When I was only five years old, my godfather Ray, died unexpectedly. He was like a father figure to me. I think that seeing my dad move out of my home one year earlier and missing him so much, may have amplified my godfather's loss to me. A dear adult friend and "Big Brother," Gary, died unexpectedly when I was eleven years old. He was indeed like a big brother to me and the unexpected loss was devastating. It seemed like important father figures to me kept disappearing! Could I depend on any of them sticking around? "Grampie," who I loved very much and is one of the biggest heroes of my life, probably because he was there for me like a father when my own father was not, died when I was a young teenager. My grandma died when I was nineteen. She was there for my siblings and me regularly and was especially important to all of us. Grandma would have us over for dinner often, which made me feel loved. My grandma was a significant person in my life after my dad left. My grandmother on my mom's side died as well. Both my grandmother and grandfather on my mom's side provided stability and love. My uncle George was also a hero to me and was my roommate for a few months prior to his tragic and sudden death. My younger brother's death was horrific and was my greatest experience of loss ever. Their untimely passing totally devastated me beyond expression through words. My aunt died and she was also an important part of my life, particularly at the end of her life. The common theme throughout these deaths and my life is that significant people I loved deeply, died unexpectedly, creating a sense that I could not count on anyone whom I loved to be with me for the long haul. My heart is broken and at times I am even very angry with God.

Within the first twenty years of my life, many events helped to mold the person who I had become. I was insecure, angry, untrusting, you bet! I began to push friendships away; I felt of little value to others because of the abuse and abandonment issues and was confused about my life purpose.

Drugs and Alcohol Abuse

At around fourteen I began experimenting with marijuana and alcohol. It started with a few friends inviting me to the high school field where everyone smoked. Several older kids that I looked up to in earlier years smoked at the field so it was natural for me to think it was okay. At first, marijuana did not seem to affect me at all. It was strange, as I look back on that time period. However, I began to smoke more and more and later began to feel a drugged and intensified effect; the result of marijuana amplified. One day I got so high on it that I went to my metal shop class and could hardly see. It was quite scary, but my friends joked about it like it was some sort of game.

I later learned that one of my friends was selling drugs. He did a pretty good job getting me hooked while he lured me and others with free drugs and later would only sell them to us. Drugs became a new way to escape for me and I would rely on them for several years as a way to numb out from the internal battle I was experiencing.

At about age fifteen I had been experimenting with alcohol. As I look back, I can see how I was searching for acceptance—the drugs and alcohol gave me the false sense of fitting in—not necessarily with the best groups, but I did fit in. At age eighteen, I expanded my use of drugs into the realm of stimulants which became a new experience as I searched for greater meaning in my life amid so much confusion.

Around eighteen, there was even greater confusion in my life. I was searching for answers to my troubles in all the wrong places. I had a deep sense of not fitting in and that was because I felt everyone looked so much better than I. I had a sense of loneliness that was beyond belief. It was an emptiness that was throughout the core of my being. My college schedule was so intense that it did not allow for a social life and that made things so much worse. Even the girlfriends I chose were bad influences on me, and I to them. Those relationships added even more confusion. The young women I dated unfortunately had some serious emotional issues of their own. They were nice people but just as emotionally damaged as I was.

Alcohol and marijuana were emotional crutches during several periods of my life. They became serious issues with me. At the beginning, drugs and alcohol were for "fitting in." Later, I used them as a way to "numb out." After some time, some of the girls I dated introduced me to speed "class" drugs like cocaine and other friends introduced me to hard liquor. The speed made me euphoric and I felt on top of the world. I often used speed not only to party, but to stay awake for college classes too. It was fortunate that I valued saving money because speed drugs like cocaine are expensive and the cost alone was enough to eventually steer me away; I thank God for that. By this time drugs and alcohol went from social consumption, partying and staying awake to private intoxication and addiction.

Loss of Another Loved One – A Decision to Change My Life

When I turned twenty, with the tragic passing of my uncle, I began to get serious about my own mortality. My uncle, and roommate at the time, had been in the hospital, recovering from surgery when out of the blue, he died suddenly. His death was difficult for me. He was only fifty years old. You can imagine my shock at losing yet another beloved, close relative. I have a very special place in my heart for him. He was perhaps the most humble man I have ever known. He loved to make people laugh. I miss him. The misery of endless pain that followed this traumatic event caused me to decide to go to the Lord. Within a few months, I made a firm decision to become a Christian, quit taking drugs, and straighten my life out.

Dashed Dreams

I had not stopped drinking socially, although I only drank on occasion. That was around ten years ago. Following the birth of my fourth child, I was so overwhelmed with life that I was getting loaded on alcohol every night. I was depressed and not able to cope with some hard decisions that I had to make regarding my goals in life. I had taken some difficult classes at a college to eventually realize my dream of becoming a professional minister. It was during those tough classes that I got the sense that I was not good enough and I was not going to be a minister after all. My dream was crushed, and again I turned to alcohol to numb the pain of this realization. I was destroying my life, and my self-worth was nowhere to be found. My wife couldn't get through to me. I was missing the first year of my little girl's life, and hanging out with people who were only contributing to my problem. I was going downhill fast. Bottoming out, I was reminded of another near overdose I had when I was a teenager, after taking marijuana laced with another illegal drug. I was very scared that the high would not end and I would possibly die.

Now I realized that alcohol could kill me just the same.

Someone must have been praying for me, because God, I believe, removed those people from my life by relocating their jobs. With no one to get drunk with anymore, it was easier to quit drinking. Fortunately, I did that very quickly on my own. It was just a matter of realizing that I wanted to be around to see my children grow up and to grow old with my wife. It was a turning point in my life when my friends were no longer in the picture.

The Bipolar Bomb – Michael's Death at Age 31

It was a beautiful spring afternoon when I drove up to the curbside of my home and was surprised to find my pastor waiting to greet me. It was a year and a half prior to my first bipolar manic episode. I stepped out of the car smiling and thought it was nice that he had dropped by. I had just taken my five kids to a doctor's appointment; they were still small—the youngest only one year old—and helped each of them out of the car. I reached out my hand and as I began to greet him, he asked me to come into the house because he had something to tell me. I insisted that he tell me, and as he sat down on the couch he suddenly said, "David, your brother Michael is dead."

"Oh My God," I cried, and without thinking, my hand swung down with full force striking the keyboard that Michael and I picked out together. It was a dream of mine to play the piano and my brother was going to teach me how to compose and play. My heart seemed to stop, and I gasped for air—as if no air were to be found. Suddenly, with a crashing sound in my mind, I awoke as if to a vivid nightmare.

I asked the pastor what happened and he said, "I don't know." My thoughts raced through my mind—was it murder, suicide, an accident, illness and where?—at the beach, his apartment, a friend's house, a car crash? All these thoughts raced through my mind at the same time. I wanted answers! My gift of being able to analyze and cross analyze, and to comprehend complex situations and deduce understanding very quickly, had just become a curse. My head was spinning. I was crying profusely as the pastor drove me to my mother's house, where the emotional trauma and questions only grew. "What in God's name was happening?"

The coroner's office had called first. The caller asked my wife if Michael was a relative and she said, "Yes." He was found dead in his apartment; he had died ten days earlier. Diane told me later that it was the most difficult phone conversation she ever had. Tears ran down her face as she heard the news, and her sobs became uncontrollable. My mom called just after she hung up the phone. It seemed like she somehow knew that there was terrible news about Michael. Someone had left a concerning message for her on her answering machine. Against her better judgment, she spoke to my mom on the phone, but because my mom became hysterical, Diane rushed over to her house. That was why she was not home when I arrived.

We didn't learn much more than that. After many discussions with the homicide investigators the investigation seemed to go nowhere and we just did not understand why he died. There was no conclusive cause of death. It was a complete mystery. My mom and I searched for months and months through records and receipts trying to make sense of things, and to create a paper trail to discover where he was, what he was doing and when he was last known to be alive. Because his body had deteriorated by the time of discovery, many questions were never answered. How could we go through this tragedy without even knowing what happened to Michael and why he died?

My thoughts surrounding my brother's horrible death occupied my mind constantly. I was obsessed to learn the truth, and no matter how hard I tried I could not figure it out. Finally, I just had to let it go. I told myself that it was over. I could not constantly dwell on it and visit the cemetery each day. The numerous dreams about Michael had begun to slow down and eventually stopped. I learned how to take a deep breath again, breathe and try to move on, although I was never the same again.

I deeply loved my brother; Michael was my baby brother and I felt like his protector. He had always been a kid at heart, loved to play practical jokes and was fun to be around. He wasn't married, and had no kids, but that didn't stop him from extending his love to all of his nieces and nephews. I am still especially thankful to him for having been a wonderful uncle for my children. His love of music had a big influence on me, and I often found him creating a new sound sample or writing a new melody. At over six foot two, he took pride in his good looks and had a style of his own. He always wanted to know more, and was intrigued with new knowledge and information, and he loved to talk, especially about the abstract and lofty. I still have a clear image of him standing in front of me with his head tilted quizzically, palms raised in a friendly, teasing gesture, as if to ask, "What?" Michael was also restless, always on the go, creating something or driving up to the city to have a good time with friends. I think that's why we didn't worry too much when he disappeared. We figured he'd be back soon; he was always there for us.

There were elements of Michael's death that were graphically disturbing. It was all so complicated, so horrible, fearful and terrorizing, that part of me seemed to die the day he died, and the part of me that lived was completely shell shocked. I felt *the darkest of dark, the fear of fears and the terror of all terrors.* I did not understand why the events of his passing still had such a strong hold on me. It is only now that I recognize the gravity of its emotional grip. I had previously felt responsible for failing to protect my brother Michael and had no idea that this protective sense of responsibility would later haunt me as it did with Angela's distress. I now realize this burden to protect was never mine to bear.

The five-year anniversary of Michael's death heightened my sensitivity and concern for a friend whom I perceived as suicidal. PTSD reared its ugly head. It was the fearful look in Angela's eyes that seemed to be the doorway, the flash, into the nightmare of Michael's horrific death. I discussed Angela earlier in this book. It is important to know that past traumatic events can resurface in your life and cause you great disturbance. I shared my brother's death and my church experience to bring into the spotlight both mixed bipolar state and how PTSD can come to life and do a person harm later.

Just as codependency can be the detonator for the bipolar bomb, so can PTSD. I hope that is now apparent to you and that you will need to work on identifying your vulnerability to provide safety to you and your circle of friends and family. Awareness of your past traumatic events with a willingness to get help when needed is crucial. In virtually every one of my major mood swings, instabilities and hospitalizations, minimal self-worth, intense worry and PTSD resulting from my brother's death, have been the apparent detonators or causes. I know that the greater the PTSD healing I can achieve, the more I can reduce the risk of another *"bipolar bomb"* exploding again. As I learn what triggers my mood swings, my risk is greatly reduced. With bipolar disorder, *I must anticipate unexpected risks and be ready for them when they come.* Even though I may have been born with a predisposition to bipolar disorder, it doesn't mean that I am powerless over the illness. Now that I am more aware of my triggers I am able to address the issues and make living with bipolar disorder safer.

I highly recommend you pursue treatments for PTSD like EMDR; it worked wonders for me. Through EMDR I have overcome numerous traumas, including Michael's death, the ordeal at church, and the sexual abuse I suffered from. I am thankful that I discovered this process; you might consider discussing EMDR with your therapist or doctor as a tool to work on your own painful memories.

Please review the "Facts about (PTSD) Post Traumatic Stress Disorder" and "(EMDR) Eye Movement Desensitization Reprocessing" in Part 3, Bipolar Survival Essentials, for more information.

WHERE IS MY ANCHOR

Oh sea of sick emotion
I travel your currents
I have seen the truth of you

Your seas appear calm
A deceiving and threatening illusion
A firm anchor with no grip

Tumultuous winds, waves swelling
Sheer rocks to my left and right
I twist and turn with great fear

I know both your calm and violence
Abandonment and anger are so near
Everything to me becomes clear

Oh sea of sick emotions
Why do your storms come and go?
Why do you seek to destroy me?

Where is my anchor for these troubled seas?
I have nearly drowned with its force
God, please rescue me!

—*David Mariant*

CHAPTER 8

Emotional Healing and Codependency

"Look not mournfully into the past. It comes not back again. Wisely improve the present. It is thine."

— Henry Wadsworth Longfellow

Sometimes I think of bipolar disorder as a lack of "emotional skin." Our physical skin is what holds our insides together and protects our bodies from outside elements. Emotional skin, then, is what holds our emotional selves together and protects them from emotionally harmful elements. Many of us with bipolar disorder have grown up without the emotional skin necessary to protect our hearts, our minds, and our souls.

Toxic relationships and harmful situations have a way of penetrating our hearts and spirits. In fact in looking back, I find that toxic relationships have precipitated each of my manic episodes. Several years ago, I began participating in online forums for bipolar disorder that allow members to poll one another. Polls that I conducted confirm that this feeling of lacking protective emotional boundaries is common among bipolar patients.

When I am around emotionally healthy people, I feel good. When I am around controlling and abusive (toxic) people for too long, I am in danger of going manic. They literally suck the joy and happiness right out of me. My parents were emotionally toxic to me at times. My sexual abusers were, of course, very toxic. Having no emotional boundaries meant having little or no protection from them.

Within the past few years, it has become apparent to me that I was codependent: I was tied to and believed others' views of me. If someone I looked up to and respected said something ugly about me, I believed that it must be true. Fortunately, I have grown emotional and spiritual skin. I have defined my boundaries, and have become my own critic and best friend. I have come to realize that I was codependent due to my lack of emotional skin. Once we develop strength, confidence and self-worth, we no longer tolerate abuse or unhealthy relationships and are much better off. I do believe however that codependency will likely be problematic for me for the rest of my life.

Healing in the area of codependency is very hard work, but it's worth the effort. After a great deal of reading about codependency I began to recognize when others tried to pass their baggage over to me. I also recognized that my old pattern was to take on the baggage of others as if it were my own. I have since learned that I do not need to respond when someone attacks me. I need to remember that their behavior is about them and it is not about me.

I don't have to be a sponge for other people's emotional messes. It doesn't mean that I don't get injured emotionally once in awhile. However, I am less likely to let it affect me the way I did before. When I do feel upset after an interaction, I know that I can just pause, take a breath, and ask myself why I feel the way I do. Try to listen to your inner self so that you can protect your vulnerable heart. In this way, we can let loving people and kind words in, but protect ourselves from abusive or toxic relationships.

It would be difficult for me to write a book on bipolar disorder without addressing codependency. Bipolar disorder and codependency appear to go hand-in-hand for so many that I know. It is very interesting that codependency in itself is a disorder, involving dysfunctional relationships. Children learn from role models when growing up; unfortunately, if their role models are emotionally unstable, the child can learn a dysfunctional way of relating to people. Codependency is so often associated with alcohol and drug abuse. It can involve sexual, physical, or mental abuse. Some of these issues came into play in my own upbringing, resulting in a confused sense of self-worth.

When I was three years old, my father left the family. I felt that I was not worthwhile and that my father didn't love me. As I grew up, I suffered other abusive behavior from my family and friends. I internalized a sense of worthlessness, which I believe was a direct result of the abuse. I have come to realize that I, like so many others, was associating love with dysfunctional relationships. If a child receives attention only in the form of being yelled at, for example, the child may begin to associate love with anger. The child may end up unable to respond to love unless it involves anger, which is obviously unhealthy.

Please review "Codependency" in Part 3, Bipolar Survival Essentials. Reviewing this chapter will help you to understand the nature of codependency.

Codependent individuals look for personal validation from others. This is a difficult pattern to change, and it can make us very vulnerable. If we base our self-worth on another person, should that person leave, we could be devastated. This has happened to me a number of times. It took long practice and patience to change my initial reactions in order to avoid triggering a manic or depressive episode.

I believe that dysfunctional relationships can have a direct correlation to bipolar responses; this has certainly been the case for me. I learned only a few years ago that my own dysfunctional relationships and codependency were closely intertwined with my bipolar responses at both ends of the spectrum. These insights have literally changed my life. I now understand that my value is not determined by others. My value comes from within, and from my belief in God. Others may think what they wish about me, but I don't have to take on their view. I am not the sum total of all my mistakes; I am who I am—a very nice person most of the time.

I once researched codependency for a friend. Looking at the diagnostic test, I can now see that my friend was indeed codependent. But when I look at it in terms of myself, I realize that I was codependent in a much more serious way! Over time this became even clearer to me when codependency later turned into an explosive emotional situation for a few friends and me.

I recommend strongly that you understand what codependency means and whether or not it relates to your life. You can talk to your therapist or doctor about it. They can read my book and others on the subject—whatever will help them help you. My views are a synthesis of hundreds of perspectives. So many with bipolar disorder have expressed a great deal of interest in codependency and its relevance to their own experiences.

Remember, if bipolar disorder were a bomb, then codependency would be one type of fuse that can detonate the bomb. Removing the fuse does not disable the bomb, but it can make the bomb much safer to be around.

My own research indicates that past emotional traumas may be linked to bipolar disorder as well. Trauma can prevent us from growing in a desired direction. It appears to have exacerbated the bipolar experience for many with the illness. So many with bipolar disorder have suffered extreme emotional traumas in childhood, and trauma has also played a huge negative role in my own life. Early childhood traumas may enable codependency by shattering our self-worth and allowing codependency to take root.

As I started to address my life issues several years ago, I began to see that there were many emotional traumas in my early childhood as well as in my adult life. For example, after my brother died, identifying his body was horribly traumatic for me. It was similar to childhood traumas that I had experienced, in that it induced similar feelings of helplessness.

In recent years, a powerful new therapy has been developed to treat trauma, called Eye Movement Desensitization Reprocessing (EMDR). I understand that EMDR treatment for post-traumatic stress disorder is effective in as high as 85 percent of cases. I first learned of and received EMDR therapy during counseling. The results were amazing. After only a few treatments, I was able to overcome serious childhood traumas, and the emotional charge associated with the experiences was gone. EMDR could be useful in overcoming your own traumatic memories. Many of those I know with bipolar disorder have found EMDR to be effective for them, as well. While I began EMDR to help me through the trauma surrounding my brother's death, I realized EMDR might be helpful for other issues as well. It allowed me to overcome the horrific experience of my brother's death, as well as the abuse I suffered as a child.

If you have past traumatic experiences that you have not worked through, you may want to consider talking to your doctor or therapist about EMDR and other treatments available. The potential benefits are enormous.

For more information, please review "Facts about Post Traumatic Stress Disorder" and "Eye Movement Desensitization Reprocessing (EMDR)" in Part 3, Bipolar Survival Essentials.

My approach for managing bipolar disorder has been to address not only the illness itself, but also other areas in my life that might trigger a bipolar response. Gaining this new perspective is one of the most important elements in my survival. I am afraid that, with so many people suffering from this illness, the focus is too often on the actual disorder, with little or no attention paid to the emotional dysfunction, codependencies and the traumas that trigger it. Imagine being free from your major stresses. What would it feel like? Would it make your life more bearable, more peaceful, and even more enjoyable?

As I began to work on my codependencies and traumas, my emotional stability increased. Dealing with our emotional baggage is hard work, but it's worth the effort. For me, even what I describe as "the journey to hell and back" was worth it, because it brought me tremendous strength. It helped me address my past and discover who I am. It helped me realize that it's OK to have boundaries and to enforce them. For these reasons, I suggest that you look into working through your own baggage, regardless of whether you have bipolar disorder or not.

Many of those with bipolar have told me that they feel terrible, worthless even, because of the stigma of being labeled with bipolar disorder. I have asked them the following questions: "How does your self-worth relate to bipolar disorder? Do you feel codependent? How does codependency tie into your experience?" Nearly everyone was interested in responding to the questions and reading the responses of others. Based on these experiences with codependency, I am convinced that this is an area that every person with bipolar should explore. Working out these issues will give you much greater stability.

When I asked this same group how codependency relates to their bipolar situation, they told me that it was the triggering aspect of their bipolar responses. Most of them reported having a poor sense of self-worth and the need for validation. They also have shared issues with childhood and adult emotional traumas that they believe have magnified the effects of this disorder.

Codependency itself implies an enormous need for validation. The sense of worthlessness associated with codependency is tremendous. If you understand that your psyche is affected by codependency and that it has helped determine who you are, you can see the potential role that codependency plays as a bipolar trigger. Stressful situations in human relationships can act as triggers to ignite the bipolar fuse. Working with issues of codependency with your therapist, therefore, makes good sense for everyone. For one with bipolar disorder, it can mean survival.

Over the past six years, I have experienced four major manic episodes. In every one of them, codependency surfaced during a stressful relationship, and was one of the triggers to the onset of mania. I have come to understand that healthy relationships are extremely important to my mental health. With appropriate therapy, interventions and understanding, we can begin to heal emotionally. We can learn how to develop more healthy relationships, and achieve greater happiness in our lives. It has certainly given my life back to me.

Of all my poetry, the following poem is my favorite. It is very special to me because it describes a spiritual event during my life, at a severe time of internal turmoil. Strength came from a new awareness of who I am, the worth that I have because of my faith in God, and the new clarified understanding of my identity in relation to God. In a moment of understanding, I realized that I am loved by God, just as I am, and that He has everything under control and loves me unconditionally. My self-worth and true identity came from the realization that I was created with a purpose by God through His intentional will. This new truth revealed my true identity—that I am a child of God.

PRICELESS MASTERPIECE

With life come many storms
Few as great as the internal storm of who we are
The inner battle between God, self, and evil

When we struggle in our heart, about not being good enough
Chances are we are listening to the lie that says
God does not love us and we are worthless

Yes we have all sinned, and yes we have all gone our own way
But we have been lied to, deceived and tricked along the way
God has no conditions except that we turn away from sin

God loved us before we were in our mother's womb
And each of us is a unique masterpiece and, oh yes, a sinner
Even with our brokenness, our beauty is beyond compare

God sent His Son to pay ransom for His beloved masterpiece
Because we have immeasurable value and
God's love is so grand
That is why He paid the ultimate price
When Jesus Christ was crucified

We were bought and paid for in full; we have a new life lease
Seek to know God and turn away from sin
Then you will see who you are
A priceless masterpiece, fashioned by God's hands
From all eternity

—David Mariant

CHAPTER 9

Forgiveness and Hope

*"Hope, the patent medicine
for disease, disaster, sin."*

—*Wallace Rice*

Over the years, I have come to realize that I owe my bipolar survival in a large part to my Christian faith. Faith in God is not easy and at times is very difficult for me but what choice do I have? I honestly do not believe I would be alive today if it were not for my personal faith in God. When things have been at their bleakest, I have always been able to turn to God for hope, although sometimes there has only been a flicker. This hope comes from the comfort I take from *knowing* deep down that there is a God, a God who is watching over me, taking care of me, loves me and forgives me. This is a perspective I choose to live by. My faith in God is my choice and my greatest survival strategy of all. It is both spiritual, practical and life saving.

My intent is not to *push* my faith on anyone else, but simply to tell my story honestly and completely. This chapter is about my Christian faith and the hope it has given me in facing my bipolar disorder and the tragic death of my brother. I have no argument with anyone who subscribes to other religious traditions or who has no belief in God. Regardless of your belief system, I hope you will find encouragement from my words.

During my first visit to a psychiatrist several years prior to my bipolar disorder diagnosis, I discussed a family situation that was weighing me down. I had an unhealthy relationship with a certain family member; I was angry and unable to forgive this person's actions. At one point in the session, we discussed forgiveness. After I shared my feelings and need for help, the psychiatrist responded by saying, "If you need help forgiving someone perhaps you should see a minister." Over the years I have done just that.

Seeking a minister may not be something you would ordinarily do and you might not feel comfortable doing this either. It might be helpful to talk with a therapist or perhaps a friend that has dealt with the issue of forgiveness with some success. Whatever your religious belief or non-belief, I encourage you to seek out positive statements of hope and forgiveness. I found it important to avoid the toxic type of person that will rehash every aspect of a situation and encourage more anger. Anger and unforgiveness may be healthy to a point and for a time. However, somewhere along the line it is necessary to let go so that you can move onward. The only way I have found to forgive serious offenses is through God. Do whatever works for you and the main point is to just let it go.

It was the help of the pastor at a new church we decided to attend that helped me begin the process of forgiving those in my past that hurt me so badly. The pastor and I could identify with one another because he had a similar experience at an earlier time in his life. Because I had tried several times to resolve the church matters with the pastor, Justin, and Angela to no avail, I was frustrated. The pastor told me that the Bible said, "Our responsibility is to do all we can to be at peace with each other." Because I knew that I did all I could do to try to resolve matters including sending apologies for my part of the mess, I felt a freedom to move on. Later, I even asked my new pastor to meet with my previous pastor to begin the reconciliation process, but that was unsuccessful.

Relationships that have unresolved issues bring added stress to our lives—stress that can damage everyone involved, especially those of us with bipolar disorder. When I began to purposefully forgive others, I experienced a level of freedom that I'd never felt before. I began forgiving others by sharing with them that, although I had been angry with them, I now forgave them. I also felt it important to ask them to forgive me for having withheld my forgiveness.

Forgiveness is an extremely powerful act; it not only allows us to release our anger, it also makes it easy for the person being forgiven to apologize. This makes them feel better, and it's nice to get the apology, although an apology is not required in order to forgive someone. The key is the act of forgiveness.

The Christian element to forgiveness is very simple. According to the Christian tradition, we have wronged God by disobeying Him, accruing a debt that prevents us from ultimately entering Heaven. God sent Jesus Christ to "pay the debt" for our disobedience, which Jesus did when He was put to death. Three days later, Jesus was raised from the dead by God, and invites others to follow Him by turning away from sin, which is disobeying God, and accepting God's love and forgiveness. God has forgiven our disobedience, and He wants us to forgive others, even if they have not asked for our forgiveness.

Forgiveness has not come easily for me. In fact, two of my greatest difficulties have been forgiving myself and forgiving those who have hurt me deeply and have not apologized. Overcoming these hurts is not easy. We often carry a great deal of pain and shame for our actions and the actions from others. My Christian faith has helped me to deal with my own need to be forgiven, has helped me to forgive others, and has assured me that I am loved by God. Hence, through my faith and by forgiving others, I have found inner peace.

Hope is important. It has helped me through some very difficult bouts of depression. I find hope and joy in my family and friends, and in the passions I enjoy. The difficulty during depressive cycles is the feeling that you are in a black hole and there is no way out of it. During those depressive cycles, it can take considerable will just to get out of bed and brush teeth, let alone have joy or hope in anything. At these times, I find great comfort in reading the Bible. When I was hospitalized during my first manic episode, I took more comfort from reading the Bible than I have experienced before or since. It has been a great reassurance to me during some very difficult times.

COMFORTING WORDS OF HOPE

As I mentioned earlier in the book, the Gideon's Bible that I read during my first hospitalization for mania brought me great comfort and helped me get through a very tough time. A number of biblical verses that speak to me in a special way are presented here. I often refer to these verses for strength and hope. If you have the inclination, please read them and see if any of the verses speak to you.

Comfort in Time of Need

Above all writings in the world it is this passage of the Bible that has provided me and so many others comfort during times of difficulty. I like to read these words substituting the word He and Lord with the word You. In this way the words feel so much more personal.

[1] The LORD is my shepherd; I have everything I need.[2] He lets me rest in green meadows; he leads me beside peaceful streams.[3] He renews my strength. He guides me along right paths, bringing honor to His name.[4] Even when I walk through the dark valley of death, I will not be afraid, for you are close beside me. Your rod and your staff protect and comfort me.[5] You prepare a feast for me in the presence of my enemies. You welcome me as a guest, anointing my head with oil. My cup overflows with blessings.[6] Surely your goodness and unfailing love will pursue me all the days of my life, and I will live in the house of the LORD forever. – Psalms 23:1-6 (NLT)

Danger

The passage below provides me so much strength knowing that God is with me and for me. It is this confidence that has aided me through danger and times of fear. I have often had to remind myself of this over and over again. I can be so forgetful even with my faith.

⁶ The LORD is for me, so I will not be afraid. What can mere mortals do to me?⁷ Yes, the LORD is for me; He will help me. I will look in triumph at those who hate me.⁸ It is better to trust the LORD than to put confidence in people. – Psalms 118:6-8 (NLT)

Depressed

This too is a favorite portion of the Bible for me. God's love is inseparable, so even when I am down and out, God is still with me. If I did not believe this in my heart of hearts I don't know what I would do. This love of God described below is a pillar of my faith in God.

³⁸ And I am convinced that nothing can ever separate us from His love. Death can't, and life can't. The angels can't, and the demons can't. Our fears for today, our worries about tomorrow, and even the powers of hell can't keep God's love away.³⁹ Whether we are high above the sky or in the deepest ocean, nothing in all creation will ever be able to separate us from the love of God that is revealed in Christ Jesus our Lord. – Romans 8:38-39 (NLT)

Far from God

I have called upon God so many times, so much so that it seems like the events of my life have been orchestrated so I would turn to God and discover Him more fully.

¹⁷ The LORD is righteous in everything He does; He is filled with kindness.¹⁸ The LORD is close to all who call on Him, yes, to all who call on Him sincerely.¹⁹ He fulfills the desires of those who fear Him; He hears their cries for help and rescues them. – Psalms 145:17-19 (NLT)

Feeling Inadequate

I have value as a person because of my faith in God. I have comfort for my soul and I know love because of God's love. Interestingly, it has been at times of feeling so inadequate that I have felt the greatest assurance of God's presence in my life.

I am holding you by your right hand—I, the LORD your God. And I say to you, "Do not be afraid. I am here to help you." – Isaiah 41:13 (NLT)

Illness and Desperation

I have been overwhelmed especially with the death of my brother Michael. I have cried a river of tears; I have faced a life threatening illness too and found comfort in God and even peace. This comfort and peace have been very small at times, however, I believe it has always been there.

[1] O God, listen to my cry! Hear my prayer! [2] From the ends of the earth, I will cry to you for help, for my heart is overwhelmed. Lead me to the towering rock of safety, [3] for you are my safe refuge, a fortress where my enemies cannot reach me. [4] Let me live forever in your sanctuary, safe beneath the shelter of your wings! – Psalms 61:1-4 (NLT)

Judgment of Others

One of the most profound things that Jesus Christ taught while he walked upon the earth was the concept of forgiveness. As I mentioned above, the Christian tradition is that everyone is a sinner and Jesus died to pay for that sin. He is the greatest example of forgiveness. The scriptures describe that we should stop judging others because we will be judged if we do. Another unusual point He makes is to help an enemy if he is in need of help. These have been difficult precepts for me to follow although I recognize that I have made many mistakes, some very serious ones, but in light of my actions and wanting my own forgiveness from God, I have learned and decided to forgive others.

[1] Stop judging others, and you will not be judged. [2] For others will treat you as you treat them. Whatever measure you use in judging others, it will be used to measure how you are judged. [3] And why worry about a speck in your friend's eye when you have a log in your own? [4] How can you think of saying, "Let me help you get rid of that speck in your eye," when you can't see past the log in your own eye? [5] Hypocrite! First get rid of the log from

154

your own eye; then perhaps you will see well enough to deal with the speck in your friend's eye. – Matt 7:1-5 (NLT)

[19] *Dear friends, never avenge yourselves. Leave that to God. For it is written, "I will take vengeance; I will repay those who deserve it," says the Lord.* [20] *Instead, do what the Scriptures say: "If your enemies are hungry, feed them. If they are thirsty, give them something to drink, and they will be ashamed of what they have done to you."* [21] *Don't let evil get the best of you, but conquer evil by doing good.* – Romans 12:19-21 (NLT)

Life Guidance

Over and over again life has brought me serious and difficult matters to deal with including illness, the death of my brother and so much more. It is my trust that God is using the events in my life for a purpose. My brother's death, for instance, has caused my bipolar disorder to manifest. It has been his death that has prompted me to write this book that I believe will help many people. I find satisfaction in my belief. I live by the following scripture because it answers the questions that I cannot.

[5] *Trust in the LORD with all your heart; do not depend on your own understanding.* [6] *Seek His will in all you do, and He will direct your paths.* [7] *Don't be impressed with your own wisdom. Instead, fear the LORD and turn your back on evil.* – Prov 3:5-7 (NLT)

Peace

It is God, and the faith that I have in Him that gives me profound peace. I have been in the midst of the worst ordeals and have literally cried out to God for help and have felt overwhelming peace come over me.

I am leaving you with a gift—peace of mind and heart. And the peace I give isn't like the peace the world gives. So don't be troubled or afraid. – John 14:27 (NLT)

[1] *I look up to the mountains— does my help come from there?* [2] *My help comes from the LORD, who made the heavens and the earth!* [3] *He will*

not let you stumble and fall; the one who watches over you will not sleep. – Psalms 121:1-3 (NLT)

Weary from Life

When my moral failures, guilt and shame became so heavy that I could not carry them any longer; after I turned to God and accepted Jesus Christ for my life, I found a rest for my soul that was very much needed.

[28] Then Jesus said, "Come to me, all of you who are weary and carry heavy burdens, and I will give you rest.[29] Take my yoke upon you. Let me teach you, because I am humble and gentle, and you will find rest for your souls.[30] For my yoke fits perfectly, and the burden I give you is light." – Matt 11:28-30 (NLT)

GOD'S FORGIVENESS

My personal relationship with God and my faith in Him is essential to my bipolar disorder survival. These Bible verses have helped me tremendously; perhaps they'll help you, too. These scripture verses deal with our direct relationship to God and may be valuable in your time of need, as they were in mine. It is important to recognize that we are all physical, emotional and spiritual beings. Without addressing spirituality in my life and finding forgiveness, it would be difficult to maintain the balance that helps me survive.

God's Love

The first Bible verse below is one of the most well-known versus in the entire world. This is true because it makes the grandest and most unique claim ever known to mankind.

For God so loved the world that He gave his only Son, so that everyone who believes in Him will not perish but have eternal life. – John 3:16 (NLT)

God showed his great love for us by sending Christ to die for us while we were still sinners. – Romans 5:8 (NLT)

We Are All Sinners

I believe that my ability to forgive myself and others is born out of my understanding and believing that I am forgiven by God. God expects me to forgive others, because He has done so for me first.

As the Scriptures say, "No one is good— not even one." – Romans 3:10 (NLT)

For all have sinned; all fall short of God's glorious standard. – Romans 3:23 (NLT)

God's Cure for Sin

It was the awareness of my immoral actions, shame and guilt that led me to God. It was through being a sinner that I learned that God loves me and forgives me. It is peculiar because it was sin that kept me away from God at first, but all the while God's intention was to reveal Himself and share His great love.

For the wages of sin is death, but the free gift of God is eternal life through Christ Jesus our Lord. – Romans 6:23 (NLT)

But to all who believed Him and accepted Him, He gave the right to become children of God. – John 1:12 (NLT)

All May Be Saved Now

As I learned and accepted Jesus Christ's death, which was payment for my sin, I became free of shame and guilt and the consequences of my actions. I still make mistakes and continue to ask God for additional forgiveness. My hope is that as I go through life, I will make better choices and become more like the person who died in payment for my sin, Jesus Christ.

⁹ For if you confess with your mouth that Jesus is Lord and believe in your heart that God raised Him from the dead, you will be saved.¹⁰ For it is by believing in your heart that you are made right with God, and it is by confessing with your mouth that you are saved.¹¹ As the Scriptures tell us, "Anyone who believes in Him will not be disappointed."¹² Jew and Gentile are the same in this respect. They all have the same Lord, who generously gives His riches to all who ask for them.¹³ For "Anyone who calls on the name of the Lord will be saved." – Romans 10:9-13 (NLT)

SUMMARY

A great deal of my emotional and spiritual healing have come from an improved view of my relationship with God. God sees everything; because of this, I have often wished to ignore His existence — but that does not mean He is not there. If I ignore His existence, then I miss the benefit of forgiveness and healing in my life through Jesus Christ. First, I needed to recognize my mistakes. I needed to humble myself before God and ask His forgiveness, and to choose to turn away from immoral and hurtful behavior.

Forgiveness also includes forgiving ourselves and, as I have said, this has been very difficult for me. Because my actions have hurt so many, it is hard for me to believe that God forgives me. It is because of this that we have trouble forgiving ourselves completely. It is as though we don't accept the forgiving power of God; we want to do something to earn it. But God's forgiveness cannot be bought; it can only be asked for. Forgiving ourselves is a byproduct of receiving God's forgiveness.

The importance of forgiving ourselves and others is simple. Most of us carry shame and guilt, which become major sources of stress in our lives. These stresses can ignite the bipolar "detonator" inside us and set off a manic or depressive cycle. Guilt and not forgiving others can weigh down our already heavy burden and put us at a greater risk of mania and depression. This has been true for me. I have done and said things while manic or depressed that I would never have said under ordinary circumstances, and when I realized my mistakes, I wound up with even more guilt, shame, and problems.

Twenty two years ago I was desperate; searching for hope and a life purpose. Friends told me of Gods love for me, His forgiveness and the hope that I could have in accepting Jesus Christ into my life. They also spoke of an open invitation for all to come to Him and find inner peace. This hope resonated in my heart and one special July day in 1984, I accepted Gods invitation and asked Jesus into my heart. I wanted to know of Gods love, experience His forgiveness and discover peace. Since that time I have known God in a special way. It hasn't been easy at times; in fact I have questioned God and have even doubted Him. One thing that has always remained is a seed of hope within my heart; it has been there through difficult times, and it has brought me through when thoughts of suicide and death have pounded on my mind. The most special thing of all is that I know that I am loved by God and He loves me and accepts me just as I am.

God can and will lift our guilt and shame if we ask Him. It has worked for me many times. I only need to believe and trust God for this to happen. One day, I will stand before God, and He will judge me based on how I have judged others. God's forgiveness is available to us all by simply asking for it. If you want to shed your guilt and stress, please consider asking for God's forgiveness today—it could greatly enhance your ability to survive bipolar disorder and live a happier life.

It really is simple to ask Jesus into your heart even if you feel you don't fully believe. You can do this with a simple prayer like mine, you can even do this now. When I pray I close my eyes and pray in a quiet place. This is a similar prayer to what I prayed when I asked for God's forgiveness:

"Dear God I know I'm a sinner. I want your forgiveness! I know I am not where I want to be. I believe that Jesus died on the cross to pay the price for my sins. Please remove my sin, shame, and guilt. I invite you

into my life Jesus to be my Lord and Savior. I ask all of this in your name Jesus. Amen!"

Having a Bible believing church has been a great support for my life at times; having Christian friends that like to discuss faith has also been important. I suggest that you seek these out. If you would like information about Christian faith and how to obtain a free Bible of your own visit the following website:

www. BipolarFaith.com

All scripture quotations marked (NLT) are taken from the Holy Bible, New Living Translation, copyright © 1996

Enemies of Love

To love my enemy
Is to learn God's nature and see
To understand God's love and mercy

To love my enemy
Is to authenticate my love towards others
To test the substance of my love

To love my enemy
Is to kill vengeance rather than to kill
To destroy the natural desire to attack

To love my enemy
Is to love the enemy I am to myself
To discover the true source of love

To love my enemy
Is to love as God loves
To emulate the greatest love of all!

—David Mariant

CHAPTER 10

The Family Perspective and the Bipolar Child

"We have lived and loved together
Through many changing years;
We have shared each other's gladness,
And wept each other's tears."

—Charles Jefferys

Bipolar disorder is like an emotional tornado, ripping through the lives of everyone in its path. Bipolar unfortunately, affects the entire family, and it affects friendships, as well. If you are a spouse or someone close to a person with bipolar disorder, you have no doubt witnessed its extreme mood swings and destructive power. Of course, our goal is to both lessen the severity of the tornado and to minimize its impact on our families. It's not easy, but by taking the important steps necessary to learn as much as we can about bipolar disorder, and by preparing ourselves as outlined throughout this book, it can be done. Ironically, the very relationships that we stress and so often destroy are the very relationships that are vital to our personal survival.

Family members and friends have a very different perspective from that of the person who actually has this disorder. By now you have seen that demonstrated through my wife's account in this book. We need to be aware of how our manic or depressed states impact the important people in our lives, like our children and spouses, because they may fear that we will go away and never come back again. During my first manic episode and hospitalization, my entire family was anxious and fearful. My five children had no idea what was happening. They only knew that their Dad had been acting very strangely and had been taken to the hospital. I remember so well their visit, and how they didn't know what to do or say.

If you have children, I recommend asking them what they remember about your bipolar episodes and how they feel about the events surrounding your illness. I have not done enough of this myself, but when I have talked to my kids, it allowed them the opportunity to express their feelings and they seemed to be much more relieved. Family counseling may also be useful. Many families would not be strong enough to put up with the things that my family has been through with my illness. Knowing this makes me all the more thankful for my wife's faithfulness and dedication, and the fact that she has stuck by me for all these years. Without her as my anchor, I'm not sure that I would have made it this far.

My hope is that this book not only speaks to those with bipolar disorder, but that it also helps family members. One of the most positive things any family member of someone with bipolar can do is to learn more about the nature of the illness. There are many excellent books on the subject of bipolar disorder, and I hope you will read as many of them as possible. The more you learn, the better able you'll be to empathize with someone close to you who has the illness and to really be there for your loved one.

Families can be a great source of support to those of us with bipolar disorder. If your loved one has bipolar, it's important to keep your relationships with that person from becoming prescriptive, dominating or overbearing. Let them know that you love them and care about them, and are interested in them as a person first. If you are the one with bipolar disorder, be aware of the potential impact of your illness on the lives of those around you, and especially family members. When our mania or depression rips through their lives, we have a responsibility to try to mend the fences and make amends. If you can do this, your life will be a lot easier; you won't be demeaning yourself and carrying the guilt that might only end up fueling another manic or depressive episode.

My wife and I have five children. They have been a great joy as a motivating force to continue moving forward in my life.

The journey between my diagnosis and the present has been a very trying experience for everyone around me, but most of all for my wife and kids. Things have gotten even more difficult since one of our children, several years ago, was tentatively diagnosed with bipolar disorder. Our child has been on medication since age ten, and exhibits many of the classic symptoms, including difficulty dealing with anger. The child is learning to live with the illness, but it has nonetheless brought even more turmoil and fear to our already stressed family. Over the past year my wife and I have reconciled many of our issues with our child, and are hopeful for an even healthier relationship in the future.

There is evidence that bipolar disorder may be hereditary. If your family has multiple members with bipolar, there may be a variety of reasons for their denial or for refusing treatment. One woman with whom I spoke had a brother with bipolar who was in complete denial about his illness. He would not take medication. Their mother had rapidly cycling bipolar disorder, and he no doubt had trouble reconciling himself to the fact that he was also bipolar.

In my family's case, my child has seen me in extreme manic states and understandably does not want to identify with that. My child with bipolar disorder has witnessed some very strange behavior on my part during mania, so it is natural that the diagnosis would be met with reluctance. Having a child diagnosed with bipolar disorder is in some ways worse than having it myself. Knowing what my child may go through in life weighs heavily on me, and I cannot help but feel responsible. Our child's behavior over the past several years has been terribly difficult to deal with. On nearly a dozen occasions, we have had to bring in the police for our own safety.

Diane: I picked up the phone, dialed 9-1-1 and placed the most difficult phone call of my life. With a shaky voice I stammered to the police dispatcher that my child was out of control and that we really needed help. I pleaded with the dispatcher to please tell the police on duty that my child was not a bad person, just a kid with bipolar disorder that was having an episode. I also told the lady to tell the police not to draw any weapons when they arrived. I really did not know what to expect. I was afraid for the safety of my child and thought that maybe the police would think that the situation was worse than it was. Of course it was bad, but I did not think that it deserved more than a stern lecture from the authorities. My husband was yelling at me to tell them to hurry as he was getting tired of restraining our child. I saw my child, the one who I had cradled in my arms as a baby, now being held in a restraining position, kicking, biting, and screaming to be released. It was obvious that this kind of hold was hurtful, but my husband had no choice but to continue to restrain our child until the police arrived. I was feeling the pain of where I had been kicked as I helped my husband hold our dear one to the ground.

It took several minutes for the police to arrive, and with tears streaming down my face, I saw them try to reason with our child, and then I saw the handcuffs come out. Seeing my child sitting in the back of a police car was more hurtful than the bruises that I was starting to feel developing on my body from the struggle that we had just had. I was afraid and did not know what the police would do now that they were involved.

Why didn't the police and the threat of being taken away make our child behave? It was as if a fighting mad spirit was in our child. I had seen this behavior many times before. It seemed to occur about every three to four weeks on the average, for about the past year or so. So what was different about this episode? We decided to draw the line, to put up a boundary, and to not allow our child to cross it. We discussed with our child what would happen if the anger that reared its ugly head was to cause bodily harm or property damage to the family in any way. We discussed with all our children that this kind of behavior would not be tolerated any more and that anyone displaying this extreme behavior would have to deal with the police and the laws of our land. We made it very clear that no matter what the reason, we would not tolerate that kind of outburst from anyone in our home again.

The first time our child was placed in the children's psyche unit was the most difficult and the scariest. The overnight stay and the shock of it all was enough to change things for a while. The mood swings seemed to lessen and the extreme behavior seemed to be much less for several months. However, it did not last that long and eventually we had to call the police again, and again, and again. With each overnight stay, our child grew more and more accepting of the consequences of being put in that place and it did not have the same impact as that first scary experience. The neighbors saw the police at our door fairly frequently and we did eventually explain to them the nature of their many visits to our house.

It was never easy for me to call the police, but it did get much less frightening each time because I witnessed how they handled the situation each time I called. Sometimes they were able to reason with our enraged child and they would not have to take him away. Other times our child would even fight with them, and they would have no choice but to take the child to the psyche unit.

The medicines that our child was taking were changed frequently as the psychiatrist tried to find the right combination of mood stabilizers and anti-psychotic drugs. It was not apparent that anything was working well, as the situation seemed to keep getting worse and worse. The behavior would lessen with some drugs, but the drugs had side effects that were not good. Our child was sleeping through classes at school and was really lethargic a lot. Those kinds of side effects were causing our normally bright child, to be rapidly failing in school. We were at a loss as to what to do.

David: Unfortunately, some of the actual medications prescribed for our child have made matters worse. Some brought on psychotic behavior, to the point that threats were made on my own life. We have had to physically restrain our child to prevent harm

167

to other family members. As a parent—especially having bipolar myself—for a time it seemed that things were completely out of control.

Diane: Eventually things got so bad that we had to press charges against our child after pulling out a butcher knife and threatening our other children with it. A report was taken by the police and serious actions followed. We believed then, and still do today, that we needed to take these more serious steps in order to save our child from a possible life behind bars someday. Younger children are generally helped much better in the court system than older teenagers. We did not want to see our child continue in a way that could eventually lead to a very long jail sentence. We also reasoned that in Juvenile Hall there might be better more thorough care since the children there are so closely watched. We hoped that they would have a psychiatrist that would be able to find the correct medications for our child that would lessen or hopefully stop the outbursts that were happening.

David: Calling the police on one's own child is extremely difficult, and pressing charges is even more so. It's something most parents will never even have to consider, let alone go through with. The charges against our child resulted in a juvenile hall sentence and a two-year program at a therapeutic group home away from the family. We desperately hope that our child will be rehabilitated.

Diane: Juvenile Hall did have psychiatrists; however, there were far too many kids there to get the individualized attention that our child and many others needed. There simply was not the resources or the staff to provide the level of medical treatment needed there. I had no idea until we went through the system, how many children suffer from mental illnesses and wind up in Juvenile Hall. The staff told me that many of the children there were diagnosed with some sort of disorder, and the doctors there could not see them more than about once or twice a month on the average. When our child was there it was a heart wrenching experience for all of us, but one that I am certain would have been far worse for an older teenager or adult. We did the right thing by pressing charges and getting our child help before something much worse happened.

The real help we received came in the form of anger management classes in a group setting with other children, and one on one counseling with a professional therapist. In order to get this help, the Juvenile Hall judge had to place our child in a group home for troubled youth. Our child has been through a lot of the system now, and we visit whenever possible and look forward to the eventual returning home of our child. We have seen dramatic changes that give us real hope that things will be very different when our family is once again reunited.

Although this is one of the hardest things that a parent can go through, it is the right way to deal with the explosive behavior of a troubled child. We encourage all parents that are going through these types of behavioral problems with their child, to get professional help and seek counseling for both their child and themselves. Things may get better if they do.

David: If you have a child with bipolar disorder, I strongly recommend joining a group for parents of children with bipolar. My wife and I have attended such groups for support from others going through and living with the same situation. Bipolar disorder manifests much differently in children than in adults. I suggest that you read the many excellent books written specifically about children with bipolar disorder. We have found them to be extremely helpful.

If your child has bipolar disorder, it is important to have an emergency plan in place and be ready to execute it. Without a plan, you won't know how to react when a crisis arises. You may allow things to go too far, putting yourself or other family members at risk. Your decision-making ability in the moment may be compromised, so deciding on a plan in advance can make all the difference. Your plan may have to be: "If our child threatens violence against a family member, we will call the police." Contact your doctor and discuss what to do in cases of an attempted suicide or violence. Make your decisions with the help of your doctor and write them down. Posting these plans by the telephone may be useful too. Sometimes we must rely on the rational decisions we have made ahead of time, because we may be tempted to change our minds during the emergency. This is precisely why it is important to plan in advance. I have been there, and I understand how your thinking may change depending on the situation, but we need to establish boundaries for the sake of our own safety and that of other family members. Call the police ahead of time and learn what procedures they follow in cases involving minors. Talk to the beat officer in your neighborhood and explain your situation. Find out where your child would go if they should be taken into custody. Would the child go to a jail or to an emergency psychiatric unit at a local hospital? Find out where the hospital is located. Ask your doctor if he or she is familiar with the facility. The more information you have, the easier it will be when an emergency situation does arise.

Your child may be contemplating suicide or a violent action. You do not want your child to become a casualty of bipolar disorder; *you need to treat the problem seriously*. Trust yourself to execute your emergency plan when the time comes. While this was one of the most difficult things we have had to do, this was actually the first step in getting the kind of help our child needed. I am glad to say that it also marked the turning point for our family. When dealing with a child with bipolar disorder, it is critically important to determine where the boundary line is. We found that our boundary kept moving because we didn't want to enforce it. We were afraid to call the police. Our child's behavior finally got so out of control that we had no choice. After experiencing police intervention, we were less reluctant to involve them. We even found comfort in knowing they were available as a last resort. Unfortunately, our child's behavior continued to escalate, and we eventually had to enlist the help of our county social services department.

Having a child with behavior issues is emotionally exhausting. At times we felt as though we had a terrorist in our home—and in a way we did. With no relief in sight, my wife and I decided that we couldn't go on exposing our other children to potential harm. If it were only my wife and I, things may have been different, but we were responsible for the safety of all of our children. When social services learned of the child's dangerous behavior, it was clear that they were not about to allow the situation to continue. We would either have to remove our child with bipolar disorder or remove our other children to keep them safe. The solution was obvious and easier to deal with. Our child with bipolar needed help beyond what my wife and I could provide.

As mentioned earlier, journaling can be very helpful in identifying relevant life events and patterns. If you have a child with bipolar disorder, I strongly recommend that you journal the events and details of your child's life, and especially note any abnormal behavior. My wife and I did this for our child, and it proved to be valuable to the doctor and therapist. Reconstructing the past is always helpful. As a parent, you know your child better than anyone. Doctors need any help you can provide to correctly diagnose and treat your child. In journaling our child's actions, we discovered patterns pointing to both behavioral issues and bipolar disorder.

Until the behavioral issues are overcome, it will be unclear as to whether bipolar is truly a factor in our child's life. Bipolar disorder in children is very difficult to diagnose, and behavioral issues only confuse the issue. It is interesting that, over the past few years, more and more bipolar diagnoses are occurring in both adults and children. I don't know if this trend is leading to a more accurate way of assessing children, or if it is simply a matter of more individuals being labeled "bipolar." As parents, we need to take ownership of our children's well-being, set boundaries and have a well thought out emergency plan of action.

The following is a short list of steps my wife and I have found to be effective in handling our child. These steps also apply to adults with bipolar disorder. This is not meant to be a substitute for creating your own list in conjunction with your doctor, but it can serve as a starting point.

1. Always call 9-1-1 in dangerous situations involving your child or an adult relative with bipolar. The police would rather be involved early, prior to the situation getting out of control.

2. Create an emergency plan and stick to it. Once we had a plan in place, it was much less difficult to contact the police when we needed to.

3. If inappropriate conduct or any other issue of concern arises, see a psychiatrist as soon as possible. Your family physician can be a good source of referrals.

4. If medications are prescribed, make sure they are taken on schedule without fail. You may want to administer the drugs personally to make sure they are being taken. This is especially important with children.

5. Therapy is essential. The same issues that apply to an adult's survival also apply to a child's. As parents, we may be able to intervene early and spare our child years of dysfunction and in many cases save their lives. Couples therapy is also recommended.

6. Take parenting classes. It may seem silly, especially if your child is a teenager, but let's face it—so many of us have children and never had any "training." Being a parent is hard work, and parents need all the help they can get.

7. Establish boundaries with your child and be firm, especially when others in the household may be at risk. Establish boundaries with adults who have bipolar disorder, too. Talk about the boundaries to make sure they're understood. If you have bipolar disorder, set boundaries for yourself as well.

8. Respect your child's feelings, and never label or belittle someone for having the illness. A strong sense of personal identity is critically important because children often have yet to establish a healthy view of themselves, and they are very sensitive to peer pressure.

9. Marriage and family counseling—with or without your child or partner—may be helpful. Dealing with teens can be very difficult, and adding a serious illness like bipolar disorder can make it all but impossible. Obtaining guidance for yourself will be helpful to the teenagers in your family.

10. Join a bipolar disorder support group. There are other parents going through the same type of issues you are. We have attended support meetings of this kind, and have found them to be very supportive, comforting and helpful.

11. If you have religious beliefs, prayer will be helpful. You may also find meditation beneficial too; this is a practice of many religious and nonreligious people. My wife and I have found tremendous comfort in seeking God's grace and attending a loving local Christian church. We find it calming to believe that all things will work out in the end; however sometimes this is very difficult to do.

12. Participate in an online support group. This will prove helpful to the entire family. It is an opportunity to ask questions of others and share hopes, concerns and strategies for success.

Go online to: www.SurvivingBipolar.Com.

Having a child with bipolar disorder can be extremely difficult, even more so if you have the illness too. Often, a child's bipolar disorder requires a group effort involving doctors, therapists, teachers, police, social services, family members and yourself. It's a significant challenge, but if you follow the suggestions presented here, you will have won half the battle. I can tell you from experience that you will get through it, one day at a time.

Please review "Bipolar Disorder" in Part 3, Bipolar Survival Essentials. Reviewing this chapter will help you learn more about bipolar disorder in children.

Thoughts of My Wife

I sat one cool afternoon
With thoughts of you on my mind

The joy we've shared with smiles
The challenges we've shared too
Our love, tested and true
Tested for a sure future together

I realized just this day
You are the most important part of me
Through you I've held on
Through you I've been encouraged
When I was down

You have rescued me during desperate times
Without you, I would not know life as I do
Without you, I wouldn't have a life today
Without fanfare, you saved my life

Your grace, faith and beauty captivate me
Your Christ-like sacrificial love amazes me
It humbles me to think of God's great generosity
You are the greatest gift a man can know

—David Mariant

LEGACY OF PROMISE

My thoughts travel, journeying beyond this page
Children of my youth, grandchildren beyond my age
My heart is weeping, for the struggling of your day
Threatening bipolar, a family burden from yesterday

Bipolar Disorder, how frightful it may be
Your destiny my children, how will you see?
Darkness and heart break, a great burden and plight
Follow me my children, I can teach you to fight

Leading you and guiding you, along the bipolar way
Seeing with new eyes, while finding a new and better day
Fighting the bipolar battle, that I continue to fight
I have exposed bipolar's power, while reducing its might

So do not be ashamed, and do not be afraid
Fighting for you, your right of passage has been paid
Continue the fighting, discovering who you are
You are not your past, you are a shining star

Seeking the faith, that dwells inside
Discovering triumph, with God we abide
We are not the illness, and we are not to blame
We are a priceless creation, made in God's name

—David Mariant

CHAPTER 11

The Journey Continues

"The race is not always to the swift,
but to those who keep on running."

—Anonymous

You have accompanied me through hell and back, through emotional meltdown, defamation of character, betrayal, anger, shame, love, faith and peace. We made it out alive. The journey continues onward for all of us. My hope is that the journey has given all readers insight and hope. It's a pleasure to have walked with you on this road. It has been a privilege and an honor to share with you my experience with bipolar disorder and my family life story. I have written this book with the intent of providing awareness, encouragement and hope to those diagnosed with bipolar disorder, and their loved ones. My hope is that it will reach interested professionals including doctors, therapists, educators, law enforcement agencies, congress, philanthropists and movie producers. I hope I have been successful in reaching you. Writing this book has been a learning experience and has aided me in the further process of my own healing and self understanding.

To my friends with bipolar disorder, you are not alone, and you are worth everything. Every day can virtually be a living hell for us. You deserve a gold medal for every day that you survive. The journey is worth the fight. Our lives were created with a purpose and that purpose is ours to discover. Beyond the journey of these pages is your own life journey . . . Regardless of what the obstacles may be, remember that we are the owners of our own lives. There is hope.

Diane: The story you have just read is all true. It has been astonishing, heart wrenching at times, and scary, but not fictional. For us it has been a journey to hell and back again. It has been filled with life lessons along the way; things that we wish we had done differently, could do over again, and simply wish didn't happen. All lives on Earth have regrets, memories that people wish they could alter, as well as happy times that they wouldn't trade for the world.

We have used every resource that we could locate to help us through the difficult struggles that come with bipolar disorder for David and for our child. There are many very worthwhile organizations available to those with bipolar and their loved ones who struggle with this disorder. These organizations can be easily located in the phone book or on various web sites, or from literature that you can pick up in hospitals or therapists' offices. We encourage you to get the help that you or your loved ones need. Bipolar disorder support groups for the individual suffering from it, or for their families, friends or relatives, can be outstanding sources of help and encouragement. They can provide the much needed hope that you will need to live with the challenges of this illness.

David: Bipolar disorder is a serious illness. As I have pointed out previously, one in five persons diagnosed with bipolar disorder take their own lives. It is essential to strike a balance in your life and lifestyle. Your very life may depend on it. Managing your bipolar disorder, and monitoring your daily activities and moods is crucial for survival. These efforts can be very important to you in order to recognize patterns in your life and take measures that will help you. With your management, the care of a doctor, a therapist and those who love you, coupled with God and His forgiveness, you can achieve safety and balance for your life.

There have been times that I have felt very angry having bipolar illness. In my case, I have been fortunate to obtain relief from drastic mood swings through the use of lithium and lamotrigine (Lamictal). If this were not the case I suppose I might be angry most of the time. Although the mood swings have been drastic at times, the depth of feeling both high and low have been insightful and meaningful. Through my experience with bipolar, I have come to learn the broad range of human emotion and plight, and for this I am actually grateful. Previously, I quoted my friend's observation: "A person with bipolar disorder seems to see with a larger palette of colors." I believe this is true. I also appreciate the ability to see the grander scheme of things and the ability to see how things are interrelated. I believe these are gifts related to bipolar disorder as well. Now that I have learned to survive, I am content to be who I am, a person who has bipolar disorder.

Diane: David and I have different viewpoints of this illness; he says that he is now able to view this illness without completely hating it, and that he can see things with a "larger palette of colors." I agree that he has that capability, but I cannot think of this disorder without hating it no matter how hard I try. The struggles are very difficult. I miss my child who I love with all my heart and want returned back home. I miss the church that used to call us members and friends. I miss the way that life used to be. Bipolar disorder changes every life that it touches. We may become stronger for going through these struggles, but it is very hard to make it through each one. The Bible says to "Pray without ceasing" and although that is not literally possible, I do pray for my family daily. I know that God will get us through each of these difficult times, and trust that He has a plan for us. The struggles that we experienced may be the very thing that you or another reader needed to read to get through your tough times. We hope that by reading our book, the reader will be helped.

I cannot view this illness without anger, but I can view it as a resource to provide help for others going through this hellish experience. It gives me hope that our life experiences may be used to help others through their own experiences with bipolar. Perhaps it will even be a book that will save lives, and you can't put a price tag on a human life. May God bless your journey.

David: The journey continues onward and from time to time may include a journey to hell and back, like mine. It is true that many challenges will come in our future; however, my hope is that the great lessons and experiences of my life will help you and give you hope for the future. Although we don't have the choice to have bipolar or not, we do have choices. Don't allow anyone to tell you otherwise, because if you truly were helpless then you might consider yourself a victim of bipolar. Remember we have control over our mood states whether great or small. If this were not so, then why do our thoughts affect our mood states so drastically at times? I can focus on the negative and in a short period of time I can feel depressed; *if I don't let up* on those thoughts, I might wind up in a full blown depressive episode. My fixation on negative thoughts, in many cases, is brought on because of the combination of anger with the negative thoughts. If I were to throw in the towel and believe I am a victim of bipolar then I have already lost the battle. Now I ask you, what purpose does that serve? It serves no purpose at all.

We can see things as we want to see them. For instance, you have heard the saying, "the glass is half full or half empty." This applies to those of us with bipolar and how we perceive the world. My thoughts, although not completely, govern my mood states. For me, it is often a matter of a *determined perspective*. If we are determined to maintain a healthy, positive perspective on life, we are the immediate recipient of its benefit. I have learned to catch myself in unhealthy thoughts and resist them the best I can. One thing that I have found helpful, is to allow myself to feel depressed consciously when something comes up that warrants it. I also allow myself to return to a level mood state, and I do. I have had to train myself to see the glass as half full. I see no other option. My thoughts depend on my positive view of life, even in the midst of difficulty, and so do yours. Even though it is terribly difficult at times, the fact remains that our thoughts are the key to what we believe, what we perceive, and our future hope.

It breaks my heart thinking about all of the relationships I have lost. Bipolar disorder seeks to almost intentionally destroy our vital loving relationships. Being in a mixed bipolar state can drive us even further to an emotionally painful existence and sometimes a suicidal death. I have decided to do everything I can to keep my bipolar disorder under control. I do not want to lose my wife, my children, my family or my life. If we don't get our bipolar disorder into check, it is possible we will lose the very people that are nourishing us and helping us stay alive. If we lose these important people, what then?

I believe that *we must understand* the dangers of bipolar and mixed bipolar state, and the many detonators, such as PTSD and codependency. By understanding these issues ourselves first, and then educating others, we can avoid the type of turmoil my family and I have encountered — which undoubtedly harmed everyone involved. My life depends on this and yours may depend on this too. By reviewing the Bipolar Survival Essentials reference material in part 3 of this book, you will be better equipped than most people diagnosed with bipolar disorder and their families. The Bibliography also contains an excellent reading list, and we highly suggest that you read the books listed.

This book is a good way to share an account of bipolar disorder and to convey an understanding of what one with bipolar goes through. We are responsible for our bipolar disorder and maintaining the relationships around us. I suggest that one way you might do so is to share this book with others and compare aspects of my experience with yours or with those in your life. Another way to inform others is to discuss bipolar and its dangers with the people you care about. Refer to the books listed in the bibliography for an excellent reading list. Visit our websites listed at the back of the book and www.SurvivingBipolar.com for information and discussion regarding a variety of bipolar topics. To my surprise, several of my friends and family read books about bipolar disorder after I was first diagnosed, so they could better understand me; I encourage your friends and family to do the same. Through sharing knowledge about this with our families and friends, they can become a vital support for us. This knowledge is important for our family, friends, employers and those who come in contact with us. We all have a stake in our emotional well being, just as my family and friends did in my story. With a healthy knowledge and understanding of bipolar disorder, I believe the events in our lives can play out differently.

This book represents the lessons Diane and I have learned, the insights we have gained and our compassion to reach out to help others with bipolar and their loved ones. There is a hope for us, a hope that requires work and persistence to realize. The title of this next poem describes my future hope, which has been born through life lessons of pain and difficulties of the past. In other words, my past has served as a teacher for a brighter personal future, and because of this I foresee a friendlier tomorrow. Please grab hold of a life perspective that gives you all the benefits for living. I encourage you to press onward, moment by moment and day by day. When you don't have the strength to continue onward, remember to look upward. God has provided me with strength during my times of weakness; He can be your strength too. Enjoy the following poem as my bidding of farewell and thanks.

Love... David & Diane Mariant

Gentle Breezes Ahead

My life, the life of a man
Tossed about by storm and wind
Marked by minutes, hours and days
Like a feather blowing in the wind

I have sailed through many storms
I have seen the winds seize
I have sailed the harsh winds
I have seen my life as if dead

Shall I sail into my past?
Shall I put my anchor down?
Shall I lower my mast?
Shall I lose hope again, in the doldrums?

Have I grown weary?
Have I surrendered my sails?
Have I closed my captain's log?
Have I given up the fight?

I shall raise my sails
I shall see hope with my eyes
I shall look to the distant horizon
I shall be courageous and not fear

Raise your sails and fear not
Seek the gentler day
Raise your eyes to the horizon
For the winds have changed

With pride and honor for your life
A new day, a new way to seize,
The new horizon draws near
With a kind and gentle breeze

—David Mariant

Part 3

Bipolar Survival Essentials

"Do not go where the path may lead; go instead where there is no path and leave a trail."

—Ralph Waldo Emerson

CHAPTER 12

Bipolar Disorder

"Madness need not be all breakdown. It may also be breakthrough. It is potential liberation and renewal as well as enslavement and existential death."

—R.D. Laing

Introduction

Bipolar disorder, also known as manic-depressive illness, is a brain disorder that causes unusual shifts in a person's mood, energy, and ability to function. Different from the normal ups and downs that everyone goes through, the symptoms of bipolar disorder are severe. They can result in damaged relationships, poor job or school performance, and even suicide. But there is good news: bipolar disorder can be treated, and people with this illness can lead full and productive lives. This information acquired from the National Institute of Mental Health provides a necessary understanding of bipolar disorder.

More than 2 million American adults,[1] or about 1 percent of the population age 18 and older in any given year,[2] have bipolar disorder. Bipolar disorder typically develops in late adolescence or early adulthood. However, some people have their first symptoms during childhood, and some develop them late in life. It is often not recognized as an illness, and people may suffer for years before it is properly diagnosed and treated. Like diabetes or heart disease, bipolar disorder is a long-term illness that must be carefully managed throughout a person's life.

"Manic-depression distorts moods and thoughts, incites dreadful

189

behaviors, destroys the basis of rational thought, and too often erodes the desire and will to live. It is an illness that is biological in its origins, yet one that feels psychological in the experience of it; an illness that is unique in conferring advantage and pleasure, yet one that brings in its wake almost unendurable suffering and, not infrequently, suicide."

"I am fortunate that I have not died from my illness, fortunate in having received the best medical care available, and fortunate in having the friends, colleagues, and family that I do."

Kay Redfield Jamison, Ph.D., *An Unquiet Mind*, 1995, p. 6.
(Reprinted with permission from Alfred A. Knopf, a division of Random House, Inc.)

What Are the Symptoms of Bipolar Disorder?

Bipolar disorder causes dramatic mood swings—from overly "high" and/or irritable to sad and hopeless, and then back again, often with periods of normal mood in between. Severe changes in energy and behavior go along with these changes in mood. The periods of highs and lows are called **episodes** of mania and depression.

Signs and symptoms of mania (or a manic episode) include:

- Increased energy, activity, and restlessness
- Excessively "high," overly good, euphoric mood
- Extreme irritability
- Racing thoughts and talking very fast, jumping from one idea to another
- Distractibility, can't concentrate well
- Little sleep needed
- Unrealistic beliefs in one's abilities and powers
- Poor judgment

190

- Spending sprees
- A lasting period of behavior that is different from usual
- Increased sexual drive
- Abuse of drugs, particularly cocaine, alcohol, and sleeping medications
- Provocative, intrusive, or aggressive behavior
- Denial that anything is wrong

A manic episode is diagnosed if elevated mood occurs with three or more of the other symptoms most of the day, nearly every day, for 1 week or longer. If the mood is irritable, four additional symptoms must be present.

Signs and symptoms of depression (or a depressive episode) include:

- Lasting sad, anxious, or empty mood
- Feelings of hopelessness or pessimism
- Feelings of guilt, worthlessness, or helplessness
- Loss of interest or pleasure in activities once enjoyed, including sex
- Decreased energy, a feeling of fatigue or of being "slowed down"
- Difficulty concentrating, remembering, making decisions
- Restlessness or irritability
- Sleeping too much, or can't sleep
- Change in appetite and/or unintended weight loss or gain
- Chronic pain or other persistent bodily symptoms that are not caused by physical illness or injury
- Thoughts of death or suicide, or suicide attempts

A depressive episode is diagnosed if five or more of these symptoms last most of the day, nearly every day, for a period of 2 weeks or longer.

A mild to moderate level of mania is called **hypomania**. Hypomania may feel good to the person who experiences it and may even be associated with good functioning and enhanced productivity. Thus even when family and friends learn to recognize the mood swings as possible bipolar disorder, the person may deny that anything is wrong. Without proper treatment, however, hypomania can become severe mania in some people or can switch into depression.

Sometimes, severe episodes of mania or depression include symptoms of **psychosis** (or psychotic symptoms). Common psychotic symptoms are hallucinations (hearing, seeing, or otherwise sensing the presence of things not actually there) and delusions (false, strongly held beliefs not influenced by logical reasoning or explained by a person's usual cultural concepts). Psychotic symptoms in bipolar disorder tend to reflect the extreme mood state at the time. For example, delusions of grandiosity, such as believing one is the President or has special powers or wealth, may occur during mania; delusions of guilt or worthlessness, such as believing that one is ruined and penniless or has committed some terrible crime, may appear during depression. People with bipolar disorder who have these symptoms are sometimes incorrectly diagnosed as having schizophrenia, another severe mental illness.

It may be helpful to think of the various mood states in bipolar disorder as a spectrum or continuous range. At one end is severe depression, above which is moderate depression and then mild low mood, which many people call "the blues" when it is short-lived but is termed "dysthymia" when it is chronic. Then there is normal or balanced mood, above which comes hypomania (mild to moderate mania), and then severe mania.

192

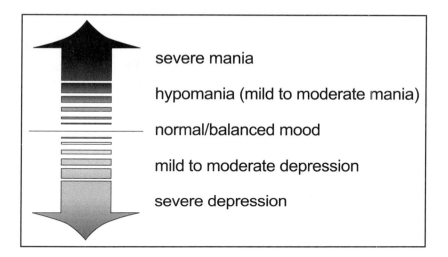

severe mania

hypomania (mild to moderate mania)

normal/balanced mood

mild to moderate depression

severe depression

In some people, however, symptoms of mania and depression may occur together in what is called a **mixed** bipolar state. Symptoms of a mixed state often include agitation, trouble sleeping, significant change in appetite, psychosis, and suicidal thinking. A person may have a very sad, hopeless mood while at the same time feeling extremely energized.

Bipolar disorder may appear to be a problem other than mental illness—for instance, alcohol or drug abuse, poor school or work performance, or strained interpersonal relationships. Such problems in fact may be signs of an underlying mood disorder.

Diagnosis of Bipolar Disorder

Like other mental illnesses, bipolar disorder cannot yet be identified physiologically—for example, through a blood test or a brain scan. Therefore, a diagnosis of bipolar disorder is made on the basis of symptoms, course of illness, and, when available, family history. The diagnostic criteria for bipolar disorder are described in the *Diagnostic and Statistical Manual for Mental Disorders, fourth edition (DSM-IV).*[3]

Descriptions offered by people with bipolar disorder give valuable insights into the various mood states associated with the illness:

> **Depression:** I doubt completely my ability to do anything well. It seems as though my mind has slowed down and burned out to the point of being virtually useless.... I am haunted... with the total, the desperate hopelessness of it all.... Others say, "It's only temporary, it will pass, you will get over it," but of course they haven't any idea of how I feel, although they are certain they do. If I can't feel, move, think or care, then what on earth is the point?

> **Hypomania:** At first when I'm high, it's tremendous... ideas are fast... like shooting stars you follow until brighter ones appear.... All shyness disappears, the right words and gestures are suddenly there... uninteresting people, things become intensely interesting. Sensuality is pervasive; the desire to seduce and be seduced is irresistible. Your marrow is infused with unbelievable feelings of ease, power, well-being, omnipotence, euphoria... you can do anything... but, somewhere this changes.

> **Mania:** The fast ideas become too fast and there are far too many... overwhelming confusion replaces clarity... you stop keeping up with it—memory goes. Infectious humor ceases to amuse. Your friends become frightened.... everything is now against the grain... you are irritable, angry, frightened, uncontrollable, and trapped.

Suicide

Some people with bipolar disorder become suicidal. **Anyone who is thinking about committing suicide needs immediate attention, preferably from a mental health professional or a physician. Anyone who talks about suicide should be taken seriously.** Risk for suicide appears to be higher earlier in the course of the illness. Therefore, recognizing bipolar disorder early and learning how best to manage it may decrease the risk of death by suicide.

Signs and symptoms that may accompany suicidal feelings include:

- talking about feeling suicidal or wanting to die
- feeling hopeless, that nothing will ever change or get better
- feeling helpless, that nothing one does makes any difference
- feeling like a burden to family and friends
- abusing alcohol or drugs
- putting affairs in order (e.g., organizing finances or giving away possessions to prepare for one's death)
- writing a suicide note
- putting oneself in harm's way, or in situations where there is a danger of being killed

If you are feeling suicidal or know someone who is:

- call a doctor, emergency room, or 911 right away to get immediate help
- make sure you, or the suicidal person, are not left alone
- make sure that access is prevented to large amounts of medication, weapons, or other items that could be used for self-harm

While some suicide attempts are carefully planned over time, others are impulsive acts that have not been well thought out; thus, the final point in the box may be a valuable long-term strategy for people with bipolar disorder. Either way, it is important to understand that suicidal feelings and actions are symptoms of an illness that can be treated. With proper treatment, suicidal feelings can be overcome.

What Is the Course of Bipolar Disorder?

Episodes of mania and depression typically recur across the life span. Between episodes, most people with bipolar disorder are free of symptoms, but as many as one-third of people have some residual symptoms. A small percentage of people experience chronic unremitting symptoms despite treatment.[4]

The classic form of the illness, which involves recurrent episodes of mania and depression, is called **bipolar I disorder**. Some people, however, never develop severe mania but instead experience milder episodes of hypomania that alternate with depression; this form of the illness is called **bipolar II disorder**. When four or more episodes of illness occur within a 12-month period, a person is said to have **rapid-cycling** bipolar disorder. Some people experience multiple episodes within a single week, or even within a single day. Rapid cycling tends to develop later in the course of the illness and is more common among women than among men.

People with bipolar disorder can lead healthy and productive lives when the illness is effectively treated (see—"How Is Bipolar Disorder Treated?"). Without treatment, however, the natural course of bipolar disorder tends to worsen. Over time a person may suffer more frequent (more rapid-cycling) and more severe manic and depressive episodes than those experienced when the illness first appeared.[5] But in most cases, proper treatment can help reduce the frequency and severity of episodes and can help people with bipolar disorder maintain a good quality of life.

Can Children and Adolescents Have Bipolar Disorder?

Both children and adolescents can develop bipolar disorder. It is more likely to affect the children of parents who have the illness.

Unlike many adults with bipolar disorder, whose episodes tend to be more clearly defined, children and young adolescents with the illness often experience very fast mood swings between depression and mania many times within a day.[6] Children with mania are more likely to be irritable and prone to destructive tantrums than to be overly happy and elated. Mixed symptoms also are common in youths with bipolar disorder. Older adolescents who develop the illness may have more classic, adult-type episodes and symptoms.

Bipolar disorder in children and adolescents can be hard to tell apart from other problems that may occur in these age groups. For example, while irritability and aggressiveness can indicate bipolar disorder, they also can be symptoms of attention deficit hyperactivity disorder, conduct disorder, oppositional defiant disorder, or other types of mental disorders more common among adults such as major depression or schizophrenia. Drug abuse also may lead to such symptoms.

For any illness, however, effective treatment depends on appropriate diagnosis. Children or adolescents with emotional and behavioral symptoms should be carefully evaluated by a mental health professional. **Any child or adolescent who has suicidal feelings, talks about suicide, or attempts suicide should be**

taken seriously and should receive immediate help from a mental health specialist.

What Causes Bipolar Disorder?

Scientists are learning about the possible causes of bipolar disorder through several kinds of studies. Most scientists now agree that there is no single cause for bipolar disorder—rather, many factors act together to produce the illness.

Because bipolar disorder tends to run in families, researchers have been searching for specific genes—the microscopic "building blocks" of DNA inside all cells that influence how the body and mind work and grow—passed down through generations that may increase a person's chance of developing the illness. But genes are not the whole story. Studies of identical twins, who share all the same genes, indicate that both genes and other factors play a role in bipolar disorder. If bipolar disorder were caused entirely by genes, then the identical twin of someone with the illness would always develop the illness, and research has shown that this is not the case. But if one twin has bipolar disorder, the other twin is more likely to develop the illness than is another sibling.[7]

In addition, findings from gene research suggest that bipolar disorder, like other mental illnesses, does not occur because of a single gene.[8] It appears likely that many different genes act together, and in combination with other factors of the person or the person's environment, to cause bipolar disorder. Finding these genes, each of which contributes only a small amount toward the vulnerability to bipolar disorder, has been extremely difficult. But scientists expect that the advanced research tools now being used will lead to these discoveries and to new and better treatments for bipolar disorder.

Brain-imaging studies are helping scientists learn what goes wrong in the brain to produce bipolar disorder and other mental illnesses.[9,10] New brain-imaging techniques allow researchers to take pictures of the living brain at work, to examine its structure and activity, without the need for surgery or other invasive procedures. These techniques include magnetic resonance imaging (MRI), positron emission tomography (PET), and functional magnetic resonance imaging (fMRI). There is evidence from imaging studies that the brains of people with bipolar disorder may differ from the brains of healthy individuals. As the differences are more clearly identified and defined through research, scientists will gain a better understanding of the underlying causes of the illness, and eventually may be able to predict which types of treatment will work most effectively.

How Is Bipolar Disorder Treated?

Most people with bipolar disorder—even those with the most severe forms—can achieve substantial stabilization of their mood swings and related symptoms with proper treatment.[11,12,13] Because bipolar disorder is a recurrent illness, long-term preventive treatment is strongly recommended and almost always indicated. A strategy that combines medication and psychosocial treatment is optimal for managing the disorder over time.

In most cases, bipolar disorder is much better controlled if treatment is continuous than if it is on and off. But even when there are no breaks in treatment, mood changes can occur and should be reported immediately to your doctor. The doctor may be able to prevent a full-blown episode by making adjustments to the treatment plan. Working closely with the doctor and communicating openly about treatment concerns and options can make a difference in treatment effectiveness.

In addition, keeping a chart of daily mood symptoms, treatments, sleep patterns, and life events may help people with bipolar disorder and their families to better understand the illness. This chart also can help the doctor track and treat the illness most effectively.

Medications

Medications for bipolar disorder are prescribed by psychiatrists—medical doctors (M.D.) with expertise in the diagnosis and treatment of mental disorders. While primary care physicians who do not specialize in psychiatry also may prescribe these medications, it is recommended that people with bipolar disorder see a psychiatrist for treatment.

Medications known as "mood stabilizers" usually are prescribed to help control bipolar disorder.[11] Several different types of mood stabilizers are available. In general, people with bipolar disorder continue treatment with mood stabilizers for extended periods of time (years). Other medications are added when necessary, typically for shorter periods, to treat episodes of mania or depression that break through despite the mood stabilizer.

- Lithium, the first mood-stabilizing medication approved by the U.S. Food and Drug Administration (FDA) for treatment of mania, is often very effective in controlling mania and preventing the recurrence of both manic and depressive episodes.
- Anticonvulsant medications, such as valproate (Depakote®) or carbamazepine (Tegretol®), also can have mood-stabilizing effects and may be especially useful for difficult-to-treat bipolar episodes. Valproate was FDA-approved in 1995 for treatment of mania.
- Newer anticonvulsant medications, including lamotrigine (Lamictal®), gabapentin (Neurontin®), and topiramate

(Topamax®), are being studied to determine how well they
work in stabilizing mood cycles.

- Anticonvulsant medications may be combined with lithium,
  or with each other, for maximum effect.
- Children and adolescents with bipolar disorder generally are
  treated with lithium, but valproate and carbamazepine also
  are used. Researchers are evaluating the safety and efficacy
  of these and other psychotropic medications in children and
  adolescents. *There is some evidence that valproate may lead
  to adverse hormone changes in teenage girls and polycystic
  ovary syndrome in women who began taking the medication
  before age 20.*[14] *Therefore, young female patients taking
  valproate should be monitored carefully by a physician.*
- Women with bipolar disorder who wish to conceive, or who
  become pregnant, face special challenges due to the possible
  harmful effects of existing mood stabilizing medications
  on the developing fetus and the nursing infant.[15] Therefore,
  the benefits and risks of all available treatment options
  should be discussed with a clinician skilled in this area. New
  treatments with reduced risks during pregnancy and lactation
  are under study.

Treatment of Bipolar Depression

Research has shown that people with bipolar disorder are at risk
of switching into mania or hypomania, or of developing rapid cycling, during treatment with antidepressant medication.[16]
Therefore, *"mood-stabilizing" medications generally are required, alone or in combination with antidepressants, to protect
people with bipolar disorder from this switch.* Lithium and valproate are the most commonly used mood-stabilizing drugs today. However, research studies continue to evaluate the potential
mood-stabilizing effects of newer medications.

- Atypical antipsychotic medications, including clozapine
  (Clozaril®), olanzapine (Zyprexa®), risperidone (Risperdal®),

quetiapine (Seroquel®), and ziprasidone (Geodon®), are being studied as possible treatments for bipolar disorder. Evidence suggests clozapine may be helpful as a mood stabilizer for people who do not respond to lithium or anticonvulsants.[17] Other research has supported the efficacy of olanzapine for acute mania, an indication that has recently received FDA approval.[18] Olanzapine may also help relieve psychotic depression.[19]

- If insomnia is a problem, a high-potency benzodiazepine medication such as clonazepam (Klonopin®) or lorazepam (Ativan®) may be helpful to promote better sleep. However, since these medications may be habit-forming, they are best prescribed on a short-term basis. Other types of sedative medications, such as zolpidem (Ambien®), are sometimes used instead.

- Changes to the treatment plan may be needed at various times during the course of bipolar disorder to manage the illness most effectively. A psychiatrist should guide any changes in type or dose of medication.

- Be sure to tell the psychiatrist about all other prescription drugs, over-the-counter medications, or natural supplements you may be taking. This is important because certain medications and supplements taken together may cause adverse reactions.

- To reduce the chance of relapse or of developing a new episode, it is important to stick to the treatment plan. Talk to your doctor if you have any concerns about the medications.

Thyroid Function

People with bipolar disorder often have abnormal thyroid gland function.[5] Because too much or too little thyroid hormone alone can lead to mood and energy changes, it is important that thyroid levels are carefully monitored by a physician.

People with rapid cycling tend to have co-occurring thyroid

problems and may need to take thyroid pills in addition to their medications for bipolar disorder. Also, lithium treatment may cause low thyroid levels in some people, resulting in the need for thyroid supplementation.

Medication Side Effects

Before starting a new medication for bipolar disorder, always talk with your psychiatrist and/or pharmacist about possible side effects. Depending on the medication, side effects may include weight gain, nausea, tremor, reduced sexual drive or performance, anxiety, hair loss, movement problems, or dry mouth. Be sure to tell the doctor about all side effects you notice during treatment. He or she may be able to change the dose or offer a different medication to relieve them. Your medication should not be changed or stopped without the psychiatrist's guidance.

Psychosocial Treatments

As an addition to medication, psychosocial treatments—including certain forms of psychotherapy (or "talk" therapy)—are helpful in providing support, education, and guidance to people with bipolar disorder and their families. Studies have shown that psychosocial interventions can lead to increased mood stability, fewer hospitalizations, and improved functioning in several areas.[13] A licensed psychologist, social worker, or counselor typically provides these therapies and often works together with the psychiatrist to monitor a patient's progress. The number, frequency, and type of sessions should be based on the treatment needs of each person.

Psychosocial interventions commonly used for bipolar disorder are cognitive behavioral therapy, psychoeducation, family therapy, and a newer technique, interpersonal and social rhythm therapy. NIMH researchers are studying how these interventions compare to one another when added to medication treatment for bipolar disorder.

- Cognitive behavioral therapy helps people with bipolar disorder learn to change inappropriate or negative thought patterns and behaviors associated with the illness.
- Psychoeducation involves teaching people with bipolar disorder about the illness and its treatment, and how to recognize signs of relapse so that early intervention can be sought before a full-blown illness episode occurs. Psychoeducation also may be helpful for family members.
- Family therapy uses strategies to reduce the level of distress within the family that may either contribute to or result from the ill person's symptoms.
- Interpersonal and social rhythm therapy helps people with bipolar disorder both to improve interpersonal relationships and to regularize their daily routines. Regular daily routines and sleep schedules may help protect against manic episodes.
- As with medication, it is important to follow the treatment plan for any psychosocial intervention to achieve the greatest benefit.

Other Treatments

- In situations where medication, psychosocial treatment, and the combination of these interventions prove ineffective, or work too slowly to relieve severe symptoms such as psychosis or suicidality, electroconvulsive therapy (ECT) may be considered. ECT may also be considered to treat acute episodes when medical conditions, including pregnancy, make the use of medications too risky. ECT is a highly effective treatment for severe depressive, manic, and/or mixed episodes. The possibility of long-lasting memory problems, although a concern in the past, has been significantly reduced with modern ECT techniques. However, the potential benefits and risks of ECT, and of available alternative interventions, should be carefully reviewed and discussed with individuals considering this treatment and, where appropriate, with family or friends.[20]

- Herbal or natural supplements, such as St. John's wort (*Hypericum perforatum*), have not been well studied, and little is known about their effects on bipolar disorder. Because the FDA does not regulate their production, different brands of these supplements can contain different amounts of active ingredient. **Before trying herbal or natural supplements, it is important to discuss them with your doctor. There is evidence that St. John's wort can reduce the effectiveness of certain medications.[21] In addition, like prescription antidepressants, St. John's wort may cause a switch into mania in some individuals with bipolar disorder, especially if no mood stabilizer is being taken.[22]**

- Omega-3 fatty acids found in fish oil are being studied to determine their usefulness, alone and when added to conventional medications, for long-term treatment of bipolar disorder.[23]

A Long-Term Illness That Can Be Effectively Treated

Even though episodes of mania and depression naturally come and go, it is important to understand that bipolar disorder is a long-term illness that currently has no cure. Staying on treatment, even during well times, can help keep the disease under control and reduce the chance of having recurrent, worsening episodes.

Do Other Illnesses Co-occur with Bipolar Disorder?

Alcohol and drug abuse are very common among people with

bipolar disorder. Research findings suggest that many factors may contribute to these substance abuse problems, including self-medication of symptoms, mood symptoms either brought on or perpetuated by substance abuse, and risk factors that may influence the occurrence of both bipolar disorder and substance use disorders.[24] Treatment for co-occurring substance abuse, when present, is an important part of the overall recommended treatment plan.

Anxiety disorders, such as post-traumatic stress disorder and obsessive-compulsive disorder, also may be common in people with bipolar disorder.[25,26] Co-occurring anxiety disorders may respond to the treatments used for bipolar disorder, or they may require separate treatment.

For more information on anxiety disorders, contact NIMH.

This information acquired from the National Institute of Mental Health provides a necessary understanding of bipolar disorder.

How Can Individuals and Families Get Help for Bipolar Disorder?

Anyone with bipolar disorder should be under the care of a psychiatrist skilled in the diagnosis and treatment of this disease. Other mental health professionals, such as psychologists, psychiatric social workers, and psychiatric nurses, can assist in providing the person and family with additional approaches to treatment.

Help can be found at:
- University, or medical school affiliated programs
- Hospital departments of psychiatry

- Private psychiatric offices and clinics
- Health maintenance organizations (HMOs)
- Offices of family physicians, internists, and pediatricians
- Public community mental health centers

People with bipolar disorder may need help to get help.

- Often people with bipolar disorder do not realize how impaired they are, or they blame their problems on some cause other than mental illness.
- A person with bipolar disorder may need strong encouragement from family and friends to seek treatment. Family physicians can play an important role in providing referral to a mental health professional.
- Sometimes a family member or friend may need to take the person with bipolar disorder for proper mental health evaluation and treatment.
- A person who is in the midst of a severe episode may need to be hospitalized for his or her own protection and for much-needed treatment. There may be times when the person must be hospitalized against his or her wishes.
- Ongoing encouragement and support are needed after a person obtains treatment, because it may take a while to find the best treatment plan for each individual.
- In some cases, individuals with bipolar disorder may agree, when the disorder is under good control, to a preferred course of action in the event of a future manic or depressive relapse.
- Like other serious illnesses, bipolar disorder is also hard on spouses, family members, friends, and employers.
- Family members of someone with bipolar disorder often have to cope with the person's serious behavioral problems, such as wild spending sprees during mania or extreme withdrawal from others during depression, and the lasting consequences of these behaviors.
- Many people with bipolar disorder benefit from joining support groups such as those sponsored by the National Depressive and Manic Depressive Association (NDMDA),

the National Alliance for the Mentally Ill (NAMI), and the National Mental Health Association (NMHA). Families and friends can also benefit from support groups offered by these organizations.

References

[1]Narrow WE. One-year prevalence of depressive disorders among adults 18 and over in the U.S.: NIMH ECA prospective data. Population estimates based on U.S. Census estimated residential population age 18 and over on July 1, 1998. Unpublished.

[2]Regier DA, Narrow WE, Rae DS, et al. The de facto mental and addictive disorders service system. Epidemiologic Catchment Area prospective 1-year prevalence rates of disorders and services. *Archives of General Psychiatry*, 1993; 50(2): 85-94.

[3]American Psychiatric Association. *Diagnostic and Statistical Manual for Mental Disorders, fourth edition (DSM-IV)*. Washington, DC: American Psychiatric Press, 1994.

[4]Hyman SE, Rudorfer MV. Depressive and bipolar mood disorders. In: Dale DC, Federman DD, eds. *Scientific American*®; Medicine. Vol. 3. New York: Healtheon/WebMD Corp., 2000; Sect. 13, Subsect. II, p. 1.

[5]Goodwin FK, Jamison KR. *Manic-depressive illness*. New York: Oxford University Press, 1990.

[6]Geller B, Luby J. Child and adolescent bipolar disorder: a review of the past 10 years. *Journal of the American Academy of Child and Adolescent Psychiatry*, 1997; 36(9): 1168-76.

[7]NIMH Genetics Workgroup. Genetics and mental disorders. NIH Publication No. 98-4268. Rockville, MD: National Institute of Mental Health, 1998.

[8]Hyman SE. Introduction to the complex genetics of mental disorders. Biological Psychiatry, 1999; 45(5): 518-21.

[9]Soares JC, Mann JJ. The anatomy of mood disorders—review of structural neuroimaging studies. *Biological Psychiatry*, 1997; 41(1): 86-106.

[10]Soares JC, Mann JJ. The functional neuroanatomy of mood disorders. *Journal of Psychiatric Research*, 1997; 31(4): 393-432.

[11]Sachs GS, Printz DJ, Kahn DA, Carpenter D, Docherty JP. The expert consensus guideline series: medication treatment of bipolar disorder 2000. *Postgraduate Medicine*, 2000; Spec No:1-104.

[12]Sachs GS, Thase ME. Bipolar disorder therapeutics: maintenance treatment. *Biological Psychiatry*, 2000; 48(6): 573-81.

[13]Huxley NA, Parikh SV, Baldessarini RJ. Effectiveness of psychosocial treatments in bipolar disorder: state of the evidence. *Harvard Review of Psychiatry*, 2000; 8(3): 126-40.

[14]Vainionpaa LK, Rattya J, Knip M, Tapanainen JS, Pakarinen AJ, Lanning P, Tekay A, Myllyla VV, Isojarvi JI. Valproate-induced hyperandrogenism during pubertal maturation in girls with epilepsy. *Annals of Neurology*, 1999; 45(4): 444-50.

[15]Llewellyn A, Stowe ZN, Strader JR Jr. The use of lithium and management of women with bipolar disorder during pregnancy and lactation. *Journal of Clinical Psychiatry*, 1998; 59(Suppl 6): 57-64; discussion 65.

[16]Thase ME, Sachs GS. Bipolar depression: pharmacotherapy and related therapeutic strategies. *Biological Psychiatry*, 2000; 48(6): 558-72.

[17]Suppes T, Webb A, Paul B, Carmody T, Kraemer H, Rush AJ. Clinical outcome in a randomized 1-year trial of clozapine versus treatment as usual for patients with treatment-resistant illness and a history of mania. American *Journal of Psychiatry*, 1999; 156(8): 1164-9.

[18]Tohen M, Sanger TM, McElroy SL, Tollefson GD, Chengappa KN, Daniel DG, Petty F, Centorrino F, Wang R, Grundy SL, Greaney MG, Jacobs TG, David SR, Toma V. Olanzapine

versus placebo in the treatment of acute mania. Olanzapine HGEH Study Group. *American Journal of Psychiatry*, 1999; 156(5): 702-9.

[19]Rothschild AJ, Bates KS, Boehringer KL, Syed A. Olanzapine response in psychotic depression. *Journal of Clinical Psychiatry*, 1999; 60(2): 116-8.

[20]U.S. Department of Health and Human Services. *Mental health: a report of the Surgeon General*. Rockville, MD: U.S. Department of Health and Human Services, Substance Abuse and Mental Health Services Administration, Center for Mental Health Services, National Institutes of Health, National Institute of Mental Health, 1999.

[21]Henney JE. Risk of drug interactions with St. John's wort. From the Food and Drug Administration. *Journal of the American Medical Association*, 2000; 283(13): 1679.

[22]Nierenberg AA, Burt T, Matthews J, Weiss AP. Mania associated with St. John's wort. *Biological Psychiatry*, 1999; 46(12): 1707-8.

[23]Stoll AL, Severus WE, Freeman MP, Rueter S, Zboyan HA, Diamond E, Cress KK, Marangell LB. Omega 3 fatty acids in bipolar disorder: a preliminary double-blind, placebo-controlled trial. *Archives of General Psychiatry*, 1999; 56(5): 407-12.

[24]Strakowski SM, DelBello MP. The co-occurrence of bipolar and substance use disorders. *Clinical Psychology Review*, 2000; 20(2): 191-206.

[25]Mueser KT, Goodman LB, Trumbetta SL, Rosenberg SD, Osher FC, Vidaver R, Auciello P, Foy DW. Trauma and posttraumatic stress disorder in severe mental illness. *Journal of Consulting and Clinical Psychology*, 1998; 66(3): 493-9.

[26]Strakowski SM, Sax KW, McElroy SL, Keck PE Jr, Hawkins JM, West SA. Course of psychiatric and substance abuse syndromes co-occurring with bipolar disorder after a first psychiatric hospitalization. *Journal of Clinical Psychiatry*, 1998; 59(9): 465-71.

This publication, written by Melissa Spearing of NIMH, is a revision and update of an earlier version by Mary Lynn Hendrix. Scientific information and review were provided by NIMH Director Steven E. Hyman, M.D., and NIMH staff members Matthew V. Rudorfer, M.D., and Jane L. Pearson, Ph.D. Editorial assistance was provided by Clarissa K. Wittenberg, Margaret Strock, and Lisa D. Alberts of NIMH.

Public Domain Source:
http://www.nimh.nih.gov/publicat/bipolar.cfm
NIH Publication No. 3679
Printed 2002

CHAPTER 13

Understanding Sleep

"Is all that we see or seem
but a dream within a dream?"

—Edgar Allen Poe

Do you ever feel sleepy or "zone out" during the day? Do you find it hard to wake up on Monday mornings? If so, you are familiar with the powerful need for sleep. However, you may not realize that sleep is as essential for your well-being as food and water and is critical to mental health. The following information acquired from the National Institute of Health provides an important understanding of sleep.

How Much Sleep Do We Need?

The amount of sleep each person needs depends on many factors, including age. Infants generally require about 16 hours a day, while teenagers need about 9 hours on average. For most adults, 7 to 8 hours a night appears to be the best amount of sleep, although some people may need as few as 5 hours or as many as 10 hours of sleep each day. Women in the first 3 months of pregnancy often need several more hours of sleep than usual. The amount of sleep a person needs also increases if he or she has been deprived of sleep in previous days. Getting too little sleep creates a "sleep debt," which is much like being overdrawn at a bank. Eventually, your body will demand that the debt be repaid. We don't seem to adapt to getting less sleep than we need; while we may get used to a sleep-depriving schedule, our judgment, reaction time, and other functions are still impaired.

People tend to sleep more lightly and for shorter time spans as they get older, although they generally need about the same amount of sleep as they needed in early adulthood. About half of all people over 65 have frequent sleeping problems, such as insomnia, and deep sleep stages in many elderly people often become very short or stop completely. This change may be a normal part of aging, or it may result from medical problems that are common in elderly people and from the medications and other treatments for those problems.

Experts say that if you feel drowsy during the day, even during boring activities, you haven't had enough sleep. If you routinely fall asleep within 5 minutes of lying down, you probably have severe sleep deprivation, possibly even a sleep disorder. *Microsleeps*, or very brief episodes of sleep in an otherwise awake person, are another mark of sleep deprivation. In many cases, people are not aware that they are experiencing microsleeps. The widespread practice of "burning the candle at both ends" in western industrialized societies has created so much sleep deprivation that what is really abnormal sleepiness is now almost the norm.

Many studies make it clear that sleep deprivation is dangerous. Sleep-deprived people who are tested by using a driving simulator or by performing a hand-eye coordination task perform as badly as or worse than those who are intoxicated. Sleep deprivation also magnifies alcohol's effects on the body, so a fatigued person who drinks will become much more impaired than someone who is well-rested. Driver fatigue is responsible for an estimated 100,000 motor vehicle accidents and 1500 deaths each year, according to the National Highway Traffic Safety Administration. Since drowsiness is the brain's last step before falling asleep, driving while drowsy can – and often does – lead to disaster. Caffeine and other stimulants cannot overcome the effects of severe sleep deprivation. The National Sleep Foundation says that if you have trouble keeping your eyes focused, if you can't stop yawning, or if you can't remember driving the last few miles, you are probably too drowsy to drive safely.

What Does Sleep Do For Us?

Although scientists are still trying to learn exactly why people need sleep, animal studies show that sleep is necessary for survival. For example, while rats normally live for two to three years, those deprived of REM sleep survive only about 5 weeks on average, and rats deprived of all sleep stages live only about 3 weeks. Sleep-deprived rats also develop abnormally low body temperatures and sores on their tail and paws. The sores may develop because the rats' immune systems become impaired. Some studies suggest that sleep deprivation affects the immune system in detrimental ways.

Sleep appears necessary for our nervous systems to work properly. Too little sleep leaves us drowsy and unable to concentrate the next day. It also leads to impaired memory and physical performance and reduced ability to carry out math calculations. If sleep deprivation continues, hallucinations and mood swings may develop. Some experts believe sleep gives neurons used while we are awake a chance to shut down and repair themselves. Without sleep, neurons may become so depleted in energy or so polluted with byproducts of normal cellular activities that they begin to malfunction. Sleep also may give the brain a chance to exercise important neuronal connections that might otherwise deteriorate from lack of activity.

Deep sleep coincides with the release of growth hormone in children and young adults. Many of the body's cells also show increased production and reduced breakdown of proteins during deep sleep. Since proteins are the building blocks needed for cell growth and for repair of damage from factors like stress and

213

ultraviolet rays, deep sleep may truly be "beauty sleep." Activity in parts of the brain that control emotions, decision-making processes, and social interactions is drastically reduced during deep sleep, suggesting that this type of sleep may help people maintain optimal emotional and social functioning while they are awake. A study in rats also showed that certain nerve-signaling patterns which the rats generated during the day were repeated during deep sleep. This pattern repetition may help encode memories and improve learning.

Dreaming and REM Sleep

We typically spend more than 2 hours each night dreaming. Scientists do not know much about how or why we dream. Sigmund Freud, who greatly influenced the field of psychology, believed dreaming was a "safety valve" for unconscious desires. Only after 1953, when researchers first described REM in sleeping infants, did scientists begin to carefully study sleep and dreaming. They soon realized that the strange, illogical experiences we call dreams almost always occur during REM sleep. While most mammals and birds show signs of REM sleep, reptiles and other cold-blooded animals do not.

Tips for a Good Night's Sleep:

Adapted from "When You Can't Sleep: The ABCs of ZZZs," by the National Sleep Foundation.

☐ Set a schedule:

Go to bed at a set time each night and get up at the same time each morning. Disrupting this schedule may lead to insomnia.

"Sleeping in" on weekends also makes it harder to wake up early on Monday morning because it re-sets your sleep cycles for a later awakening.

☐ Exercise:

Try to exercise 20 to 30 minutes a day. Daily exercise often helps people sleep, although a workout soon before bedtime may interfere with sleep. For maximum benefit, try to get your exercise about 5 to 6 hours before going to bed.

☐ Avoid caffeine, nicotine, and alcohol:

Avoid drinks that contain caffeine, which acts as a stimulant and keeps people awake. Sources of caffeine include coffee, chocolate, soft drinks, non-herbal teas, diet drugs, and some pain relievers. Smokers tend to sleep very lightly and often wake up in the early morning due to nicotine withdrawal. Alcohol robs people of deep sleep and REM sleep and keeps them in the lighter stages of sleep.

☐ Relax before bed:

A warm bath, reading, or another relaxing routine can make it easier to fall sleep. You can train yourself to associate certain restful activities with sleep and make them part of your bedtime ritual.

☐ Sleep until sunlight:

If possible, wake up with the sun, or use very bright lights in the morning. Sunlight helps the body's internal biological clock reset itself each day. Sleep experts recommend exposure to an hour of morning sunlight for people having problems falling asleep.

☐ Don't lie in bed awake:

If you can't get to sleep, don't just lie in bed. Do something else, like reading, watching television, or listening to music, until you feel tired. The anxiety of being unable to fall asleep can actually contribute to insomnia.

☐ Control your room temperature:

Maintain a comfortable temperature in the bedroom. Extreme temperatures may disrupt sleep or prevent you from falling asleep.

☐ See a doctor if your sleeping problem continues:

If you have trouble falling asleep night after night, or if you always feel tired the next day, then you may have a sleep disorder and should see a physician. Your primary care physician may be able to help you; if not, you can probably find a sleep specialist at a major hospital near you. Most sleep disorders can be treated effectively, so you can finally get that good night's sleep you need.

NINDS health-related material is provided for information purposes only and does not necessarily represent endorsement by or an official position of the National Institute of Neurological Disorders and Stroke or any other Federal agency. Advice on the treatment or care of an individual patient should be obtained through consultation with a physician who has examined that patient or is familiar with that patient's medical history.
Prepared by:
Office of Communications and Public Liaison
National Institute of Neurological Disorders and Stroke
National Institutes of Health
Bethesda, MD 20892

Public Domain Source:
www.ninds.nih.gov
Reviewed July 3, 2003

CHAPTER 14

Introduction to Stress Management

"It's okay to get jacked up and head out onto the highway, but I've been there and I can tell you that the fast lane is littered with countless smoldering wrecks."

—Hunter S. Thomas

Stress is the trigger for the onset of bipolar disorder mood swings; the more stress in your life the greater danger in which you will find yourself. Understanding stress and stress relief can minimize the potentially dangerous threat of bipolar disorder in your life. Managing stress can make way for a happier and healthier lifestyle. The following information is provided with permission by the American Institute for Preventative Medicine and provides important stress reduction techniques.

Introduction to Stress Management

Systematic Stress Management® is a structured program designed to prevent and minimize the damaging effects of stress. The techniques presented are easy to learn and can be included in normal day to day activities. The *system* to **Systematic Stress Management** is made up of five simple steps:

1. Capture an increased understanding of stress theory as we know it today. This knowledge is key to making the remaining steps worthwhile.
2. Remember to pay attention to distress signals and symptoms.
3. Identify personal stressors. This takes a high level of

awareness plus honesty, and leads to the responsible and effective management of stress.

4. Seek out tools and skills that work to prevent, eliminate, and recover from distress.

5. Practice all of the above steps regularly in order to become and remain stress-fit.

> *"Stress is essentially reflected by the rate of all the*
> *wear and tear caused by life.*
> *..... although we cannot avoid stress as long as we live,*
> *we can learn a great deal about how to keep*
> *its' damaging side-effects, distress, to a minimum."*
> *Hans Selye, M.D.*

Introduction to thinking differently

The inner messages you tell yourself are frequently the real producers of stress, rather than the situation itself.

A key factor in whether you experience stress relates to what you say to yourself about stress triggers in the environment.

1. What do you say to yourself when you're stuck in traffic?

2. What do you say to yourself when your boss is critical of your work?

3. What are your thoughts when your children leave a messy bedroom after repeated warnings to clean up?

4. The inner messages you tell yourself are frequently the real producers of stress, rather than the situation itself.

Most situations are neutral. It is our thoughts about them that create negative or positive feelings. Their stress value is generated within the mind. These thoughts determine if a situation becomes difficult to handle. In other words, being stuck in traffic can be extremely stressful for one person and only a mild nuisance for another.

This section:

- Looks at controlling thoughts that are repetitive or self-defeating.
- Explains how you can distract yourself from having negative thoughts and instead relate to things in a calmer, more relaxed manner.

Correcting distorted thinking patterns is also addressed because they, too, produce stress.

Irrational thinking

The expression "nothing is either good or bad but thinking makes it so," explains the important role that thoughts play in stress management. When thinking is clear, stress is minimized. Often, people are stressed by thoughts that are false or unrealistic. Irrational thinking is at the root of a lot of unhappiness.

Learning to beat negative thoughts

Negative thinking is stressful. The following three techniques work in controlling stressful thoughts that are repetitive, self-defeating and cause "psychological pollution." People mistakenly ruin their own best efforts with negative thinking. These exercises distract or lessen such thinking. They provide the ability to choose and control what thought is about.

Thought Control Techniques

Now Awareness

This is a technique developed by Alcoholics Anonymous and

used by members who need to wipe out thoughts about drinking. It can be used to control other negative thoughts as well. The procedure works because it puts time and space between you and your original self-defeating thought.

1. An unpleasant or unwanted thought occurs.
2. Distract yourself by saying out loud the words, "Now I am aware of _____." Complete the sentence by naming objects that you can actually see like, "Now I am aware of the door; now I am aware of the pencil holder; now I am aware of the picture; now I am aware of the carpet; now I am aware of the desk; now I am aware of the telephone."
3. Continue repeating the expression and naming things in your immediate surroundings. You can repeat things you have already mentioned. Should the thought return, repeat the procedure.

One can also choose to focus on a single item rather than multiple items.

Thought Stopping

This technique was developed to stop recurring or compulsive thoughts. It has been used to correct self-defeating thoughts, too. The technique utilizes the startle response. We experience this when we are deep in thought and someone startles us by saying something or making a loud noise. When you try to return to your thought, it becomes difficult.

Verbal Version

1. An unpleasant thought occurs.

2. Close your eyes and focus on the thought.
3. Count to three.
4. Yell the word **"STOP!"** as loud as you can.
5. Pair a behavior such as pulling your earlobe, scratching your head, or pinching yourself along with the yelling. This enhances the technique over time because we begin to associate that behavior with effective thought stopping.
6. Repeat the procedure if the thought reoccurs.

Silent Version

This version is to be used in situations where you don't want to be obvious about doing the technique. This is effective only after conditioning yourself with the verbal version several times.

1. An unpleasant thought occurs.
2. Close your eyes and focus on the thought.
3. Count to three.
4. Imagine yelling **"STOP!"** or imagine the word **STOP!** in large red letters, picture a flashing red light, see a **STOP** sign.
5. Pull your earlobe, scratch your head, or pinch yourself as you imagine yelling **"STOP!"**

Thought Zapper

This technique involves the use of mild physical punishment when unwanted self-talk occurs. It is based upon a very simple behavior change concept – any behavior that is followed by a punishment will occur less often. This technique is also very effective when combined with thought stopping.

Steps

1. Place an elastic or rubber band around your wrist.
2. You decide to stop your current self-talk because you decide it is unnecessary and not realistic at the present moment. Perhaps it is creating what you believe to be distress. You choose to spend less time and emotional energy with a belief about a certain person, place, or thing. You choose to be in control.
3. Give yourself a zap by pulling a rubber or elastic band.
4. Repeat as necessary.

Ten Forms of Distorted Thinking

Distorted thinking results from making faulty conclusions about the outside world. What we say to ourselves or how we interpret situations may not be logical. Faulty conclusions lead to anxiety, pain or other negative emotions. When people interpret experiences more clearly, their attitudes improve.

Distorted thinking is a habit that can be changed, but it takes practice. Devote several weeks to recognizing and refuting thoughts that are distorted from reality. Read the definition of each type of distorted thinking that follows. Then place a check in front of those distorted thoughts you tend to use. Cite examples of your own distorted thinking that you can recall and write them down.

1. **All or Nothing** -The tendency to see situations as either all black or white. There is no middle ground.
2. **Overgeneralization** - Drawing a conclusion based on a single event or small piece of evidence.
3. **Filters** - We only see what we want to see in a situation. We filter out other parts.
4. **Magnification** - Making mountains out of molehills. Everything is a potential tragedy.

5. **Labeling** - Putting tags on people or situations that are one-sided. Stereotyping.
6. **Jumping to Conclusions** - Making snap judgments or assumptions based on incomplete evidence.
7. **Shoulds** - Following an inflexible rule list about how the world "should" act.
8. **Blaming** - Always looking for blame either in yourself or others. Situations seem easier if you can blame someone.
9. **Disqualifying** - A person reverses a compliment so that it is perceived as an insult.
10. **Mistake of Control** - Feeling totally helpless or totally powerful in a given situation.

Quickie Qualm Quieters

How do you get some relief from the stress of daily life? Sometimes all you need is a refreshing break involving some pleasurable activity. Once the stress is gone, you can now handle the problem that faced you earlier. The following activities are incompatible with high stress levels. Place a check next to those you'd like to try.

- ☐ Take an early morning stroll
- ☐ Pull weeds in your garden
- ☐ Arise earlier than usual
- ☐ Spend playtime with children
- ☐ Write a letter to a friend
- ☐ Take a steam bath
- ☐ Take a bubble bath
- ☐ Plan a vacation – whether you take it or not
- ☐ Take in a funny movie
- ☐ Wear beat-up old jeans
- ☐ Drink an herbal tea

- ☐ Sing a favorite song.
- ☐ Take a nap
- ☐ Go swimming
- ☐ Prune a tree or bush
- ☐ Watch the sunset
- ☐ Consciously smile a lot
- ☐ Play classical music
- ☐ Go barefoot
- ☐ Tend to houseplants
- ☐ Watch birds
- ☐ Shop in boutiques
- ☐ Go to the lake
- ☐ Compile a list for household repair jobs
- ☐ Enjoy a story
- ☐ Sit in the yard
- ☐ Take photographs
- ☐ Bake yeast bread
- ☐ Jog or speed walk
- ☐ Play the piano
- ☐ Do needlework
- ☐ Eat a bowl of hot soup

Suggestions on how to handle stress

Here are some alternative ideas to include in your stress management activities. Read each and see which ones will be helpful to you.

1. **Physical Exercise** - Many people who exercise will tell you that nothing relieves tension like exercise. Not only does it promote physical fitness, but it also frees your mind and body from stress.
2. **Take Walks** - Walking is an excellent way to overcome stress. It is a good form of physical activity, and when

done in pleasant surroundings like a park, country lane or lake, your mind can wander as your feet do.

3. **Scramble Your Day** - Alter your stress triggers by doing things differently. Mix up your daily routines. If, for example, driving to work causes you stress, then alter your driving routine; wear gloves; try a new radio station; open the windows; take a new route. Familiar stress triggers from a variety of daily routines can be weakened by scrambling.

4. **Stay Well Rested** - Get plenty of sleep.

5. **Warm Water** - Shower or bathe with warm water to soothe and calm your nerves. Do this twice daily if desired and give yourself some extra time in the water.

6. **Learn Acceptance** - Sometimes a difficult problem is out of your control. When this happens, accept it until changes can be made. This is better than worrying and getting nowhere.

7. **Give In** - If the source of your stress comes from disagreements with other people, try giving in. Fighting will only create additional stress. Know when to give in.

8. **Balance Work and Play** - All work and no play can make you pretty uptight. Plan some time for hobbies and recreation. These activities relax your mind and are a good escape from life's worries.

9. **Help Others** - We concentrate on ourselves when we're distressed. Sometimes helping another person is the perfect remedy for whatever is troubling us.

10. **Talk Out Troubles** - It sometimes helps to talk with a friend, relative, clergyman or a professional therapist. Another person can help you see a problem from a different point of view.

11. **Temporary Escape** - When you feel you are getting nowhere with a problem, a temporary diversion can help. Going to a movie, reading a book, visiting a museum or taking a drive can help you get out of a

rut. Temporarily leaving a difficult situation can help develop new attitudes.

12. **Clock Watch** - When you feel stressed, stop all activity and watch the second hand of a clock for one full minute. It is relaxing.

13. **Listen Well** - Focus in on some dull sound in your environment. Examples are: an air conditioner, a copying machine, passing cars, or a typewriter. Only think about the sound. Close your eyes and just listen.

14. **Count to Ten** - This is an old technique, but it does work. Remember when you were told to hold your breath and count to ten when you were upset? Well, it still works to help tone down anger, screaming and ranting.

15. **Self-Help Books** - The following books help you develop a positive attitude. Read one or more of them.

   - *Super Joy: Learning to Celebrate Everyday Life* by Paul Pearsall
   - *Psychocybernetics* by Maxwell Maltz
   - *Your Erroneous Zones* by Wayne Dyer
   - *How to be Your Own Best Friend* by Newman & Berkowitz
   - *I'm O.K., You're O.K.* by T. Harris
   - *Creative Coping* by Julius Fast

16. **Mirror Talk** - Have a heart to heart talk with yourself while standing in front of a mirror. Use positive self-statements and convince yourself that you can handle stressful situations and be in control.

17. **Self-Reward** - Starting today, reward yourself with little things that make you feel good. Treat yourself to a bubble bath, buy the hard cover edition of a book, call an old friend long distance, buy a flower, picnic in the park during lunchtime, try a new perfume or cologne, or give yourself some "me-time."

18. **Daydreaming** - Research has shown normal amounts

of daydreaming to be healthy. A lack of daydreaming can cause emotional problems. It's a relaxation technique that helps imagination and intellectual growth.

19. Sense of Humor - When events seem too overwhelming, keep a sense of humor. Laughter makes our muscles go limp and releases tension. It's difficult to feel stress in the middle of a belly laugh. Learn to laugh as a relaxation technique.

Information provided with permission:

American Institute for Preventative Medicine

30445 Northwestern Hwy., Suite 350, Farmington Hills, MI 48334
248.539.1800   Fax 248.539.1808
www.HealthyLife.com

CHAPTER 15

Codependency

"Compassion is the antitoxin of the soul: where there is compassion even the most poisonous impulses remain relatively harmless"

—Eric Hoffer

Through codependency we develop a deformed sense of worth as a person. Because of this our self image or self view is also distorted. We develop a needing of other people's approval so that we can have a sense of self-worth. This is not healthy however, and can be quite dangerous. Broken and dysfunctional relationships can trigger the onset of bipolar disorder mood swings. The following information provided with permission by Robert Burney, the author of, "Codependence: The Dance of Wounded Souls," will help you better understand codependency and the tremendous stress and danger that it can cause.

What is Codependency / Codependence

The dance of Codependence is a dance of dysfunctional relationships, of relationships that do not work to meet our needs. That does not mean just romantic relationships, or family relationships, or even human relationships in general. The fact that dysfunction exists in our romantic, family, and human relationships is a symptom of the dysfunction that exists in our relationship with life - with being human. It is a symptom of the dysfunction which exists in our relationships with ourselves as human beings.

Codependency is about having a dysfunctional relationship with self! With our own bodies, minds, emotions, and spirits. With our own gender and sexuality. With being human. Because we have dysfunctional relationships internally, we have dysfunctional relationships externally.

Codependency is an emotional and behavioral defense system which our egos adapted in early childhood to help us survive. We were raised in shame based, emotionally dishonest, Spiritually hostile environments by parents who were wounded in their childhoods by patriarchal, shame based civilization that treated children and women as property. We formed our core relationship with self in early childhood - and built our relationship with self, life, and other humans based on that foundation. Programmed to feel shame about being imperfect humans, and trained to be emotionally dishonest, we were set up to live life reacting to the emotional trauma and dysfunctional intellectual programming of childhood. Because we feel shame about being human, we have a relationship with life that does not work to bring us Joy or inner peace.

We do not have the power to change others - we do have the power to change our relationship with self by healing our codependency / wounded souls. We can access the capacity to accept, embrace, forgive, have compassion for, and set boundaries with, all parts of self. Learning to Love our self will allow us to gain the capacity to Love others in a healthy way. Changing our relationship with life can transform life into an exciting adventure.

Codependency Described

Codependency is at its core, a dysfunctional relationship with self. We do not know how to Love our self in healthy ways because our parents did not know how to Love themselves. We were raised in shame-based societies that taught us that there is something wrong with being human. The messages we got often included that there is something wrong: with making mistakes; with not being perfect; with being sexual; with being emotional; with being too fat or too thin or too tall or too short or too whatever. As children we were taught to determine our worth in comparison with others. If we were smarter than, prettier than, to receive better grades than, faster than, etc. - then we were validated and got the message that we had worth. In a codependent society everyone has to have someone to look down on in order to feel good about themselves. And, conversely, there is always someone we can compare ourselves to that can cause us to not feel good enough.

Codependency could more accurately be called outer or external dependence. The condition of codependence is about giving power over our self-esteem to outside sources/agencies or external manifestations. We were taught to look outside of our selves to people, places, and things - to money, property and prestige, to determine if we have worth. That causes us to put false gods before us. We make money or achievement or popularity or material possessions or the "right" marriage the Higher Power that determines if we have worth. We take our self-definition and self-worth from external manifestations of our own being so that looks or talent or intelligence becomes the Higher Power that we look to in determining if we have worth. "All outside and external conditions are temporary and could change in a moment. If we make a temporary condition our Higher Power we are setting ourselves up to be a victim - and, in blind devotion to that Higher Power we are pursuing, we often victimize other people on our way to proving we have worth.

Codependency is a particularly vicious form of delayed stress syndrome. Instead of being traumatized in a foreign country against an identified enemy during a war, as soldiers who have delayed stress are - we were traumatized in our sanctuaries by

the people we loved the most.   Instead of having experienced
that trauma for a year or two as a soldier might - we experienced
it on a daily basis for 16 or 17 or 18 years. A soldier has to shut
down emotionally in order to survive in a war zone. We had to
shut down emotionally because we were surrounded by adults
who were emotional cripples of one sort or another.

Codependency is a dysfunctional emotional and behavioral
defense system. When a society is emotionally dishonest, the
people of that society are set up to be emotionally dysfunctional.
In this society being emotional is described as falling apart, losing it, going to pieces, coming unglued, etc. (Other cultures
give more permission to be emotional but then the emotions are
usually expressed in ways that are out of balance to the extreme
of letting the emotions control. The goal is balance between
emotional and mental - between the intuitive and the rational.)

Traditionally in this society men have been taught that anger is
the only acceptable emotion for a man to express, while women
are taught that it is not acceptable for them to be angry. If it is
not ok to own all of our emotions then we can not know who
we are as emotional beings. Traditionally women are taught to
be codependent. Their self-definition and self-worth are derived
from relationships with men, while men are taught to be codependent on their work/career/ability to produce and from their
presumed superiority to women.

Codependency is a disease of lost self. If we are not validated
and affirmed for who we are in childhood then we don't believe
we are worthy or lovable. Often we got validated and affirmed
by one parent and put down by the other. When the parent who is
"loving" does not protect us - or themselves - from the parent that
is abusive, it is a betrayal that sets us up to have low self-esteem
because the affirmation we received was invalidated right in our
own homes. And being affirmed for being who we are is very
different than being affirmed for who our parents wanted us to

be - if they could not see themselves clearly then they sure could not see us clearly. In order to survive, children adapt whatever behavior will work best in helping them get their survival needs met. We then grow up to be adults who don't know our self and keep dancing the dance we learned as children.

"A dysfunctional relationship is one that does not work to make us happy."

Codependency is about having a dysfunctional relationship with self. With our own bodies, minds, emotions, and spirits. With our own gender and sexuality. With being human. Because we have dysfunctional relationships internally we have dysfunctional relationships externally. We try to fill the hole we feel inside of our self with something or someone outside of us - it does not work.

The Condition of Codependency

The word changed and evolved further after the start of the modern Codependence movement in Arizona in the mid-eighties. Codependents Anonymous had its first meeting in October of 1986, and books on Codependence as a disease in and of itself started appearing at about the same time. These Codependence books were the next generation evolved from the books on the Adult Child Syndrome of the early eighties. Children now are being taught in school and through the media, that it is good to have boundaries (just say no) and to talk about their feelings. There are books and classes now in healthy parenting. This is a major leap forward for society.

It was not long ago, that the philosophy of child raising was based upon a "this is right and this is wrong - and you better do right or else. Unfortunately it still is for many families. And even more unfortunately, most of the kids that are being given healthier messages are still not getting healthy role modeling. Role modeling is just as important - if not more important - in the developmental process for children than direct messages. "Do as I say, and not as I do," does not work when it comes to parenting. The reality of human development is that we form the foundation dynamics of our relationships with self, with life, and with other people in early childhood. Our relationship patterns are pretty embedded by the time we are 4 or 5 years old.

Since there is no integration of the human developmental process into society - no real training of how to be healthy adults or real ceremonies / initiation rites to mark vital milestones / passages in development, such as puberty (junior high school as it is experienced in society is not a celebration of adolescence) - and no culturally approved grieving to take the emotional charge away from wounds caused by childhood trauma, we are stuck with those early childhood patterns.

We are trained in childhood to be emotionally and intellectually dishonest, through both direct messages and watching our role models. We learned that it was very important to keep up appearances - to wear a mask. We watched out parents say nasty, judgmental things about a person when they weren't around and then be nice to them in person. We got told that it was not okay to speak our truth. There was an old song I always thought described how I saw people interacting, that went something to the effect "The games people play now, every night and every day now, never saying what they mean - never meaning what they say." We were trained to be dishonest. We also got taught to be emotionally dishonest. We got told not to feel our feelings with messages like, don't cry, don't be afraid - at the same time we saw how our parents lived life out of fear. We got messages that it was not okay to be too happy when our exuberance was embarrassing to our parents. Many of us grew up in environments where it was not okay to be curious, or adventurous, or playful. It was not okay to be a child.

A society is unhealthy when:

> **Emotional dishonesty** is not just the standard but the goal (keep up appearances, don't show vulnerability);

> **As children we learn that we have power over other people's feelings** (you make me angry, you hurt my feelings, etc.);

> **Being emotional is considered negative** (falling apart, loosing it, coming unglued, etc.);

> **Gender stereotypes set twisted, unhealthy models for acceptable emotional behavior** (real men don't cry or get scared, it is not ladylike to get angry);

> **Parents without healthy self-esteem see their children as extensions of self** that can be either assets or deficits in their own quest for self-worth;

> **Families are isolated from any true reality of community or tribal support**;

> **Shame, manipulation, verbal and emotional abuse are considered standard tools** for behavior modification in a loving relationship;

> **Long embedded societal attitudes support the belief that it is shameful to be human** (make mistakes, not be perfect, to be selfish, etc.);

> **Any human being is denigrated and held to be less worthy for any inherent characteristic** (gender, race, looks, etc.).

We were Setup to be Codependent

We were trained and programmed in childhood to be dishonest with ourselves and others. We were taught false, dysfunctional concepts of success, romance, love, life. We could not have lived our lives differently because there was no one to teach us how to be healthy. We were doing the best we knew how with the tools, beliefs, and definitions we had - just as our parents were doing the best they knew how. We have new tools now. We have information and knowledge that was not available until recently.

We can change the way we live our lives. It is important to stop shaming ourselves for living life the way we were programmed to live, in order to start learning how to live in a way that is more functional - in a way that works to help us have some peace and happiness in our lives. The only way to be free of the past is to start seeing it more clearly - without shame and judgment - so that we can take advantage of this wonderful time of healing that has begun.

Codependency has been the human condition.

We now have the knowledge and power to change our relationship with ourselves. That is how we can change the human condition.

Codependence vs. Interdependence

Codependence and interdependence are two very different dynamics. Codependence is about giving away power over our self-esteem. . . . Interdependence is about making allies, forming partnerships. It is about forming connections with other beings.

The disease of Codependence causes us to keep repeating patterns that are familiar. So we pick untrustworthy people to trust, undependable people to depend on, unavailable people to love. By healing our emotional wounds and changing our intellectual programming we can start to practice discernment in our choices so that we can change our patterns and learn to trust ourselves.

The way to healthy interdependence is to be able to see things clearly - to see people, situations, life dynamics and most of all ourselves clearly. If we are not working on healing our childhood wounds and changing our childhood programming then we cannot begin to see ourselves clearly let alone anything else in life.

Emotional abuse is Heart and Soul Mutilation

Emotional abuse is underneath all other types of abuse - the most damaging aspect of physical, sexual, mental, etc. abuse is the trauma to our hearts and souls from being betrayed by the people that we love and trust. Our parents were emotionally abused in childhood because their parents were emotionally abused in childhood. Our parents were our role models who taught us how to relate to ourselves and our own emotions. The most destructive emotional abuse is the emotional abuse we learned to inflict upon ourselves. We formed our core relationship with self in early childhood and have been judging and shaming ourselves ever since. The most destructive thing about the emotional abuse we suffered, because our parents were wounded, was that we incorporated the messages we got from their behavior into our relationship with self. We emotionally abuse ourselves on a daily basis.

LOVE is the fabric from which we are woven

LOVE is the answer. And in order to start finding my way home to LOVE - I first had to start awakening to what Love is not. Here are a few things that I have learned, and believe, are not part of the True nature of Love.

Love is not

Critical	Shaming	Abusive	Controlling	Manipulative
Demeaning	Humiliating	Separating	Discounting	Diminishing
Belittling	Negative	Traumatic	Painful	

Love is also not an addiction

It is not taking a hostage or being taken hostage. The type of romantic love that I learned about growing is a form of toxic love. The "I can't smile without you," "Can't live without you." "You are my everything," "You are not whole until you find your prince/princess" messages that I learned in relationship to romantic love in childhood are not descriptions of Love - they are descriptions of drug of choice, of someone who is a higher power/false god.

Love is not being a doormat

Love does not entail sacrificing your self on the altar of martyrdom - because one cannot consciously choose to sacrifice self if they have never Truly had a self that they felt was Lovable and worthy. If we do not know how to Love our self, how to show respect and honor for our self - then we have no self to sacrifice. We are then sacrificing in order to try to prove to ourselves that we are lovable and worthy - that is not giving from the heart, that is codependently manipulative, controlling, and dishonest.

Unconditional Love is not being a self-sacrificing doormat

Unconditional Love begins with Loving self enough to protect our self from the people we Love if that is necessary. Until we start Loving, honoring, and respecting our self, we are not Truly **giving** - we are attempting to **take** self-worth from others by being compliant in our behavior towards them. - The True Nature of Love - what Love is not

Any kind of physical, verbal, mental, sexual abuse is also emotionally abusive

Any attitudes or behaviors that convey a message that the other is less than a being who deserves to be treated with respect and dignity - including objectifying and stereotyping - are emotionally abusive.

The overt forms of abuse are often much more readily identifiable

It is relatively easy for most people to see that raging and yelling are emotionally abusive. That name calling and verbal put downs are emotionally abusive. It can be hard to identify some of the more passive aggressive forms as being just as wounding - as being abusive and damaging. Passive-aggressive behavior is the expression of anger indirectly. This happens because we got the message one way or another in childhood that it was not OK to express anger.

Emotional Honesty and Emotional Responsibility

Because we were discounted and invalidated in childhood (and for most of our adult lives due to our repeating patterns); because we were taught not to trust our own feelings and perceptions; because we learned to have twisted, distorted relationships with ourselves and our own emotions; we need validation from other

241

people that what we are awakening to is in fact real and not some product of our defective, shameful self image.

At the same time, it is a codependent pattern to gather allies. To have people to complain to, who will sympathize with us and tell us how awful the other person/people were for abusing us. We gather allies that will give their approval to our self righteous indignation. When we are feeling self righteous indignation we are buying into a victim perspective.

Anytime that we are focusing on the situation at hand and giving power to the belief that we are victims of the situation/people we have just interacted with, without looking at how that situation is connected to our childhood wounds - we are not being honest with ourselves. We will feel like victims - because we have been abused. But feeling like a victim and giving power to the belief in victimization are two completely different things.

I have often told clients that going from feeling suicidal to feeling homicidal is a step of progress. It is a stage of the recovery process that we will move into - and then at some later point will move beyond. An incest victim transforms into an incest survivor. Owning the anger is an important part of pulling ourselves out of the depression that turning the anger back on ourselves has created. It is often necessary to own the anger before we can get in touch with the grief in a clean and healthy way. If we haven't owned our right to be angry, it is possible to get stuck in a victim place of self-pity and martyrdom, of complaining and gathering sympathetic allies - instead of taking action to change."

Setting Personal Boundaries - protecting self

The purpose of having boundaries is to protect and take care of ourselves. We need to be able to tell other people when they are acting in ways that are not acceptable to us. A first step is starting to know that we have a right to protect and defend ourselves.

That we have not only the right, but the duty to take responsibility for how we allow others to treat us.

It is important to state our feelings out loud, and to precede the feeling with 'I feel.' (When we say "I am angry, I'm hurt, etc." we are stating that the feeling is who we are. Emotions do not define us, they are a form of internal communication that help us to understand ourselves. They are a vital part of our being - as a component of the whole.) This is owning the feeling. It is important to do for ourselves. By stating the feeling out loud we are affirming that we have a right to feelings. We are affirming it to ourselves - and taking responsibility for owning ourselves and our reality. Rather the other person can hear us and understand is not as important as hearing ourselves and understanding that we have a right to our feelings. It is vitally important to own our own voice. To own our right to speak up for ourselves.

Setting boundaries is not a more sophisticated way of manipulation - although some people will say they are setting boundaries, when in fact they are attempting to manipulate. The difference between setting a boundary in a healthy way and manipulating is: when we set a boundary we let go of the outcome. It is impossible to have a healthy relationship with someone who has no boundaries, with someone who cannot communicate directly, and honestly. Learning how to set boundaries is a necessary step in learning to be a friend to ourselves. It is our responsibility to take care of ourselves - to protect ourselves when it is necessary. It is impossible to learn to be Loving to ourselves without owning our self - and owning our rights and responsibilities as co-creators of our lives."

Learning to Love our self

Codependence is a dysfunctional defense system that was built in reaction to feeling unlovable and unworthy - because our parents were wounded codependents who didn't know how to love themselves. We grew up in environments that were emotionally dishonest, Spiritually hostile, and shame based. Our relationship with ourselves (and all the different parts of our self: emotions, gender, spirit, etc.) got twisted and distorted in order to survive in our particular dysfunctional environment.

We need to take the shame and judgment out of the process on a personal level. It is vitally important to stop listening and giving power to that critical place within us that tells us that we are bad and wrong and shameful.

That "critical parent" voice in our head is the disease lying to us. ... This healing is a long gradual process - the goal is progress, not perfection. What we are learning about is unconditional Love. Unconditional Love means no judgment, no shame.

The critical parent voice keeps us from relaxing and enjoying life, and from loving our self. We need to own that we have the power to choose where to focus our mind. We can consciously start viewing ourselves from the "witness" perspective.

Inner Child Healing = a path to freedom, serenity, and empowerment

It is through healing our inner child, our inner children, by griev-ing the wounds that we suffered, that we can change our behav-ior patterns and clear our emotional process. We can release the grief with its pent-up rage, shame, terror, and pain from those feeling places which exist within us. Because of our broken hearts, our emotional wounds, and our scrambled minds, our subconscious programming, what the disease of Codependence causes us to do is abandon ourselves. It causes the abandonment of self, the abandonment of our own inner child - and that inner child is the gateway to our channel to the Higher Self.

The one who betrayed us and abandoned and abused us the most was ourselves. That is how the emotional defense system that is

Codependence works. The battle cry of Codependence is "I'll show you - I'll get me. We need to rescue and nurture and Love our inner children - and STOP them from controlling our lives. STOP them from driving the bus! Children are not supposed to drive, they are not supposed to be in control. And they are not supposed to be abused and abandoned. We have been doing it backwards. We abandoned and abused our inner children. Locked them in a dark place within us. And at the same time let the children drive the bus - let the children's wounds dictate our lives. It is necessary to own and honor the child who we were in order to Love the person we are. And the only way to do that is to own that child's experiences, honor that child's feelings, and release the emotional grief energy that we are still carrying around.

Robert Burney

Spiritual Teacher and Codependency Therapist and Author Robert Burney, whose work has been compared to John Bradshaw's except much more spiritual and described as taking inner child healing to a new level. He has developed a unique approach to emotional healing that is the next level of recovery from codependency that so many people have been seeking. He has pioneered an inner child healing paradigm that offers a powerful, life changing formula for integrating Love, Spiritual Truth, and intellectual knowledge of healthy behavior into one's emotional experience of life - a blueprint for individuals to transform their core relationship with self and life.

Roberts process is firmly grounded on twelve step recovery principles and emotional energy release / grief process therapy, specializes in teaching individuals how to become empowered to have internal boundaries so they can learn to relax and enjoy life in the moment while healing. It is the unique approach and application of the concept of internal boundaries, coupled with a Loving Spiritual belief system, that make the work so innovative and effective.

*In his book **Codependence: The Dance of Wounded Souls** "A Cosmic Perspective on Codependence and the Human Condition" he postulates that Codependence (i.e. outer or external dependence) is The Human Condition."*

Codependence: The Dance of Wounded Souls
By Robert Burney copyright 1995
Library of Congress Catalog Card Number: 95-95029
ISBN: 0-9648383-1-1 ~
Published by
Joy to You & Me Enterprises
PO Box 977
Cambria CA 93428
www.joy2meu.com

CHAPTER 16

Facts about Post-Traumatic Stress Disorder

*"Untwisting all the chains that tie
the hidden soul of harmony."*

—John Milton

Post-traumatic stress disorder (PTSD) is an anxiety disorder that can develop after exposure to a terrifying event or ordeal in which grave physical harm occurred or was threatened. Traumatic events that can trigger PTSD include violent personal assaults such as rape or mugging, natural or human-caused disasters, accidents, or military combat. PTSD can be extremely disabling, and magnify the affect of bipolar disorder. The following information acquired from the National Institute of Health, provides an important understanding of PTSD.

Military troops who served in the Vietnam and Gulf Wars; rescue workers involved in the aftermath of disasters like the terrorist attacks on New York City and Washington, D.C.; survivors of the Oklahoma City bombing; survivors of accidents, rape, physical and sexual abuse, and other crimes; immigrants fleeing violence in their countries; survivors of the 1994 California earthquake, the 1997 North and South Dakota floods, and hurricanes Hugo and Andrew; and people who witness traumatic events are among those at risk for developing PTSD. Families of victims can also develop the disorder.

Fortunately, through research supported by the National Institute of Mental Health (NIMH) and the Department of Veterans Affairs (VA), effective treatments have been developed to help people with PTSD. Research is also helping scientists better understand the condition and how it affects the brain and the rest of the body.

What Are the Symptoms of PTSD?

Many people with PTSD repeatedly re-experience the ordeal in the form of flashback episodes, memories, nightmares, or frightening thoughts, especially when they are exposed to events or objects reminiscent of the trauma. Anniversaries of the event can also trigger symptoms. People with PTSD also experience emotional numbness and sleep disturbances, depression, anxiety, and irritability or outbursts of anger. Feelings of intense guilt are also common. Most people with PTSD try to avoid any reminders or thoughts of the ordeal. PTSD is diagnosed when symptoms last more than 1 month.

How Common Is PTSD?

About 3.6 percent of U.S. adults ages 18 to 54 (5.2 million people) have PTSD during the course of a given year. About 30 percent of the men and women who have spent time in war zones experience PTSD. One million war veterans developed PTSD after serving in Vietnam. PTSD has also been detected among veterans of the Persian Gulf War, with some estimates running as high as 8 percent.

When Does PTSD First Occur?

PTSD can develop at any age, including in childhood. Symptoms typically begin within 3 months of a traumatic event, although occasionally they do not begin until years later. Once PTSD occurs, the severity and duration of the illness varies. Some people recover within 6 months, while others suffer much longer.

What Treatments Are Available for PTSD?

Research has demonstrated the effectiveness of cognitive-behavioral therapy, group therapy, and exposure therapy, in which the patient gradually and repeatedly relives the frightening experience under controlled conditions to help him or her work through the trauma. Studies have also shown that medications help ease associated symptoms of depression and anxiety and help promote sleep. Scientists are attempting to determine which treatments work best for which type of trauma.

Some studies show that giving people an opportunity to talk about their experiences very soon after a catastrophic event may reduce some of the symptoms of PTSD. A study of 12,000 schoolchildren who lived through a hurricane in Hawaii found that those who got counseling early on were doing much better 2 years later than those who did not.

Do Other Illnesses Tend to Accompany PTSD?

Co-occurring depression, alcohol or other substance abuse, or another anxiety disorder are not uncommon. The likelihood of treatment success is increased when these other conditions are appropriately identified and treated as well.

Headaches, gastrointestinal complaints, immune system problems, dizziness, chest pain, or discomfort in other parts of the body are common. Often, doctors treat the symptoms without being aware that they stem from PTSD. NIMH encourages primary care providers to ask patients about experiences with violence, recent losses, and traumatic events, especially if symptoms keep recurring. When PTSD is diagnosed, referral to a mental health professional who has had experience treating people with the disorder is recommended.

Who Is Most Likely to Develop PTSD?

People who have suffered abuse as children or who have had other previous traumatic experiences are more likely to develop the disorder. Research is continuing to pinpoint other factors that may lead to PTSD.

It used to be believed that people who tend to be emotionally numb after a trauma were showing a healthy response, but now some researchers suspect that people who experience this emotional distancing may be more prone to PTSD.

What Are Scientists Learning From Research?

NIMH and the VA sponsor a wide range of basic, clinical, and genetic studies of PTSD. In addition, NIMH has a special funding mechanism, called RAPID Grants, that allows researchers to immediately visit the scenes of disasters, such as plane crashes or floods and hurricanes, to study the acute effects of the event and the effectiveness of early intervention.

Studies in animals and humans have focused on pinpointing the specific brain areas and circuits involved in anxiety and fear, which are important for understanding anxiety disorders such as PTSD. Fear, an emotion that evolved to deal with danger, causes an automatic, rapid protective response in many systems of the body. It has been found that the body's fear response is coordinated by a small structure deep inside the brain, called the amygdala. The amygdala, although relatively small, is a very complicated structure, and recent research suggests that different anxiety disorders may be associated with abnormal activation of the amygdala.

The following are also recent research findings:

- In brain imaging studies, researchers have found that the hippocampus—a part of the brain critical to memory and emotion—appears to be different in cases of PTSD. Scientists are investigating whether this is related to short-term memory problems. Changes in the hippocampus are thought to be responsible for intrusive memories and flashbacks that occur in people with this disorder.
- People with PTSD tend to have abnormal levels of key hormones involved in response to stress. Some studies have shown that cortisol levels are lower than normal and epinephrine and norepinephrine are higher than normal.
- When people are in danger, they produce high levels of natural opiates, which can temporarily mask pain. Scientists have found that people with PTSD continue to produce those higher levels even after the danger has passed; this may lead to the blunted emotions associated with the condition.
- Research to understand the neurotransmitter systems involved in memories of emotionally charged events may lead to discovery of medications or psychosocial interventions that, if given early, could block the development of PTSD symptoms.

Public Domain Source:
National Institute of Mental Health. Facts about Post-Traumatic Stress Disorder. Bethesda (MD):
National Institute of Mental Health, National Institutes of Health, US Department of Health and
Human Services; 2001 [reprinted 2002; cited 2004 May 19]. (NIH Publication Number: NIH
OM-99 4157). 3 web pages. Available from: http://www.nimh.nih.gov/publicat/ptsdfacts.cfm

CHAPTER 17

Eye Movement Desensitization and Reprocessing (EMDR)

*"Voyage through death
to life upon these shores."*

—Robert Earle Hayden

Eye Movement Desensitization Reprocessing (EMDR) is a treatment for some forms of PTSD. EMDR was very helpful in overcoming many childhood and adult issues that traumatized me for years. If you are struggling with life issues that really hold you down, then I suggest that you discuss EMDR and other treatments available for PTSD with your therapist or doctor. Information acquired from the National Center for Post Traumatic Stress Syndrome.

What is EMDR?

Eye Movement Desensitization and Reprocessing (EMDR) is a relatively new clinical treatment that has been scientifically evaluated primarily with trauma survivors. EMDR's originator, Dr. Francine Shapiro, describes the procedure in detail in a recent book, and advises that therapists use EMDR only after completing an authorized advanced training in EMDR. When considering the possibility that EMDR may be helpful for you or someone you know, an important first step is to speak with therapist(s) who have had advanced EMDR training and are experienced in selecting clients and successfully conducting EMDR. For information on qualified EMDR therapists, contact the International EMDR Network (P.O. Box 51038, Pacific Grove, California 93950).

Who are treated?

EMDR is widely used by psychotherapists with adult trauma survivors, including war veterans, abuse and rape survivors, and accident and disaster survivors. EMDR also is used with traumatized children and with adults suffering from severe anxiety or depression.

How does EMDR work?

Briefly, in EMDR a qualified therapist guides the client in vividly but safely recalling distressing past experiences ("desensitization") and gaining new understanding ("reprocessing") of the events, the bodily and emotional feelings, and the thoughts and self-images associated with them. The "eye movement" aspect of EMDR involves the client moving his/her eyes in a back-and-forth ("saccadic") manner while recalling the event(s).

How Effective is EMDR?

EMDR has shown evidence of therapeutic effectiveness in several recent scientific studies. After receiving between one and twelve sessions of EMDR, many (but not all) adolescents and adult clients have reported a variety of benefits. EMDR recipients in these studies have included adult and adolescent child and domestic abuse survivors, combat veterans, rape and violent assault survivors, victims of life-threatening accidents and disasters, and individuals with severe panic attacks or depression. Some of these individuals were seeking help from the VA, from their HMO medical plan, or from mental health specialists at clinics or counseling centers, while others were not actively seeking healthcare or mental health treatment, but agreed to participate in a research study in order to receive treatment.

The benefits reported following EMDR include:

- Feeling less troubled by trauma memories and reminders while awake and in their dreams (PTSD intrusive re-experiencing symptoms)
- Feeling able to cope with trauma memories and reminders without simply trying to avoid troubling thoughts, conversations, people, activities, or places (PTSD avoidance symptoms)
- Feeling more able to enjoy pleasurable activities and to be emotionally involved in relationships, as well as feeling that there is a future to look forward to (PTSD numbing and detachment symptoms)
- Feeling less tense, stressed, irritable or angry, easily startled, and on-guard, and more able to sleep restfully, concentrate on activities, and deal with pressure and conflict (PTSD hyperarousal / hypervigilance symptoms)
- Feeling less anxious, worried, fearful or phobic, and prone to panic attacks
- Feeling less depressed (down and blue, hopeless, worthless, emotionally drained, or suicidal)
- Feeling an increased sense of self-esteem and self-confidence

---

Are treatment effects maintained over time?

A few studies have checked to see how participants were doing several months or more than a year after completing EMDR, generally finding that the benefits persisted over these time periods.

However, EMDR is not a certain cure, nor always effective. In even the most successful studies approximately 25-33% of participants report no clear benefit. EMDR's most consistent benefit is helping clients to feel better about themselves because they feel less troubled by and more able to cope with trauma memories. EMDR is less likely to actually change how much bodily arousal and mental hypervigilance trauma survivors experience—although such changes do occur at times.

EMDR also is not always the best treatment to deal with PTSD or related psychological problems. One study with Vietnam military veterans diagnosed with PTSD showed EMDR to be no better than other widely used forms of counseling. Another study with spider phobic children showed EMDR to be less helpful than an "in vivo exposure" treatment in which the children gradually and safely saw and touched a variety of real or artificial spiders.

EMDR involves carefully but intensively confronting very frightening or disturbing memories. Some clients report that the eye movement feature of EMDR helped them to rapidly feel less terrified, intimidated, or hopeless while undergoing this therapeutic "exposure" to sources of fear, anxiety, or depression. However, several studies suggest that "direct therapeutic exposure" by vividly and safely confronting stressors without eye movements is equally as effective as EMDR. These studies, with combat veterans or civilian trauma survivors diagnosed with PTSD, and with adults with phobias or panic disorder, raise the question of whether eye movements are essential to the positive results that can occur following EMDR. That question remains unanswered.

What you should know about EMDR

If you or someone you know are considering undergoing EMDR, you should be aware, however, that PTSD is a complex and devastating disorder. No single procedure can "cure" PTSD. The best treatment plan is based upon a thorough professional assessment, and may include individual therapies such as EMDR or therapeutic exposure, but also a range of other appropriate services such as group and family therapy, addiction care, medication, stress and anger management, vocational therapy, and healthcare. EMDR, like any other therapy, should be done with these basic guidelines:

1. With a goal of helping the survivor make sense of confusing disturbing experiences
2. With an emphasis on gaining self-esteem and personal empowerment
3. Vividly and without avoiding any aspect of the experience, however stressful
4. Guided by the survivor's desire for healing, not as a test of strength or stamina
5. With an emphasis upon helping the survivor find realistic new hope and optimism
6. Free from pressure, demands, manipulation, or criticism from the therapist
7. With a goal of helping the survivor develop accurate and realistic self-understanding
8. Guided by the survivor's bodily and emotional feelings and awarenesses
9. At an intensity and pace that the survivor feels is helpful, not overwhelming
10. Guided by an active and involved therapist

Suggested Readings
* Lee Hyer and Jeffrey M. Brandsma, "EMDR Minus Eye Movements Equals Good Psychotherapy," *Journal of Traumatic Stress* 10(3): 515-522 (July 1997).

* Francine Shapiro, *Eye Movement Desensitization and Reprocessing: Basic Principles, Protocols, and Procedures* (Guilford Press, 1995, ISBN 0-89862-960-8)

Public domain source:
National Center for Post Traumatic Stress Syndrome. Accessed 2004
http://www.ncptsd.va.gov/index.html

CHAPTER 18

Neurofeedback

"The question was put to him, what hope is;
and his answer was, "The dream of a waking man."
— Diogenes Laertius

Learning to be aware of and control our thoughts as well as our feelings can provide us with a great deal of power over our mood swings. Understanding how the brain works and how to control it is essential since thoughts are at the root of how we feel. Neurofeedback is new to me and yet I have already gained some important insights about how my mind reacts to different stressors. Through this new therapy I am learning how to lessen a depressive mental state and I am learning how to go to sleep quicker upon my mental command. Both my quality of sleep and my mental state are critical factors which can determine whether I go manic or become depressed. The following information has been provided with permission by Susan E. Klear Ph.D., Licensed Psychologist for the purposes of better understanding Neurofeedback and its possible benefits to those with bipolar disorder.

Introduction to Neurofeedback

Also known as EEG Biofeedback or Brainwave Biofeedback, this treatment has been shown to be highly effective in training many physical and psychological disorders.

Neurofeedback was originally used successfully to help individuals suffering from epilepsy. It was then found to be applicable to many other disorders. It is not the *cure-all, end-all* treatment with millions of promises but it is a new and exciting treatment that has shown clinical success on a variety of disorders.

The famed Menninger Clinic has used Neurofeedback for the successful treatment of alcohol and drug addiction. Many businesses in the United States and Japan trained their management personnel in peak performance protocols to enhance creativity, coping skills, and critical thinking.

The Model

I have my roots in person-centered psychotherapy and self-regulation. I feel that the healthy brain has the versatility to modulate states of arousal and attention styles as demanded by specific situations. The disordered brain has diminished ability to respond to these specific demands. The immature, injured, or disordered brain seems to lack the normal elasticity of the healthy brain. There appear to be discontinuities in cortical processes or breakdowns in intra-cortical communications. The disordered brain seems to get "stuck" and exhibits inappropriate brain waves for the immediate situation. For example, the ADD child tends to exhibit more day dreaming type brainwaves with less than normal concentrating type brainwaves.

Neurofeedback training teaches a person what specific brain wave states feel like and how to turn those states on at will. The trainee can "move" to different physiological states depending on what the immediate situation requires. *We claim no more than that a person can learn through training to change to a different physiological state.* People have been learning to change their physiological states through temperature and EMG training. We are simply using the more *"central"* information of EEG correlates of physiological states rather than peripheral measures.

We feel that if we can make the brain more flexible it may have a generalizing effect on other functions such as the full nervous system, the immune system, the endocrine systems, the body's ability to heal itself and general cognitive functioning.

Self-healing is what biofeedback is all about. We do not do anything to anybody except teach them to listen in on themselves. We are teachers which is what any good therapist is. We can teach people to listen in on their own physiology and to change their physiological and psycho-logical states.

What is Biofeedback?

Biofeedback is like eavesdropping on our body's internal conversations and using this information to change negative patterns that are contributing to poor physical and mental health. Our bodies are a sea of information and communication, every organ talking to every other organ. As a general rule, we do not pay attention to these inside-the-skin conversations. With sophisticated listening devices we can collect this information and feed it back to our brains through our ears, eyes, and touch. With practice, we can then begin to change inside-the-skin events to make us healthier. You already use biofeedback. If you charge up the steps noticing your heart rate and respiration go up, you slow down.

Now medical science is able to help us listen in to the quieter messages that otherwise go unnoticed until we have medical or emotional problems. With biofeedback we can change temperature, heart rate, blood pressure, muscle tension, chemical responses, electrical impulses, and even brainwaves.

What is Neurofeedback?

By recording electrical activity produced by the brain and correlating this activity into frequency bands we are able to determine different subjective states of consciousness, such as relaxation, by using the EEG feedback. The individual is able to either enhance this state or change the state. Therefore, a person can learn to do a much more efficient job at such tasks as concentrating or relaxing. Neurofeedback is, again, taking a very subtle inside-the-skin event and using it to change our level of functioning. This is the me art of self-mastery-making one less dependent on others, drugs, machines, or medical technology.

The Learning Process

All biofeedback is a learning process that involves both physical and mental skills. It is learning how to change your body by listening to your body's messages. Some biofeedback processes, like temperature training, may take only a few sessions whereas brainwave feedback may take ten to twenty sessions before a person begins to grasp what a particular brainwave state "feels" like. Then, more sessions will be needed to perfect the process. Learning to modify a brainwave state in the correct direction to sustain a desired mental state is a "discovery" process, a process of gaining more and more control over your thoughts, feelings, and behaviors.

The following syndromes have published evidence of effectiveness using Neurofeedback:

    * ADHD/ADD
    * Anxiety and Relaxation

* Addiction
* Depression
* Learning Disabilities
* Peak Performance (athletes,
  business professionals)
* Post Traumatic Stress Disorder
* Sleep Disorders

The following syndromes have clinical reports of effectiveness using Neurofeedback:

* Attachment Disorder
* Chronic Fatigue Syndrome
* Chronic Pain
* Cognitive Decline in the Elderly
* Eating Disorders
* Fibromyalgia
* Obsessive-Compulsive Disorder
* Parkinson's Disease
* Tourette's Syndrome
* Traumatic Brain Injury

Note: 75-90% of all healthcare visits are stress related. (National Institute of Health)

Susan E. Klear Ph.D.
Licensed Psychologist, PSY 19510

Member of the American Psychological Association
Affiliate of EEG Spectrum, Intl
1588 Homestead Rd, Suite 11 Santa Clara, CA 95050
408-249-3270 office, 408-984-1035 fax
sueklear@earthlink.net

CHAPTER 19

Frequently Asked Questions about Suicide

"The real voyage of discovery consists not in seeking new landscapes but in having new eyes."

—Marcel Proust

Suicide is an unfortunate outcome for many who have been diagnosed with bipolar disorder. It is essential that the person with bipolar disorder and their circle of family and friends understand the nature and danger of suicidal thinking.

What should you do if someone tells you they are thinking about suicide?

If someone tells you they are thinking about suicide, you should take their distress seriously, listen nonjudgmentally, and help them get to a professional for evaluation and treatment. People consider suicide when they are hopeless and unable to see alternative solutions to problems. Suicidal behavior is most often related to a mental disorder (depression) or to alcohol or other substance abuse. Suicidal behavior is also more likely to occur when people experience stressful events (major losses, incarceration). If someone is in imminent danger of harming himself or herself, do not leave the person alone. You may need to take emergency steps to get help, such as calling 911. When someone is in a suicidal crisis, it is important to limit access to firearms or other lethal means of committing suicide.

What are the most common methods of suicide?

Firearms are the most commonly used method of suicide for men and women, accounting for 60 percent of all suicides. Nearly 80 percent of all firearm suicides are committed by white males. The second most common method for men is hanging; for women, the second most common method is self-poisoning including drug overdose. The presence of a firearm in the home has been found to be an independent, additional risk factor for suicide. Thus, when a family member or health care provider is faced with an individual at risk for suicide, they should make sure that firearms are removed from the home.

Why do men commit suicide more often than women do?

More than four times as many men as women die by suicide; but women attempt suicide more often during their lives than do men, and women report higher rates of depression. Men and women use different suicide methods. Women in all countries are more likely to ingest poisons than men. In countries where the poisons are highly lethal and/or where treatment resources scarce, rescue is rare and hence female suicides outnumber males.

Who is at the highest risk for suicide in the U.S.?

There is a common perception that suicide rates are highest among the young. However, it is the elderly, particularly older white males that have the highest rates. And among white males 65 and older, risk goes up with age. White men 85 and older have a suicide rate that is six times that of the overall national rate. Some older persons are less likely to survive attempts because they are less likely to recuperate. Over 70 percent of older suicide victims have been to their primary care physician within the month of their death, many did not tell their doctors they were depressed nor did the doctor detect it. This has led to research efforts to determine how to best improve physician's abilities to detect and treat depression in older adults.

Is suicide related to impulsiveness?

Impulsiveness is the tendency to act without thinking through a plan or its consequences. It is a symptom of a number of mental disorders, and therefore, it has been linked to suicidal behavior usually through its association with mental disorders and/or substance abuse. The mental disorders with impulsiveness most linked to suicide include borderline personality disorder among young females, conduct disorder among young males and antisocial behavior in adult males, and alcohol and substance abuse among young and middle-aged males. Impulsiveness appears to have a lesser role in older adult suicides. Attention deficit hyperactivity disorder that has impulsiveness as a characteristic is not a strong risk factor for suicide by itself. Impulsiveness has been linked with aggressive and violent behaviors including homicide and suicide. However, impulsiveness without aggression or violence present has also been found to contribute to the risk for suicide.

Is there such a thing as "rational" suicide?

Some right-to-die advocacy groups promote the idea that suicide, including assisted suicide, can be a rational decision. Others have argued that suicide is never a rational decision and that it is the result of depression, anxiety, and fear of being dependent or a burden. Surveys of terminally ill persons indicate that very few consider taking their own life, and when they do, it is in the context of depression. Attitude surveys suggest that assisted suicide is more acceptable by the public and health providers for the old who are ill or disabled, compared to the young who are ill or disabled. At this time, there is limited research on the frequency with which persons with terminal illness have depression and suicidal ideation, whether they would consider assisted suicide, the characteristics of such persons, and the context of their depression and suicidal thoughts, such as family stress, or availability of palliative care. Neither is it yet clear what effect other factors such as the availability of social support, access to care, and pain relief may have on end-of-life preferences. This public debate will be better informed after such research is conducted.

What biological factors increase risk for suicide?

Researchers believe that both depression and suicidal behavior can be linked to decreased serotonin in the brain. Low levels of a serotonin metabolite, 5-HIAA, have been detected in cerebral spinal fluid in persons who have attempted suicide, as well as by postmortem studies examining certain brain regions of suicide victims. One of the goals of understanding the biology of suicidal behavior is to improve treatments. Scientists have learned that serotonin receptors in the brain increase their activity in persons with major depression and suicidality, which explains why medications that desensitize or down-regulate these receptors (such as the serotonin reuptake inhibitors, or SSRIs) have been found effective in treating depression. Currently, studies are underway to examine to what extent medications like SSRIs can reduce suicidal behavior.

Can the risk for suicide be inherited?

There is growing evidence that familial and genetic factors contribute to the risk for suicidal behavior. Major psychiatric illnesses, including bipolar disorder, major depression, schizophrenia, alcoholism and substance abuse, and certain personality disorders, which run in families, increase the risk for suicidal behavior. This does not mean that suicidal behavior is inevitable for individuals with this family history; it simply means that such persons may be more vulnerable and should take steps to reduce their risk, such as getting evaluation and treatment at the first sign of mental illness.

Does depression increase the risk for suicide?

Although the majority of people who have depression do not die by suicide, having major depression does increase suicide risk compared to people without depression. The risk of death by suicide may, in part, be related to the severity of the depression. New data on depression that has followed people over long periods of time suggests that about 2 percent of those people ever treated for depression in an outpatient setting will die by suicide. Among those ever treated for depression in an inpatient hospital setting, the rate of death by suicide is twice as high (4 percent). Those treated for depression as inpatients following suicide ideation or suicide attempts are about three times as likely to die by suicide (6 percent) as those who were only treated as outpatients. There are also dramatic gender differences in lifetime risk of suicide in depression. Whereas about 7 percent of men with a lifetime history of depression will die by suicide, only 1 percent of women with a lifetime history of depression will die by suicide.

Another way about thinking of suicide risk and depression is to examine the lives of people who have died by suicide and see what proportion of them were depressed. From that perspective, it is estimated that about 60 percent of people who commit suicide have had a mood disorder (e.g., major depression, bipolar disorder, dysthymia). Younger persons who kill themselves often have a substance abuse disorder in addition to being depressed.

Does alcohol and other drug abuse increase the risk for suicide?

A number of recent national surveys have helped shed light on the relationship between alcohol and other drug use and suicidal behavior. A review of minimum-age drinking laws and suicides among youths age 18 to 20 found that lower minimum-age drinking laws was associated with higher youth suicide rates. In a large study following adults who drink alcohol, suicide ideation was reported among persons with depression. In another survey, persons who reported that they had made a suicide attempt during their lifetime were more likely to have had a depressive disorder, and many also had an alcohol and/or substance abuse disorder. In a study of all nontraffic injury deaths associated with alcohol intoxication, over 20 percent were suicides.

In studies that examine risk factors among people who have completed suicide, substance use and abuse occurs more frequently among youth and adults, compared to older persons. For particular groups at risk, such as American Indians and Alaskan Natives, depression and alcohol use and abuse are the most common risk factors for completed suicide. Alcohol and substance abuse problems contribute to suicidal behavior in several ways. Persons who are dependent on substances often have a number of other risk factors for suicide. In addition to being depressed, they are also likely to have social and financial problems. Substance use and abuse can be common among persons prone to be impulsive, and among persons who engage in many types of high risk behaviors that result in self-harm. Fortunately, there are a number of effective prevention efforts that reduce risk for substance abuse in youth, and there are effective treatments for alcohol and substance use problems. Researchers are currently testing treatments specifically for persons with substance abuse problems who are also suicidal, or have attempted suicide in the past.

What does "suicide contagion" mean, and what can be done to prevent it?

Suicide contagion is the exposure to suicide or suicidal behaviors within one's family, one's peer group, or through media reports of suicide and can result in an increase in suicide and suicidal behaviors. Direct and indirect exposure to suicidal behavior has been shown to precede an increase in suicidal behavior in persons at risk for suicide, especially in adolescents and young adults.

The risk for suicide contagion as a result of media reporting can be minimized by factual and concise media reports of suicide. Reports of suicide should not be repetitive, as prolonged exposure can increase the likelihood of suicide contagion. Suicide is the result of many complex factors; therefore media coverage should not report oversimplified explanations such as recent negative life events or acute stressors. Reports should not divulge detailed descriptions of the method used to avoid possible duplication. Reports should not glorify the victim and should not imply that suicide was effective in achieving a personal goal such as gaining media attention. In addition, information such as hotlines or emergency contacts should be provided for those at risk for suicide.

Following exposure to suicide or suicidal behaviors within one's family or peer group, suicide risk can be minimized by having family members, friends, peers, and colleagues of the victim evaluated by a mental health professional. Persons deemed at risk for suicide should then be referred for additional mental health services.

Is it possible to predict suicide?

At the current time there is no definitive measure to predict suicide or suicidal behavior. Researchers have identified factors that place individuals at higher risk for suicide, but very few persons with these risk factors will actually commit suicide. Risk factors include mental illness, substance abuse, previous suicide attempts, family history of suicide, history of being sexually abused, and impulsive or aggressive tendencies. Suicide is a relatively rare event and it is therefore difficult to predict which persons with these risk factors will ultimately commit suicide.

Public domain source:

National Institute of Mental Health
http://www.nimh.nih.gov/suicideprevention/suicidefaq.cfm
Posted December 1999
Accessed 2004

Acknowledgements

I would like to thank you, Frank, for your listening ear, words of wisdom and for walking with me along my journey. You are a *true* friend.

Ever since we were kids, Brian, you were always there for me as a friend, and you are like a brother to me. Thanks for your love. A Silver Lining friends, Mela and especially Pat who brought out the poet and writer in me, thanks for your love and encouragement to write.

Lynne, you helped me see — "The only way out is through."

Your experience and guidance, Pastor John, significantly helped see me through my journey.

Thanks, Mom, for your love, your ideas, editing work and encouragement especially during the final stretch of the book when I needed it the most.

Thanks, Thomas, for supporting and encouraging me during a critical time in the genesis of my book. You helped me see the finish line from such a long distance away.

Thanks, Dave, for working your magic on the critical edits of the book. You helped me see what this book could become and helped me press on.

Jean, you are awesome! You are so much more than my editor. Your vast knowledge has been more than helpful. This book would not have been possible without you; I am truly grateful.

Thank you Anne for your incredible patience and interior book design.

Cathi, thanks for your creativity and the incredible cover design.

Al and Shirley D., Cathy W., Annette B., Michelle T., Sarah W., Pastor John, David M., and Jonathan Russ M.D., your feedback was so essential to the formation of this book and what it has become.

Carol K., Thanks for the transcription work during the early development of this book.

Dr. Wayne Dyer, your book, *Erroneous Zones*, is incredible and is among the greatest works I have ever read.

Robert Burney, you have helped me overcome my life's greatest challenges, and thanks for your tremendous contribution to this book.

I am infected with your passion, Tony Robbins— I have chosen to live life with passion too!

John L., Robert B., Catherine W., Adelina H., Julie C., Suri H. and Dr. Klear: your guidance has been priceless.

Kaiser Permanente HMO doctors and surgeons—In the face of potential blindness and possible death, you have given me life, breath and sight and provided me the opportunity to complete this book.

Jonathan Russ, M.D.—*I am surviving bipolar disorder and am living because of you.*

David Goya, D.O.—*I have lungs that can breathe and sustain my life because of you.*

Hang Ly, M.D. and surgeon Lyndell Wang, M.D.—*I can see because of you, and learned the value of sight when you gave it back to me. I thank God for your passions and gifts of healing.*

Select Bibliography

Books

Beattie, Melody. *Codependent No More*. San Francisco: Harper & Row, 1987.
Burney, Robert. *Codependence: The Dance of the Wounded Souls*. Cambria, California: Joy to You & Me Enterprises, 1995.
Campbell, Bebe Moore. *72 Hour Hold*. New York: Alfred A. Knopf. Distributed by Random House, 2005.
Carlson, Trudy. *The Life of a Bipolar Child: What Every Parent and Professional Needs to Know*. Duluth, Minnesota: Benline Press, 2000
Copeland, Mary Ellen. *The Depression Workbook: A Guide for Living with Depression and Manic Depression*. Oakland, California: New Harbinger Pub, 1992.
Cymbala, Jim. *Fresh Wind, Fresh Fire*. Grand Rapids, Michigan: Zondervan, 1997.
Dobson, James C. *When God Doesn't Make Sense*. Wheaton, Illinois: Tyndale House Publishers, 1997.
Duke, Patty and Gloria Hochman. *A Brilliant Madness: Living with Manic Depressive Illness*. New York: Bantam Books, 1992.
Dyer, Wayne W. *Your Erroneous Zones: Step by Step Advice for Escaping the Trap of Negative Thinking*. New York: HarperPerrenial, 1991.
Glass, Lillian. Toxic People: *10 Ways of Dealing with People Who Make Your Life Miserable*. New York: St. Martin's Press, 1995.
Jamison, Kay Redfield. *An Unquiet Mind*. New York: Vintage Books, 1996, c1995.
— — — *Touched With Fire: Manic Depressive Illness and the Artistic Temperament*. New York: Free Press; Toronto: Maxwell Macmillan International, 1993.
Kushner, Harold S. *When Bad Things Happen to Good People*. New York: Schocken Books, 2001.
Mellody, Pia and Andrea Wells Miller and J. Keith Miller. *Facing Codependency: What It Is, Where It Comes From, How It Sabotages Our Lives*. New York: HarperCollins Publishers, 1989.
Miklowitz, David J., Ph.D. *The Bipolar Disorder Survival Guide: What You and Your Family Need to Know*. New York: Milford Press, 2002.

Potter-Efron, Ron T. and Pat Potter-Efron. *Letting Go of Anger: The 10 Most Common Anger Styles and What to Do About Them*. Oakland, California: Harbinger Publications, Inc., 1995.

Articles on the World Wide Web

American Institute for Preventive Medicine. "Introduction to Stress Management." Accessed 15 July 2006. http://www.healthylife.com/Checkin.asp?Id=10.

Gardner, Amanda. "Many Cambodians Still Bear Scars of Khmer Rouge." *In DepressionIssues.com*. 2 August, 2005. http://www.depressionissues.com/ms/news/527189/main.html

McManamy, John. "Ethnopolar: Ethnicity and Depression and Bipolar." *In McMan's Depression and Bipolar Website*. Accessed 29 May 2006. http://www.mcmanweb.com/article-151.htm

National Institute of Mental Health (NIMH). "Facts About Post-Traumatic Stress Disorder." Accessed 15 July, 2006. http://www.nimh.nih.gov/healthinformation/ptsdmenu.cfm

— — —. "Frequently Asked Questions About Suicide." Accessed 15 July 2006. http://www.nimh.nih.gov/suicideprevention/suicidefaq.cfm

National Institute of Neurological Disorders and Stroke. Accessed 15 July 2006. "Brain Basics: Understanding Sleep." http://www.ninds.nih.gov/disorders/brain_basics/understanding_sleep.htm

National Sleep Foundation. "The ABCs of ZZZs." In National Sleep Foundation Website. Accessed 16 July, 2006. http://www.sleepfoundation.org/sleeplibrary/index.php?secid=&id=53

Ponton, Lynn, Ph.D. "Coping With Bipolar Disorder." *In Dr. John Grohol's Psych Central*. 16 February, 2006. http://psychcentral.com/lib/2006/02/coping-with-bipolar-disorder/

Spearing, Melissa. "Bipolar Disorder." *The National Institute of Mental Health (NIMH)*. Accessed 15 July 2006. http://www.nimh.nih.gov/publicat/bipolar.cfm

United States Department of Veterans Affairs. "Facts About PTSD." National Center for PTSD. Accessed 15 July 2006. http://www.ncptsd.va.gov/facts/index.html

VISIT OUR WEBSITE

Information, Chat, Love and Support

It's Free

Stop by any time and find a meeting place for those with bipolar disorder, family, friends and community who participate in meaningful discussions about bipolar disorder, survival strategies and provide loving support to one another. SurvivingBipolar.com website which includes a Community of Hope forum, provides the bipolar community open and anonymous forums in which to share ideas, research, success strategies, and provide a safe place to share feelings. Our purpose is to foster hope and the self-worth needed for a brighter tomorrow.

We hope to see you there—You make a difference!

www.SurvivingBipolar.com

Bipolar Website Resources and Chat Forums

Website	Subject Matter
www.SurvivingBipolar.com	Bipolar Survival and Hope
www.BipolarArts.com	The Bipolar Artistic Expression
www.BipolarCodo.com	Codependency and Bipolar
www.BipolarCongress.com	Congressional Strategies Action Bipolar
www.BipolarFaith.com	Faith and Bipolar, Care and Support
www.BipolarFund.com	Philanthropic opportunities
www.BipolarHope.com	Bipolar Magazine
www.BipolarJob.com	Bipolar in the Work Place
www.BipolarJustice.com	Justice, Crime and the Future
www.BipolarLaw.com	Law Enforcement Issues
www.BipolarMedical.com	Medical Care Best Practices
www.BipolarPeople.com	Famous People with Bipolar
www.BipolarPoets.com	The Bipolar Poetic Expression
www.BipolarPTSD.com	PTSD and Bipolar
www.BipolarSleep.com	Sleep and Bipolar
www.BipolarSuicide.com	Suicide Prevention and Support
www.BipolarWriters.com	The Bipolar Written Expression
www.DrugsBipolar.com	Medication Information
www.EducateBipolar.com	Education, Training, Facilitation
www.FamilyBipolar.com	Bipolar in the family
www. HealBipolar.com	Pursuit of a cure
www.ImBipolar.com	Share your Story - Stand up and be Counted
www.KidsBipolar.com	Children's bipolar issues
www.MentalHealthHope.com	Mental Health Community of Hope
www.MovieBipolar.com	Promoting Movie Ideas and Production
www.NewsBipolar.com	Bipolar News and Views
www.ResearchBipolar.com	Researching the Truth about Bipolar
www.Speakbipolar.com	Bipolar Motivational Speakers
www.TreatBipolar.Com	Treatment Best Practices and Options

Make a difference and stop by today!

MARIANT
ENTERPRISES

Other Publications

Surviving Bipolar's Fatal Grip
The Journey to Hell and Back
Print, and E-book
Full Length Audio CD
Audio CD Condensed Version

Joyous Sadness
Poetry from a Bipolar Perspective
Print, and E-book
Audio CD

Your Bipolar Workbook
Survival Guide – Made Simple
Print, and E-book

Professional Services

Bipolar Awareness

Bipolar Solutions Consulting

Motivational Speaking Engagements

Program Management

Workshops and Facilitation

For More Information Contact Us at:
www.SurvivingBipolar.com

SURVIVING BIPOLAR'S FATAL GRIP

Order online at: www.SurvivingBipolar.com

Use This Form to Order Additional Copies

Please Print:

Name _____

Address _____

City_____ State_____

Zip_____

Phone Number(   )_____

Email Address_____

<u>Quantity</u>			<u>Price Each</u>
1 –	20	copies of book @	$ 20.00 each
21 –	100	copies of book @	$ 19.00 each
101 –	250	copies of book @	$ 18.00 each

For larger quantities contact www.Mariant.com

_____ copies of book @ _____each $_____

CA residents add ___% sales tax $_____

Postage and Handling @ $4.00 per book $_____
(Media Rate - U.S. Destinations Only)
(Go online for international rates)

Total Amount $_____

Charge to: VISA___ MASTERCARD____ AMEX____OTHER_____

Account# _____

Expiration Date _____

Signature _____

Check enclosed_____Make checks payable to Mariant Enterprises Inc.

Send to: Mariant Enterprises, Inc.
P.O. Box 2026, Santa Clara, CA 95055

SURVIVING BIPOLAR'S FATAL GRIP
BOOK ORDER FORM

NOTICE

To preserve your privacy, books will be shipped in a plain packaging (with no reference to Bipolar.)

All customers will automatically be added to our regular emailing list.

☐ Check here if you would like to be removed from our emailing list.

SURVIVING BIPOLAR'S FATAL GRIP

Order online at: www.SurvivingBipolar.com

Use This Form to Order Additional Copies

Please Print:

Name _____

Address _____

City_____ **State**_____

Zip_____

Phone Number(**)**_____

Email Address_____

Quantity		Price Each
1 – 20	copies of book @	$ 20.00 each
21 – 100	copies of book @	$ 19.00 each
101 – 250	copies of book @	$ 18.00 each

For larger quantities contact www.Mariant.com

_____ copies of book @ _____each $_____

CA residents add ___% sales tax $_____

Postage and Handling @ $4.00 per book $_____
(Media Rate - U.S. Destinations Only)
(Go online for international rates)

Total Amount $_____

Charge to: VISA___ MASTERCARD____ AMEX____OTHER_____

Account# _____

Expiration Date _____

Signature _____

Check enclosed_____Make checks payable to Mariant Enterprises Inc.

Send to: Mariant Enterprises, Inc.
P.O. Box 2026, Santa Clara, CA 95055

SURVIVING BIPOLAR'S FATAL GRIP
BOOK ORDER FORM

NOTICE

To preserve your privacy, books will be shipped in a plain packaging (with no reference to Bipolar.)

All customers will automatically be added to our regular emailing list.

☐ Check here if you would like to be removed from our emailing list.

Those who wait for the LORD,
Will gain new strength;
They will mount up with wings like eagles,
They will run and not get tired,
They will walk and not become weary.
Isaiah 40:31 (NLT)